Palestinians in Israel

The Politics of Faith after Oslo

While the international community and regional powers in the Middle East are focusing on finding a solution to Israel's "external problem" – the future of the occupied West Bank and Gaza Strip – another political conflict is emerging on the domestic Israel scene: the question of the future status of Israel's Palestinian minority within the 1967 borders. The Palestinian minority in Israel are currently experiencing a new trend in their political development. Here, Ghanem and Mustafa term that development "The Politics of Faith", referring to the demographic, religious and social transformations among the Palestinian minority that have facilitated and strengthened their self-confidence. Such heightened self-confidence is also the basis for key changes in their cultural and social life, as well as political activity. This book traces the emergence of a new and diverse generation of political leadership, how Palestinian society has developed and empowered itself within Israel, and the politicization of Islamic activism in Israel.

AS'AD GHANEM is Professor of Comparative Politics at the University of Haifa. His theoretical work has explored the legal, institutional and political conditions in ethnic states and conflict studies. He has published eight books and numerous articles about ethnic politics in divided societies, including about ethnic divisions and Arab–Jewish relations in Israel. He has been the initiator and designer of several policy schemes and empowerment programs for Arabs in Israel.

MOHANAD MUSTAFA is a senior lecturer at Beit Berl College and lecturer of the Middle East Politics program at the University of Haifa. He specializes in political Islam, Arab regimes, democratization, and politics in Palestine and Israel. He has published various articles in referred journals about these issues.

Palestinians in Israel

The Politics of Faith after Oslo

AS'AD GHANEM
University of Haifa

MOHANAD MUSTAFA
Beit Berl College

CAMBRIDGE
UNIVERSITY PRESS

CAMBRIDGE
UNIVERSITY PRESS

University Printing House, Cambridge CB2 8BS, United Kingdom

One Liberty Plaza, 20th Floor, New York, NY 10006, USA

477 Williamstown Road, Port Melbourne, VIC 3207, Australia

314-321, 3rd Floor, Plot 3, Splendor Forum, Jasola District Centre, New Delhi - 110025, India

79 Anson Road, #06-04/06, Singapore 079906

Cambridge University Press is part of the University of Cambridge.

It furthers the University's mission by disseminating knowledge in the pursuit of
education, learning and research at the highest international levels of excellence.

www.cambridge.org
Information on this title: www.cambridge.org/9781108701051
DOI: 10.1017/9781108641647

© As'ad Ghanem and Mohanad Mustafa 2018

First published 2018
First paperback edition 2020

A catalogue record for this publication is available from the British Library

Library of Congress Cataloging in Publication data
Names: Ganim, Asad, author. | Mustafa, Muhannad, author.
Title: Palestinians in Israel : the politics of faith after Oslo / Asad Ghanem,
    University of Haifa, Israel, Mohanad Mustafa, University of Haifa, Israel.
Description: Cambridge, United Kingdom ; New York, NY, USA : Cambridge
    University Press, [2018] | Includes bibliographical references and index.
Identifiers: LCCN 2018022940 | ISBN 9781108476560 (hardback : alk. paper) |
    ISBN 9781108701051 (pbk. : alk. paper)
Subjects: LCSH: Palestinian Arabs–Israel–Politics and government–20th century. |
    Palestinian Arabs–Israel–Politics and government–21st century. | Palestinian Arabs–
    Israel–Ethnic identity. | Israel–Ethnic relations.
Classification: LCC DS113.7 .G384 2018 | DDC 305.892/7405694–dc23
    LC record available at https://lccn.loc.gov/2018022940

ISBN 978-1-108-47656-0 Hardback
ISBN 978-1-108-70105-1 Paperback

Contents

Figures and Tables

Introduction: Historical Background and Analytical Framework

While the international community and regional powers in the Middle East are concentrated on finding a solution to Israel's "external" problem, the future of the West Bank and Gaza Strip, occupied since 1967, another political conflict is emerging internally: the future status of the Palestinian minority living in pre-1967 Israel. There were around 1.5 million Palestinians in Israel in 2015,[1] or 18% of the population.[2] Their birth rate was 4.3, down from nine in the 1960s and five in the early 1980s (the average birth rate among Jews is 2.6 [Haider, 2005: 30]). Thus despite the decrease in the Palestinian birth rate it remains higher than that of the Jewish sector.

The demographic changes among the Palestinian minority have bolstered their self-confidence since the 1970s. This has served as the basis for new developments in cultural life and politics. But despite the increased desire to develop a separate economy in Palestinian towns and cities, the efforts have yet to bear significant fruit.

With regard to age distribution, the Palestinians in Israel are younger than the Jews. In 2003, for example, 41% of Palestinians were below the age of 15; the corresponding figure in the Jewish sector was 25.5%. Similarly, only 3.2% of Palestinians in Israel are 65 years or older, compared to 11.8% of the Jews (Ghanem and Mustafa, 2009a).

The Palestinians in Israel are concentrated in three districts. A majority (56.6%) live in the Galilee, which stretches from Haifa in the west to Beisan (Beit She'an) in the east and north to the Lebanese border. The Triangle, which runs adjacent to the border with the West Bank and along the Mediterranean coastline and extends from southeast of Haifa to east of Tel Aviv, is home to 23% of them. Another 12% of

---

[1] The literature refers to them in many ways: "Palestinians in Israel," "Arabs in Israel," "Arab citizens of Israel," "the Palestinian minority," and "1948 Palestinians."

[2] These data are more reliable as they do not include the Palestinians in East Jerusalem or the residents of the Golan Heights. See Ghanem *et al.*, 2015.

1

Palestinians live in the Naqab (Negev), specifically in the area of Be'er al-Sabe' (Beersheva). The balance (about 8.5%) live in the mixed cities – Akka (Acre), Haifa, Lydd (Lod), Ramla, and Jaffa (Haider, 2005: 28).

The Palestinians in Israel are affiliated with three religions. The majority, around 80%, are Muslims. They live in most of the Palestinian villages and cities and in all the areas. Christians account for 10%, with the vast majority in the Galilee, and belong to several denominations, mainly Catholic, Orthodox, Maronite, Armenian and several Protestant groups. Druze constitute another 10%, all of them in the Galilee and the Carmel (see Ghanem *et al.*, 2015).

The Palestinians in Israel are absent or excluded from the attention and perception of most of their reference groups (including Jews in Israel and Palestinians in the West Bank, Gaza, and Palestinian diaspora). This situation is a product of their unique situation as residents of a state that was forced on them and that has never represented them.

The Palestinians in Israel: Historical Background

On the eve of the *Nakba* in 1948, nearly two million people lived in Palestine, two-thirds Arab and one-third Jews. Most of the former (about 940,000) and the vast majority of Jews lived in the areas that later became the State of Israel. As a result of mass expulsions, ethnic cleansing, and flight from the Jewish forces, only 160,000 Palestinians remained within Israel's borders when the fighting ended. They comprised only 10% of all Palestinians at the time. The subsequent deterioration in the Palestinians' status was a direct result of the war (Ghanem and Mustafa, 2009a: 25). The main difference between the Palestinians in Israel and those elsewhere is that the former remained on their land and became Israeli citizens. This was not of great benefit to them, however, because the Israeli authorities and security agencies viewed them as an enemy that posed a security threat and strategic threat. Israel took harsh measures to deter, subdue, and control them.

Bäuml writes that the Zionist leaders saw "transfer" as an ideal and practical solution for dealing with the Palestinian minority that remained in the Jewish state. It was the dominant solution they toyed with in the late 1950s. It lost momentum after residents of Kufr Qassem stayed put despite the massacre of 1956 (Bäuml, 2007: 35), and gave way to alternative ideas in the late 1960s.

Bäuml notes that in the 1950s and 1960s Israeli policies towards the Palestinians centered on the following principles: treating the Palestinians as a security threat and fifth column; confiscating land and preventing geographic continuity between Palestinian population centers; not drafting Palestinians into the armed forces; discriminating against them in all aspects of life; amplifying their internal regional and sectarian tensions; preventing the formation of a Palestinian leadership; rejecting their identification as a national group; and stymieing the emergence of a local Palestinian economy.

Three events played a decisive role in the development of the Palestinians in Israel and affected them culturally, socially, and economically. The first regional event was the war of 1948. It is often referred to as the *Nakba* [Catastrophe] in Palestinian literature, political discourse, and historical memory. The second event was the war of June 1967. The third was the Oslo Accords, after which the politics and discourse of Palestinians in Israel emerged on a new track.

The *Nakba* caused the exodus of a majority of the Palestinians, the destruction of their cities, and devastation of their farms, along with the expulsion of the political and social leadership that had emerged in earlier decades. Most of the Palestinians who remained in Israel were rural. The military government that lasted until 1966 destroyed pre-existing social ties and geographic contiguity. A new system of laws was created by military orders and decrees. A new Palestinian leadership coalesced that was quite different from the historical leadership before 1948 (Kimmerling and Migdal, 1993).

Despite being an indigenous people and a minority in their own homeland, the political reality that germinated in the aftermath of the *Nakba* did not permit the Palestinian minority to organize and rebuild itself politically. Theirs was a society in ruins, with few financial and cultural resources and devoid of political and social elites (Lustick, 1980).

The period of the military government (1949–1966) had a strong impact on the political development and organization of the Palestinians in Israel. It clamped tight control on the Palestinian minority in the new state (Bäuml, 2007) in ways that impeded political activity and organization within Palestinian society. The urbanization process that began in the 1930s and 1940s was suspended. Always subject to "security considerations," the military administration used clan and traditional leaders as the primary channel for granting favors in various fields, including education, employment, and travel permits.

The Palestinians in Israel lost not only their political and cultural elite, but also their middle class. The transformation of a rural agrarian society into a proletarian one was the most significant socioeconomic change affecting the Palestinian minority during the years of the military government. Zureik would later describe it as "deserting agriculture" (Zureik, 1979). In the absence of a Palestinian national economy and with no Palestinian bourgeoisie, laborers moved from working the land in their villages to the manual-labor market in Jewish cities. The Israeli Palestinians' isolation from the outside world, and the Arab world in particular, led to their dual marginalization: on the one hand they were marginal in the State of Israel; on the other hand, they became marginal in the Palestinian national movement as well (Al-Haj, 1993).

Two parallel systems emerged during the years of the military government: a democratic system for the Jews and a non-democratic system for the Palestinians. Although the state granted the Palestinians some political rights – citizenship and the franchise – it restricted or suppressed other political rights inherent to democracy. The most flagrant examples are the right of political organization and the right of movement and assembly. Even though citizens, the Palestinians came under the jurisdiction of military courts. Under the segregation practiced in Israel, Jews had collective and national rights, whereas Palestinians enjoyed only individual (and unequal) rights (Boimel, 2007).

The military government established state control of three aspects considered essential to the success of the Zionist project and the building of the state: land expropriation, a system of permits to control Palestinian participation in the Israeli job market, and preventing the Palestinians in Israel from having contact with their compatriots and relatives abroad. Palestinians in Israel were also prohibited from engaging in active and organized political efforts to change their situation and status.

The military administration and the authorities dominated the political development of the Palestinians in Israel. Palestinians were isolated from the political, administrative, and social structure, in pursuit of more effective political monitoring. Israeli historian Tom Segev summed up the political goals of the military administration during its first years as follows:

The policies of the state sought to divide the Palestinian residents into sects and regions, ... creating municipal authorities in Palestinian villages, coupled with the competitive environment that existed during elections to the local municipality and deepened the division inside villages. These factors acted in unison to prevent unity among Palestinian residents. (Segev, cited by Ghanem and Mustafa, 2009a)

In conclusion, the Palestinian political discourse that took shape during the period of the military government (1949–1966) overlooked the reality of defeat to ensure that people stayed in their homeland after the war. There was an overemphasis on civil discourse, focused on achieving the bare minimum of rights and freedoms to provide a semblance of existential security. The military government isolated the Palestinians in Israel from their Palestinian, Arab, and Muslim surroundings. The main focus of their struggle was the call for the unconditional abolition of the military government. In other words, the bulk of the Palestinian discourse during those years related to the civil domain; it was detached from the political and national discourse that sees the Palestinians in Israel as part of the Palestinian case and one of its consequences. But the Land Movement (al-Ard) of the 1960s emphasized the national affiliation of the Palestinians in Israel and affirmed their place in the Palestinian national movement and its aspirations (Ghanem and Mustafa, 2009a).

The 1967 war was the second regional event with far-reaching consequences for the development of Palestinian society in Israel. The occupation of the West Bank and Gaza that followed had both direct and indirect effects on the Palestinians in Israel. The war came shortly after the abolition of the military government. Contemporary publications focused primarily on the effects of the occupation on Palestinian identity in Israel (Al-Haj, 1993). Much of this literature asserts that the war helped ingrain the Palestinian component in the collective identity of Palestinian society in Israel. The Palestinian component began to compete with the Israeli civilian component in the Palestinians' self-definition and identity.

The occupation also affected the patterns and forms of political organization among Palestinians in Israel. Two new movements appeared, representing the secular national trend and the Islamic trend in the Occupied Palestinian Territories – the "Sons of the Village" and the Islamic Movement, respectively.

The 1967 war affected the economic status of the Palestinians in Israel. They were no longer on the lowest rung of the Israeli economic ladder, replaced in the job market by the cheaper labor of Palestinians from the occupied territories. The economic betterment of the Palestinians in Israel had extensive social ramifications, including the emergence of a new educated and middle class (Haida, 1990).

The political, economic, and social transformation generated an increase in the national awareness of the Palestinians in Israel and the establishment of national institutions. The early 1970s saw the initial emergence of an educated sector and the expansion of the middle class; this in turn produced national or regional institutions to organize Palestinian society in Israel. They included the National Committee of the Heads of Arab Local Authorities, founded in 1974, and the next year, the Regional Alliance for Palestinian University Students, the Regional Alliance for Palestinian High School Students, and the Committee for Defense of Palestinian Lands. These institutions were a strong force in the reorganization and rebuilding of Palestinian society in Israel (Rekhess, 1993).

Mar'i believes that the new interaction with the Palestinian people created the conditions for politicization of the Palestinian masses in Israel. He explains that,

the Palestinians in Israel did not succeed in merely maintaining their identity while in Israel, but actively worked to infuse Palestinian identity into every spoken and written word, into poems and novels and during the practical exercise of their social and political struggle. It was a process akin to opening the flood gates of Palestinian political awareness and refining it so as to meet the challenges of every stage in the development process of the Palestinian case. (Mar'i, 1988: 35)

A growing class of educated Palestinians emerged in the aftermath of the 1967 war, mainly due to an emphasis in the early 1970s on college prep course for Palestinians who wished to attend university (Al-Haj, 1995).

The 1967 war and the increased contact between Palestinians living on both sides of the Green Line produced a sense of a shared destiny and the feeling that Palestinians in Israel are part of the Palestinian cause. Evidence of this was Israeli Palestinians' increased involvement in paramilitary resistance operations. Between the end of the war in

June 1967 and July 1970, Israeli courts tried 120 Palestinian citizens of Israel on security charges; another 27 were placed in administrative detention. According to other sources, 48 Palestinians were arrested through October 1968, for participation in operations against Israeli security targets; a year later the figure was 115. Between 1967 and 1973, 320 Palestinians were arrested and tried for participating in resistance operations (Rekhess, 1993: 114).

In addition to fostering a stronger sense of national identity in the late 1960s and early 1970s, the process of institution-building culminated in the events of Land Day, on March 30, 1976. For the first time, Palestinians in Israel behaved as an organized and a cohesive national group. The events that day were the crest of a long struggle by social and popular movements, which intensified in the nine months prior to February 29, 1976. That was the day when Israeli authorities confiscated close to 21,000 dunams (about 5,200 acres) of land from several Palestinian villages in central Galilee, including Arrabeh, Sakhnin, Deir-Hannah, and Arab al-Sawa'ed, in order to build Jewish settlements and further the Judaization of the Galilee.

The political and literary transformations that appeared in the aftermath of the 1967 war indicate a fundamental change in the relationship between two aspects, the civil and the national, in the political discourse of the Palestinians in Israel. The Palestinians in Israel thought that solving the problem of the occupation in the West Bank and Gaza would improve their civil status, because, as an integral part of the Palestinian people, that depends on the national issue. This is evident from the approach to citizenship in the Palestinian political discourse. The components of this citizenship do not depend solely on the struggle by the Palestinians in Israel, but also on a solution to the overall Palestinian question.

The signing of the Oslo Accords in September 1993 between the Palestinian Liberation Organization (PLO) and the State of Israel, and the mutual recognition that followed, constitute the third regional event of significance for the Palestinians in Israel, with regard to their relationship with the state, their political discourse, and their political activity. The signing of the Oslo Accords coincided with major global transformations that affected Palestinian society in Israel, especially globalization and international economic and political changes. These developments have affected political development among the Palestinians in Israel over the last two decades.

Oslo came in the wake of the first Palestinian Intifada, which began in 1987, and the declaration of a Palestinian state in 1988. Numerous events and developments in these years that affected the evolution of Palestinians were merely the start of dramatic changes. The 1990s brought a new set of changes, including the collapse of the Soviet Union and entire Eastern bloc, the signing of the Oslo Accords, the accelerated pace of globalization and openness produced by the internet and mass media, the Aqsa Intifada of 2000 (commonly referred to as the second Intifada), the Lebanon war in July 2006, and the Gaza war in December 2008. All these events left an imprint on the Palestinian minority in Israel.

For the Palestinians in Israel, this period can be divided into two phases. The first, which lasted from the mid-1980s until the mid-1990s, was an extension of a previous phase that began after the end of military rule (1966). But it was also marked by democratization and liberalization on the Israeli national level.

Until the mid-1990s the Palestinians in Israel felt a growing urgency to assert their Israeli citizenship. It became essential for that minority to involve itself in the state on a par with the Jewish majority. This was evident in various ways, including the declaration of Equality Day in June 1987, participation in demonstrations against the suppression of the first Intifada, and monetary support for the Palestinians under occupation. They took a role in the political process and accepted their role as part of the "Blocking Coalition."[3]

In the next phase, after Oslo, it became clear that the hope for full and equal citizenship and full integration into Israeli society and politics was misplaced. The Israeli government and people were opposed to such an idea. Later developments saw a major rise in ethnic discrimination against the Palestinians in Israel and an increase in official policies that aimed to isolate and confine the Palestinians.[4] The discriminatory measures included land confiscation, particularly in the Naqab (southern Israel). The climax came with the carnage of October

---

[3] The Blocking Coalition refers to the Arab political parties in the Knesset in 1992–1995. At a time when Rabin's coalition did not have the necessary votes to approve agreements, it provided support from the outside to win approval of the Oslo Accords.

[4] See Sikkuy reports (www.sikkuy.org.il/english/reports.html).

2000, when 13 Palestinian citizens of Israel were shot and killed while demonstrating against the government's discriminatory policies.[5]

This led to a new phase and new approach to the Israeli framework and the possibility of realizing their prospects as a group and as individuals through their Israeli citizenship. The Palestinians reassessed and modified the methods of dissent they had employed through the late 1990s. They realized that the Oslo era was over and that solutions based on international resolutions in support of the Palestinian cause were fruitless.

An Islamic stream appeared and called for the establishment of a "separate society." Similarly, the idea of boycotting the Israeli national elections gained traction and was adopted by several political and nationalist movements (Ghanem and Mustafa, 2007). This led to the embrace of the concept of a shared homeland, not established on the basis of a Jewish state, and an exploration of the impact of the *Nakba* on the Palestinian situation in Israel.

In the last two decades, the majority of Palestinian political and scholarly efforts have been dedicated to exposing the incompatibility of the Jewish character of the state with democracy. This became the rallying cry of the Palestinian minority in Israel, to the extent that the head of the General Security Service (GSS), Yuval Diskin, considered this demand a strategic danger to the state. He stated that the GSS would sabotage every attempt, however democratic, to alter the state's Jewish character.[6]

The most significant changes since the mid-1990s, which reveal the relationship between the Palestinian minority, the State of Israel, and the Jewish majority, can be summarized as follows:

From the Perspective of the "Jewish State"

From Assimilation without Equality to Segregation without Autonomy

The majority and the state had held to the "integration narrative" as part of an attempt to absorb the Palestinians into Israel, even though

---

[5] See Orr Commission report (http://elyon1.court.gov.il/heb/veadot/or/inside_index.htm).
[6] *Ha'aretz*, March 16, 2007.

that narrative does not include equality for the Palestinian collective, but only diminished individual equality. The majority still refuses to recognize the Palestinians as a national minority and prefers to deal with it as fragmented communities. The refusal to recognize the collective national rights of the Palestinians in Israel led to the new calls for separation, without giving the Palestinians any rights as a collective. The state seeks to maintain its Jewish identity and character through segregation, achieved through statutory and political means. In some mixed towns, like Lydd (Lod) and Ramla, walls have been built to isolate some Palestinian neighborhoods from adjacent Jewish neighborhoods.

The Emergence of a Politics of Ethnic Superiority

Globalization did not affect the politics of citizenship in Israel. The Israeli case was cited as a model for how globalization affirmed the state's identity and character. Throughout the last two decades, Israel has intensified the ethnic focus of its politics. Israel defines itself as a democratic Jewish state, but the Jewish sphere has encroached on the democratic sphere and in many instances effectively nullifies the citizenship of the Palestinian minority. The most notable example of this is the legislative moves to enhance the Jewishness of the state, particularly with regard to the citizenship law.

From Individual Rights to Collective Duties

In the Jewish state, rights are not derived from citizenship but from membership of the hegemonic (Jewish) group. Nor are they derived from the public sphere. Despite the dissociation between rights and duties in a democratic system, the Jewish state attempts to link individual rights with certain duties. In this framework, the proposal to require young people to do civilian service was presented as a link between rights and duties. But in fact it makes the rights essential normal daily life conditional on abdicating national identity and dignity and perverting the culture. Civilian service runs counter to the long struggle by the Palestinian minority and its cultural and political elite to achieve the delicate balance between collective identity and civic affairs, in which the demand for civil rights becomes part of the glorification of national identity (Ghanem and Mustafa, 2009a).

From the Perspective of the Palestinians in Israel

From the Politics of Coexistence to the Politics of Rights

Over the last two decades, the Palestinian political discourse in Israel has moved from the politics of coexistence to the politics of rights. Coexistence stems from dialogue between the two sides. The discourse of rights emerges from the demand for group-specific rights and utilizes the tools of litigation and political dissent.

In the politics of coexistence, the two sides meet face to face and are exposed to the entire social collective of the other. By contrast, in the politics of rights each side sees the other through the lens of gains, without the need to be exposed to it. Each side perceives the other only through the prism of its own interests.

From Identity Politics to the Politics of Identity

The politics of identity is considered to be common among marginalized groups (see Aronowitz, 1992). Here there has been a change in the political discourse of Palestinians in Israel over the last two decades. The politics of identity is wielded, intentionally or unintentionally, to buttress the collective self and reinforce the "I" against the "Other." Identity is in turn defined by "Otherness" and not in its own right. Identity is not fixed or complete; it would wither if it were. Writing about identity is political and ideological in nature; the writing affects the author's identity as well. In contrast, the politics of identity aims to better the status of the marginalized group by its consolidation as a group against another and hegemonic group. The entire Palestinian political movement in Israel practices the politics of identity: the Islamic movement, the politics of identity that stem from Islamic identity; and the national movement, the politics of identity stemming from the Palestinian–Arab identity.

From the Politics of Representation to Political Representation

Within the framework of the state's refusal to recognize the Palestinians as a national group with collective rights, the politics of representation is one of the methods used to control and contain weak ethnic groups (Phillips, 1995). The politics of representation involves the appointment of minority representatives to official positions, or as token gestures, an indicator that the minority or marginalized group is represented in state institutions. Often those representatives do not represent the political trends among the minority, but those of the majority and the state instead. They are used as a symbol for the minority group's equality in government institutions. The politics of representation can mean the appointment of Palestinian deputy ministers or selection of Palestinians for official positions in the Israeli bureaucracy, such as the education system. The politics of representation is part of the state's public relations effort to showcase the improved status of the minority and its assimilate into the state.

The politics of representation is considered to be part of the "primary" discourse of equality among the Palestinians as well. But this discourse has started to give way to a new discourse of political representation. Political representation is based on the premise that Palestinian representatives must express the positions and opinions of the marginalized group, not those of the hegemonic majority. The discourse of political representation is part of the collective demand for a change in the nature of the Jewish state and its replacement by a bi-national state or a state of all its citizens. The demand is based on the idea that political representation in state institutions is devoid of meaning when the ethnic character of the state is such a strong presence.

The Politics of Difference and the Politics of Recognition

Two competing political discourses have been growing in parallel among the Palestinians in Israel – the discourse of difference and the discourse of recognition. The politics of recognition, which calls on the majority to respect the minority and its unique traits (see Taylor, 1994), has become part of the political Palestinian discourse over the last two decades. It calls for recognition of the Palestinians in Israel as a national minority with the attendant rights. Integral to this discourse is the demand for recognition of the historical narrative of the Palestinian minority in textbooks. At the very least, it calls on the majority to carry out projects that affirm the minority's historical narrative.

The politics of recognition, which stems from collective rights, is accompanied by the politics of difference, initiatives that demand recognition by the state or the majority. A collective of political, cultural, social, and institutional actions appear and attempt to exercise the collective rights.

The Study of the Palestinians in Israel

Political studies about the status of the Palestinians in Israel have tended to rely primarily on political and sociopolitical developments and their relationship with the state and the majority, using theoretical formulas derived from the basic concept that the Palestinians in Israel are a relatively traditional minority in a Western and democratic state.

Many Israeli researchers have used the term "Modernization Theory" or "modernity" to analyze the development of the Palestinians in Israel. Their methods rely on the basic premise that the "Palestinian minority," because a "different" ethnic group and part of the East – a hemisphere that is still in the process of political development – has developed politically, socially, culturally, and economically through modernization. A minority that is fortunate to be interacting with the "modern and advanced" majority and the state's policies undertaken to "modernize" said minority.

The most prominent models in this theoretical framework are those of the Israeli sociologist Shmuel Eisenstadt and historians Yakov Landau and Elie Rekhess. The modernity theory appears in the works of Cohen (1990), Landau (1993), and Rekhess (1993) all of whom believe that the Palestinian minority in Israel underwent rapid modernization. That hypothesis, they explain, is supported by the rise in the standard of living and educational level, which leads in turn to higher expectations. Palestinian society evaluates its status according to the following criteria: the extent of development and the Jewish majority's degree of accomplishment in the state; and the existence of gaps between the two groups in various areas, including industrialization of the Palestinian village, housing for young couples, the allocation of water for agriculture, and assimilation and immersion in the Israeli economy. These factors and others have led to depression and bitterness among the Palestinians in Israel, and these feelings have pushed them towards radical positions and politics. This began the June 1967 war. Until then, due to their isolation from the Palestinian world and the close monitoring by the military government, the various circles of affiliation of Palestinians in Israel were kept in balance.

Antipodal to the "modernization" approach, the political sociologist Sammy Smooha advanced the theoretical framework of "pluralism and conflict," in which the Palestinians in Israel gained a better understanding of the rules of the Israeli political system. They did so by molding their collective identity and nurturing the components of this identity, both the national-Palestinian and the civil-Israeli. This process received a boost as a result of their interaction with the Palestinians from the West Bank and Gaza after the 1967 war. This model – like Lustick's (1980) – claims that there is a pluralistic society in Israel, divided along religious lines (religious vs. secular), sectarian lines (Ashkenazi vs. Eastern Jews), and national lines (Jews vs. Palestinian Arabs). As part of the national pluralism, the Palestinians in Israel are undergoing a complex process of politicization composed of three main parts. The first is Israelization, meaning the intensive assimilation of the Palestinian minority into Israeli society in all aspects, including the values and traditions prevalent among Jews. The second part is internal divisions into Accommodationists, Reservationists, Oppositionists, and Rejectionists.[7] The third part is militancy. Here the Palestinians in Israel embrace the Palestinian national identity and exhibit solidarity with the idea of the establishment of a Palestinian state alongside Israel. The process also encompasses a stronger campaign to establish a Palestinian state and improve their status within Israel.

A process of politicization has taken place in light of the democratic transformations within Israeli society, a diminishing Arab–Israeli conflict, in general, and a diminishing Palestinian Israeli conflict, in particular. Majid Al-Haj (1993) used this model to explain the political status of Palestinians in Israel. He believes that "the Palestinians in Israel have developed over time a special adaptation strategy as a result of contextual circumstances related to their position in the State of Israel and related to changes in various aspects of life, a process that started during the establishment of the state."

Those strategies include the Palestinians' adoption of lawful methods of struggle. Al-Haj concludes that although the solidarity of the Palestinians in Israel with the Palestinian struggle in the West Bank and the Gaza Strip intensified during the First Intifada (1987–1992), their demands for equality within Israel increased as well. In the same study, Al-Haj proposed the notion of a "Double Periphery." According to

---

[7] The Accommodationists accept the inferior status of Palestinians in Israel as a Jewish state. The Reservationists have accepted the Jewish character of the state but struggle to improve the status of Palestinians in Israel. The Oppositionists demand a changed in the Jewish character of the state and consequent change in the status of Palestinians. The Rejectionists are opposed to Israel's existence.

him, the Palestinians in Israel were pushed to the margins after the Intifada. Their marginalization took two forms: in Israel they were marginalized for their support of the Intifada and other associated actions; and within the Palestinian national movement they were marginalized because they did not actively participate in the Intifada, which was a step towards Palestinian national liberation. According to Al-Haj, these forms of marginalization complicated the status of Palestinians in Israel more than ever.

The politicization model asserts that the Palestinians in Israel accept the state and their minority status. In fact, they reject the Jewish Zionist character of the state and the consequent discrimination against them, including the majority's ideas for resolving the Palestinian case. To achieve favorable changes in their status, they employ legal means, both parliamentary and extra-parliamentary. Smooha (1992) finds evidence for those claims in Knesset voting patterns for Jewish Zionist parties and non-Jewish parties. In addition, there is an extensive network of independent political organizations and movements that participate in extra-parliamentary politics through demonstrations, protests, and strikes.

Building on the studies conducted by these scholars, Palestinian sociologist Elia Zureik has proposed an Internal Colonialism model, borrowed from Hechter, the English sociologist. This model analyzes the minority's development in terms of the relationships among the economic, social, and cultural affiliations imposed on the minority by the majority. These relationships are primarily directed at maintaining the majority's dominance and the minority's subordination and inferiority.

The Internal Colonialism model was employed by Nakhleh (1979) and Zureik (1979). In their attempt to demonstrate Israel's colonialist nature, they focus on the status of Palestinians and Jews before the founding of Israel. This, they assert, proves the colonial roots of Jewish settlement in the land. Following the same path, they analyze the interactions between Jews and Palestinians and between the state and its Palestinian citizens. Zureik asserts that even before 1948 the Zionist movement had invested extensive effort to strip Palestinians of their land and build Jewish settlements there, with the support and assistance of Britain and the other imperialist powers. He further explains that since 1948, and as a result of the *Nakba*, Israeli has a Palestinian minority dominated by a Jewish majority. This minority constitutes a cheap labor force that serves the Jewish financial elite.

This model rests primarily on government policies towards Palestinians in Israel. It sees their political development as a reaction to the policies of land expropriation and discrimination against the Palestinian citizens. From these studies, one concludes that the Palestinians in Israel developed "Palestinian" approaches and applied them – up to and including armed conflict – in response to the policies directed at them. If some of these methods have yet to be utilized, that is merely the result of the pressure and intensive monitoring directed against them.

Lustick introduced the Control Model as a basis for understanding the development of the Palestinian minority in the Jewish state. He argued that in the current conditions of ethnic separation in Israel, the majority has full control over the minority, including the pace of that minority's development. Lustick (1980) asserts that despite the reality of a divided society in Israel, composed of a Jewish majority and a hostile Palestinian minority, the majority has been able to implement a monitoring system to police and control the minority. He explains that this control apparatus has three components: separation, dependence, and cooptation. Separation is achieved by isolating the Palestinian minority from the Jewish majority while also deploying divide-and-control policies against that minority. Dependence involves heightening the Palestinian minority's dependence on the Jewish majority, so that it cannot amass the political and economic resources available to other citizens. Cooptation is manifested in a vast system of privileges dangled before the Palestinian elite (bribes) as a way to contain their protest.

As is the case with Internal Colonialism, the Control Model relies primarily on Israel's policies towards its Palestinian citizens. However, this monitoring means that the Palestinians' political participation in Israel is limited. As a result of restrictions placed on political activity, the Palestinians in Israel might well adopt methods of struggle similar to those methods employed by the Palestinians in the occupied territories and diaspora against Israel during the 1970s and 1980s.

The control approach has been implemented in both the public and the planning spheres. Geographer Oren Yiftachel argues that Israel seeks to control land and land use by means of the Jewish-dominated planning institutions, which intentionally produce plans that perpetuate Jewish control and deprive Palestinians in Israel from benefiting from their land. Such state-sanctioned practices lead to an increase in Palestinian Arab political dissent. Occasionally, the protests end in

violent confrontations. State intervention through control and Judaization of Palestinian land could lead to an escalation of conflict between
Palestinians and Jews in Israel and polarization of society (Yiftachel
and Ghanem, 2004).

Al-Haj, in his earlier studies of the Palestinian education system in
Israel, advanced the "domination model." In recent years (Al-Haj,
2006) he has suggested multiculturalism as a theoretical framework
for understanding Israeli society and other subordinate multicultural
groups and a way to understand the development of Palestinians in
Israel. Most studies on the Palestinians in Israel have based their
analysis on minorities in democratic states. Their failure to explain
the complex situation of Palestinians in Israel has prompted scholars to
seek alternative theoretical models, such as those applied to conflicts
between indigenous communities and colonial powers.

Recent Studies

Over the last decade, the number of publications on the situation of the
Palestinians in Israel has increased dramatically: hundreds of articles
have appeared, several conferences have discussed their situation, and
a number of important books have focused on the issue.

Peleg and Waxman (2011) refer to the interaction between the
external Arab–Israeli conflict as the main explanation for the political
transformation of Palestinians in Israel. In their words: "Our fundamental claim in the book is that the growing ethno-national conflict
within Israel today between Israeli Jews and Palestinian Arabs should
be viewed as part of the larger conflict between Israel and the Palestinians" (Peleg and Waxman, 2011: 4). They conclude that "this [the case
of Palestinians in Israel] is not just an issue of domestic importance to
Israel that threatens the country's internal stability and even its democratic regime. It is also an issue that is inextricably linked to the Israel–
Palestinian conflict, a conflict with massive regional and even global
repercussions" (ibid., 217). The main argument demonstrates how the
external conflict is the internal conflict, and vice versa, a linkage that
underscores the explosive potential of the situation.

Haklai (2011) offers state–society models to explain the ethno-
national political awakening among the Palestinians in Israel. He
rejects both the "grievances model" and the "resourceful leadership

model" as suitable explanations for their shift towards ethno-national politics. From his perspective, these two explanations contain elements that have been part of the Palestinians' situation during the creation of Israel and consequently cannot explain the more recent changes in the modes of political mobilization (Haklai, 2011: 22–23). He avers that Palestinian politics in Israel has gone through three main phases since 1948. First was the quiescent period, when the military government severely limited the political activism of Palestinians in Israel. In the ethno-class period of the 1970s and 1980s, most political mobilization was channeled through the Communist Party. Since then, in the ethno-national period, independent Palestinian political organizations and civil society organizations have been the main agents for political mobilization. The key explanation for the political activism of the Palestinian minority involves changes that have occurred on the national level; changes in the relationship between the state and society in general are the main factors behind the changes among the minority:

To a large extent Israeli politics, economy, and society have undergone a tremendous liberalization process since the 1980s, shifting the balance of power away from the central government and towards other institutions and organized social forces. At the same time, one key institutional characteristic has not liberalized: the formal ownership of the state by the Jewish majority. Israel is a state that lacks autonomy from the Jewish majority. It is the impact of these institutional contours that largely explains transitions in the [Palestinian Arab citizens of Israel's] politics. (Haklai, 2011: 14)

In other words, changes during the last three decades of Palestinian minority politics "mirror changes in Israeli politics in large" (Haklai, 2011: 8).

Jamal (2011) argues that the rising politics of indigeneity is the main source of the growing demand for collective rights by the Palestinians in Israel – their main political expression in the last two decades. Referring to the increasing political mobilization of the Palestinians in Israel, he asserts:

The major factors responsible for this change are the disillusionment with the liberal conception of equality, especially its substantive dimensions within the "Jewish and democratic" definition of the state, the rise of a global Palestinian elite that is fully aware of developments in the international arena related to minority rights, and the return of the politics of Palestinian indigeneity as the moral and political basis for rights the Palestinians population in Israel, as a result of the growing national sentiments among them. (Jamal, 2011: 11)

In his comprehensive book, Jamal refers to various manifestations of Palestinian politics, including political demands, political participation, development of civil society development, leadership, and of course the "Future Vision," as the core of Palestinian politics in Israel over the last decade.

Pappe's book (2011) is a general and comprehensive review of the history of the Palestinian minority in Israel. According to him, the Palestinians in Israel are the "forgotten Palestinians," because they have lived and developed inside Israel, while internal Israeli politics, Palestinian politics, and regional and international interest focus on the core of the Palestinian problem – the future of the refugees and the Israeli occupation in the West Bank and Gaza Strip.

After a general presentation of models presented in previous works about developments among the Palestinian minority and its relationship with the majority and the state, Pappe proposed the term "Mukhabarat State" as an analytical framework for understanding the reciprocal relations between the Israeli state and its Palestinian citizens. The Mukhabarat State is a unique form of oppressive regime, in which the police, intelligence, and security forces are mobilized to maintain what the ruling group considers to be "quiet and order" in a way that serves its needs. This model, according to Pappe, is precisely that employed by Arab regimes to control their citizens. Thus Israel is just one more example of the autocratic Middle Eastern state that is a regular phenomenon in the Arab world, hiding behind a "mask of democracy."

Our Previous Contribution

In our previous studies about the Palestinians in Israel (for example, Ghanem and Mustafa, 2009a, 2011), we asserted that the main hurdle facing them is their lack of a collective status. This affects their situation and rights on both the group and individual levels. Clarifying and defining its status is the most important step towards defining the options available to a minority (including an indigenous minority) for cultivating a positive relationship with the state and with the majority (Kymlicka, 1995). In the case of the Palestinians in Israel, their rights and circumstances do not depend on citizenship, but on the polar relationship between their growing consciousness as a native minority and the intensified ethnicization of the colonial entity. Thus, the theoretical framework must be revised to accommodate the indigenous minority, the colonial framework, and the latter's relationship with the native population.

The Palestinians in Israel and their growing awareness of themselves as an Indigenous Minority

Sometimes, the term "minority" is used as a synonym for "national, ethnic, racial, and religious groups." According to the definition of the Subcommission for Human Rights and the Subcommission on Prevention of Discrimination and Protection of Minorities, a "minority" is a group that holds the citizenship of the state in which it lives, but whose unique ethnic, religious, and linguistic attributes differentiate it from the majority group. "Indigenous minority" is a new term, referring to a population that still resides in its own homeland, where immigrant groups have settled or founded a new state. Such a minority often becomes a political and numerical minority (Jamal, 2005, 2011).

The Palestinian minority in Israel meets most of the criteria to be considered indigenous (Kimmerling and Migdal, 1993), as enumerated by the United Nations Subcommission on Prevention of Discrimination and Protection of Minorities. These are: early presence; voluntary conservation of cultural uniqueness; self-definition as an indigenous people; and a refusal to be subjugated, trivialized, marginalized, expelled, or discriminated against by the hegemonic society. In addition, indigenousness emerges from the relationship between, the presence of a group of people as a society and their attachment to a specific area (Jamal, 2005, 2011).

Our main concern here is the ability of the indigenous minority to preserve its political, social, and cultural uniqueness and remain distinct from the hegemonic majority. International declarations have affirmed the rights of indigenous groups. For example, ILO Convention 169, concerning Indigenous and Tribal Peoples in Independent Countries, calls on governments to adopt measures for "promoting the full realization of the social, economic and cultural rights of these peoples with respect for their social and cultural identity, their customs and traditions and their institutions" (Article 2(2)). "No form of force

or coercion shall be used in violation of the human rights and fundamental freedoms of the peoples concerned" (Article 3(2)). "In applying
the provisions of this Convention, the social, cultural, religious and
spiritual values and practices of these peoples shall be recognized and
protected, and due account shall be taken of the nature of the problems
which face them both as groups and as individuals" (Article 5(a)).[8]
According to the UN Declaration on the Rights of Persons Belonging to National or Ethnic, Religious and Linguistic Minorities, "States
shall protect the existence and the national or ethnic, cultural, religious
and linguistic identity of minorities within their respective territories
and shall encourage conditions for the promotion of that identity."[9]

Thus indigenousness peoples are entitled to preserve their culture
and identity. They also have the right to reject policies that threaten
their identity and culture. These rights form the foundation for fair
relationships between the minorities of the world, especially indigenous ones, and the states in which they live (see Gurr, 1993).

The Ethnicization of Israel and the Palestinian Minority

The theoretical framework that views Israel as a colonial state triggered a lively debate in academia. According to the "colonial model,"
colonialism is the theoretical framework that best explains and analyzes the development of Israeli society from the first wave of Jewish
immigration to Palestine in 1881 until the present. Other researchers
consider its colonial character to be the key to understanding Israeli
society (Shafir and Peled, 2002), which carried out the "destruction of
another people" (see Ghanem and Mustafa, 2009a).

Three cases can help illustrate the relationship between the indigenous local community and the settler society. First: exterminating the
indigenous local population and settling in its place after gaining control of the area (e.g., the United States and Australia). Second: blending
the settler society with the indigenous population and creating one
society (South America). Third, which applies to the Israeli–Zionist
case: establishing a settler society alongside the local indigenous population, so that the region is divided between the two groups. The settler
society can be distinguished by its expansionist policies and gradual

---

[8] www.ilo.org/dyn/normlex/en/f?p=NORMLEXPUB:12100:0::NO::P12100_ILO_
CODE:C169.

[9] www.un.org/documents/ga/res/47/a47r135.htm. This declaration is based on
General Assembly Resolution 47/135 of December 1992.

confinement of the indigenous population (Kimmerling and Migdal 1993; Peled and Shafir, 2002).

When it comes to Zionism, separating the territory from the ideology is an intricate task, because the two exist in a symbiotic relationship. The linkage to settlement, control over an area, and its subsequent Judaization is the essence of Zionism, as a colonial settlement movement. Zionist ideology defined the instrument of settlement and its objectives. Thus understanding the ideology requires an explanation of the settlement practices. The Zionist project relied on a connection with the land, while the land was connected to the ideology. This gave Zionism the intellectual and political legitimacy it sought. The process of rescuing or redeeming the land is one of the three intellectual foundations on which Zionist thought relies. The second and third are working the land and building on the land. Taken together, these strategies complete the process of Judaization (Yiftachel and Ghanem, 2004).

The Judaization idea is far removed from the democratic system. Oren Yiftachel calls it "ethnocracy"; the ethnocratic regime is founded on a national project that imposes ethnic national hegemony on the domain through the processes of expansion and settlement. In the case of Zionism, the Judaization of the domain and the land produced an ethnocratic regime. Spatial control is an important pillar of the ethnocratic regime. Its goal is the "creation of a new ethno-political geography." The process of "ethnicizing" a disputed region evolves in the following stages: first, separation of settlements is used to propagate the majority's control of the land. The minority is labeled a threat to the ethnic control of land. This is followed by land planning, which enables the ethnic control of the land. Finally, there is structural discrimination against the minority, denying it access to development projects and to the distribution of resources (ibid.).

Israel is presented by Israeli and Western academia as a state founded in response to the Jewish (Zionist) nationalist call for self-determination. This view was supported by the international community through the United Nations Partition Plan and direct support from various countries. It is also maintained by public opinion and the political elite in Israel and even by some Palestinian elites there. Furthermore, the Israeli regime is often presented as a stable democracy that embodies the main elements of Western political democracy. However, it is possible to analyze these main components using theories developed in the West to help understand state-building processes and the dynamics that underlie them (see Yakobson and Rubenstein, 2003).

For another group of scholars, Israel was founded on the principles of colonialism and has maintained a bi-ethnic system, one that favors the interests of the founding ethnic group. Among those scholars are Nakhleh (1979) and Zureik (1979), who have published a series of studies to demonstrate that Israel is a typical manifestation of classic colonialism. They add that internal contradictions in Israel are typical of colonial experiences elsewhere. Still another group of scholars has studied the stratification of Israeli society and its relationship to ethnic groups in the state. Ghanem argued that the Israeli system has the characteristics of the tyranny of the majority. Later, Yiftachel developed an alternative theoretical model of Israel's ethnocratic nature and other cases around the globe (Yiftachel, 2006a; Yiftachel and Ghanem, 2004).

The starting point of our previous studies of the relationship between Israel and the indigenous population in Palestine is based on several principles (see Ghanem and Mustafa, 2011). First, our analysis is comprehensive and discusses the Palestinian case in Israel while looking at Israel as a whole, including Jews and Palestinians. Second, our assumption is that historical processes are determined by interests, values, and social criteria. Third, it is the reality on the ground, and not the intentions of political leaders or the documented ideas of the elite in the state, that determines the nature of analysis.

The two claims are linked by two historical processes. One, Israel emerged as a colonial settler society aiming to displace the indigenous population and replace it with Jewish and non-Jewish immigrants. This colonial settler enterprise removes the indigenous population from its land. Two, Israel has been shaped and is still in the process of shaping itself as an ethnic society in which the state maintains Jewish ethnic superiority. Hence the claim that the regime in Israel is based on the contradictions and balance between the two elements, Jewish and democratic (see Smooha, 1990) has no basis in reality. In fact, the state promotes the character and content of its ethnic Jewish nature. Understanding what happened to Palestinians in Israel is associated with our understanding of how the Palestinians in general are treated under the colonial system. This model analyzes the Zionist movement as both an entity and as an ideology that has and continues to implement colonial methods against its own citizens.

The system in which the Palestinians in Israel found themselves has led to their marginalization. The Israeli political apparatus has distanced the Palestinians from both decision-making and the distribution of national resources (see Ghanem, 1998; Ghanem and Mustafa, 2011). However, in light of changes that began in the late 1990s and peaked during the Al-Aqsa Intifada in October 2000, Palestinians have begun searching for alternative political means and a new discourse to end their decades-long ignition stage and move towards the launching stage in pursuit of a unified national and group agenda and new methods of political activism that can redefine the concept of citizenship in Israel. This book explains the new discourse and politics of the Palestinians in Israel in the last two decades.

The Analytical Framework: The Palestinians in Israel and the "Politics of Faith"

The term "politics of faith," in contrast to the "politics of skepticism," was introduced by Michael Oakeshott in his brilliant book, *The Politics of Faith and the Politics of Skepticism* (1996). Oakeshott, who was the chair of the Department of Government at the London School of Economics, is considered to be one of the most important philosophers of the twentieth century.[10] In contrast to "faith" as a religious concept, Oakeshott uses it to describe a political and manmade design for the sake of human wealth and a "perfect" life. In his words,

Human perfection is to be achieved by human efforts, and confidence in the evanescence of imperfection springs here from faith in human power and not trust in divine providence. We may, perhaps, be permitted to encourage ourselves by believing that our efforts have the approval and even the support of providence, but we are to understand that the achievement of perfection depends upon our own unrelaxed efforts, and that if those efforts are unrelaxed, perfection will appear. (Oakeshott, 1996: 23)

Politics in this context is the will of the leaders to achieve the maximum for their followers and community, thanks to their faith in their own "human capabilities" and their desire to perfect life on earth. This is a positive description of politics at variance with the politics of "skepticism" that is suspicious of leaders' intentions and their ability to achieve the maximum for the community and citizens (Oakeshott, 1996: 30).

---

[10] See www.newstatesman.com/politics/2014/04/michael-oakeshott-conservative-thinker-who-went-beyond-politics (accessed April 4, 2017).

The Politics of Faith is the desire to achieve the collective goals of society, rather than the individual interests; the stakes are the interest of the community. Leaders' conduct should be measured by their achievements for their communities and the depth of the "perfection" they provide the community. To quote Oakeshott again:

One of the characteristics assumptions … of the politics of faith is that human power is sufficient, or may become sufficient, to produce salvation. A second assumption is that the word "perfection" (and its synonyms) denotes a single, comprehensive condition of human circumstances. This condition may not be able to premeditate it with any great degree of distinctness, but we can at least discern its general outline; it is the goal of political activity, and there is no alternative to it. Consequently, this style of politics requires a double confidence: the conviction that the necessary power is available or can be generated, and the conviction that, even if we do not know what constitutes perfection, at least we know the road that leads to it … Confidence that we are on the right road may be acquired in various ways. It may be a visionary certainty, or, alternatively, it may be the fruit of research, reflection, and argument. In the politics of faith, political decision and enterprise may be understood as a response to an inspired perception of what the common good is. (Oakeshott, 1996: 26–27)

According to Oakeshott, achieving the political, social, and economic goals depends on the "human efforts, and confidence … and faith in human power" (ibid., 23, 114). This "Politics of Faith" is related to three basic principles. First, the belief that "man is redeemable in history"; i.e., perfection is a political option on earth, and not only in the next life, in Heaven, as religions promise. Second, achieving perfection on earth depends on "human circumstances" that are created by humans"; i.e., the ability to organize human capabilities and efforts in order to be able to act for the sake of human interests and perfection. Third, achieving the goals and perfection on earth is the task and duty of the leaders (and political institutions), which should act to organize the resources and prioritize the goals in a feasible action plan that make use of the community's strong points (ibid., 23–25). In Oakeshott's words,

clearly, it – the politics of faith – to this style of politics to welcome power rather than to be embarrassed by it; and no quantity of power will be considered excessive. Indeed, to brood over every activity, to keep every enterprise in line, not to be behindhand in expressing its approval of every undertaking, and, in short, to concentrate all the power and resources of the community upon the project of perfection, making certain that none is unexploited or wasted. (ibid., 28–29)

In the context of the politics of dominated groups – and minorities – in divided societies, the "Politics of Faith" is related to minorities' ability to challenge the dominant groups and majority. According to Ghanem (2012), this minority politics depends on several variables that can lead a minority to consolidate and intensify its ability to achieve its needs and demands, of which the three most critical are the demographic and territorial factor, the level of cohesion among the minority, and the performance of its leadership.

The first is a two-pronged factor, namely, the minority's territorial concentration and demographic weight in the country. To address the latter first, the greater the minority's relative size as compared to the majority, the greater its ability to exert pressure on the political system to achieve its goals. Demographic weight helps minorities participate in the political process and can have some influence on the course of events. It is difficult for a minority to play an active role in modifying its situation if it represents only a small percentage of the population; but when the minority's share of the population enters double digits, its voice begins to be heard and it amasses increasing influence.

The geographical factor, too, is important. If the minority is scattered throughout the country, its ability to mobilize for effective political action is impaired. Indeed, territorial concentration has a significant impact on both the minority's and the majority's sense of their own power. The case of Quebec is a classic example in which demographic and geographic factors combined to help Canada's Francophone minority gain a measure of institutional autonomy.

A second factor is the minority's internal cohesion – that is, its ability to function as a unified ethnic or national group, despite differences in its members' views and ideas. A united minority has a common platform and a shared vision of its future role in the state or its position vis-à-vis the majority. Minorities in general are subject to a "divide and conquer" approach, in which the regime aims to split the minority in order to weaken its bargaining power (Lustick, 1980). Whether this strategy succeeds depends on structural factors associated with the minority, such as ideological rifts, geographic or ethnic affiliations, and so on. The state may also try to weaken the local leadership and divert it from the collective national objectives to rivalries and political dissension. This deprives the minority of the ability to present a unified front and distracts it from the struggle towards a clear goal. The minority's internal cohesion is also affected by whether it has collective national institutions that can regulate internal conflicts and forge a shared political vision and platform.

Finally, and crucially, there is the human factor – that is, the nature and functional ability of the minority's (and the majority's) leadership. It is the leadership of the minority – whether a single individual or a group – that must devise and implement its strategy. Both the nature of the minority's demands and the manner and timing of their presentation are key factors that depend on the minority's political leadership and how well it functions. A minority will make no gains if its political leadership is dysfunctional. An effective national leadership is therefore at least as important as a shared collective vision.

Our main argument in this work builds on the "Politics of Faith" as introduced by Oakeshott. The political development of the Palestinians in Israel reflects a basic "faith" in this community's ability to work in an organized fashion in order to achieve its collective interests. We will show that the three basic principles of Oakeshott's "Politics of Faith" are present in the political activity initiated by the Palestinian leadership in Israel: a basic confidence in their ability to achieve positive change for their community; organized and coordinated efforts to maximize the use of their human resources; and prioritization of their goals and interests.

In this book we argue that the demographic and social transformations of the Palestinians in Israel have bolstered their self-confidence. This heightened self-confidence is the basis for important changes in cultural and social life as well as political activity. For example, the desire and ability to create a separate economy is greater than ever in Arab towns and cities. In sum, Palestinian society today is much stronger than ever, with a clear social, political, and cultural structure; it is an important element in Israel's future and the future of the Israeli–Palestinian encounter. These developments – and many others to be presented in the book – have created the foundation of the "Politics of Faith" and empowerment among the Palestinians in Israel.

In the following chapters we will present and analyze the "pillars" of the politics of faith and empowerment. The emergence of the "Politics of Faith" among the Palestinians in Israel was accompanied by a set of new forms and strategies for political action. This includes the consolidation of the main pillars of transformative politics: (1) the consolidation of the political demands of the Palestinian minority in Israel, including challenging the Jewish hegemony; (2) the emergence of a new and diverse generation of political leadership; (3) the Palestinians' empowerment in Israeli civil society; (4) the politicization of Islamic activism in Israel; (5) the publication of the Future Vision document, as a manifestation of collective identity politics; and (6) the establishment of the Joint List as a new stage in the consolidation of collective political action among the Palestinians in Israel. Each pillar is the subject of one chapter of this book.

1 The Political Aspirations and Demands of the Palestinian Minority in Israel after Oslo: Challenging the "Hegemonic Ethnocracy"

The situation of the Palestinian minority in Israel is that of a marginal minority in an ethnic hegemonic state (see Peleg, 2007). That is to say that Israel has a strong commitment to procedural democracy but preserves the ethnic hegemony of the majority that systematically dominates the minority groups. In this system, the majority controls the various organs and branches of government and uses its power to prevent the minority from attaining personal or collective equality. Public agencies give primacy to ethnic affiliation over citizenship as the criterion for dealing with citizens and their rights, and display favoritism for one group and its members over the other groups that make up society. Interest in this type of state has increased recently within the social sciences. Different sources refer to these states in various ways: Smooha (1990, 1998, 2004) uses the term "ethnic democracy"; Yiftachel (1997, 2000, 2006a) refers to them as "ethnocracies"; Rouhana (1997) writes "exclusive ethnic state"; and Peleg (2007) uses "hegemonic state." The literature is replete with examples of minorities that live in "hegemonic states" where the dominant group has offered "partial democracy" to the minority while upholding its own superiority and sovereignty.

The Palestinians' status worsened as a direct result of the 1948 war. The main difference between the Palestinians in Israel and Palestinians elsewhere is that the former stayed on their land and became Israeli citizens. Although some were able to keep their land, the Israeli government and its various security branches considered them an "enemy," a security threat and a strategic threat. Israel took harsh measures to deter, control, and subdue them.

The aspirations of the Palestinians in Israel range from "integration" within the state to full autonomy as a national minority. Minorities in similar situations can be found in other "ethnic hegemony" systems,

29

such as Estonia, Latvia, Lithuania, Romania, Turkey, Malaysia, Macedonia until the Ohrid Agreement of 2001, and Northern Ireland until the Belfast Agreement in 1998.

A hallmark of the "ethnic hegemony" system is its ability to maintain the dominance of the leading ethno-national group while excluding ethnic or national minorities.

An ethnic hegemony conducts a continuous "ethnic project" that attempts to construct an informal public image of separate and unequal groups. This image is diffused into most societal arenas (public culture, politics, academia, the economy), causing long-term reproduction of ethno-class inequalities. However, the Hegemonic State's self-representation as democratic creates structural tensions, because it requires the state to go beyond lip service and to grant minorities some (though less than equal) formal political powers. The cracks and crevices between the overt claim of democracy and the denial of equality to the minority fans the tensions and conflicts typical of ethnic hegemonic regimes (see Ghanem, 1998; Mann, 1999).

The status of the minority in the hegemonic state is shaped by reciprocal and confrontational relationships. The former is fashioned by the status of the majority and its aspiration to dominate, while the latter refers to the minority and its aspirations, demands, and mobilization (for more, see Gurr, 1993; Horowitz, 1985; Kymlicka, 1995; Lijphart, 1977, 1984, 1999, 2002). Understanding the minority's aspirations concerning its future status is the key to understanding the reaction of the state and majority and the nature of relations between the groups. The minority's aspirations appear in two different forms. The first is separation or irredentism. This method has been attempted in some conflicts or situations in which societies were divided among groups. Geographic or regional division can produce equality between societies. In these circumstances, the groups in conflict (usually violent) have the choice of struggle with external parties or geographic division into two political entities, where each entity retains the vast majority of the members of its group. This method ensures equality between the groups by allowing each group to manage its own political system through its representatives (see Smooha and Hanf, 1992). One can point to positive results of this model, such as the division of Cyprus along ethno-religious lines, the division of India along religious lines, with a large Muslim minority remaining, or the partition of the former

Yugoslavia on ethno-religious lines. This model, however, differs from the solutions aimed at resolving ethnic problems in a shared territory.

The second form of minority aspirations aims to actualize equality among the groups within the state by abolishing the hegemony of one group and its monopoly on state authority, giving full equality to all groups in the state as part of a "consociational arrangement." In this situation, the state becomes neutral in the competition between the groups. This option can be actualized in two ways. The first is establishing a federation or a confederation between the groups, where representatives of the groups agree to the equal distribution of the centers of power, symbols, budgets, and social, cultural, and monetary rewards among the groups. The distribution can be based on grouping, ratio, or equity, where the numbers and powers of the various groups are taken into consideration. This model was implemented in Cyprus (until 1963) and is currently employed in Belgium, Switzerland, Lebanon, Northern Ireland since the Belfast Agreement in 1998 (see Lijphart, 1977, 2002; O'Leary, 2002), and in Macedonia since the Ohrid agreement in 2001.

Actualizing the consociational option depends on consensual agreements stemming from an agreed upon formula about the system's structure and bureaucracies. The various groups continue to use their respective languages and gain legitimacy in the process. They are supported by the state in developing their own cultures and managing their own affairs, including religious identity and social affairs. Similarly, the groups agree to share the centers of power in the state (in government, local institutions, mass communication, etc.) in relative forms (see Gurr, 1993; Kymlicka, 1995).

This second possibility completely abolishes one group's hegemony and exclusive control of the state and its political apparatus by establishing a liberal democratic system. This system views the individual as an independent entity based on his or her status as a citizen, and not as a member of a particular group. In a liberal democracy, such as the United States, equal citizens compete, without reference to their ethnic affiliation, to define the "public interest" of the state. In a consensual democracy such as Belgium, tensions may rise between groups, not between individuals as citizens, but as affiliates of a certain group, regarding issues that define the public interest (see Smooha, 1990).

Israel's treatment of the Palestinian minority after 1948 is typical of a hegemonic ethnocratic state. The system in which the Palestinians in Israel found themselves led to their marginalization. At the core of this system, with its goal of perfecting control over its Palestinian citizens, is the discourse of ethnic control, democracy, and equality. Similarly, the Israeli political apparatus has sought to distance the Palestinians from both decision-making and the distribution of national resources. In light of several few changes that began in the late 1990s and peaked during the last two decades, the Palestinians in Israel are searching for alternative political means and a new discourse that can empower them to end their marginality. The essence of their demand is that the Israeli hegemonic system be transformed into one with collective equal rights and binationalism. This will be shown below as we examine the public demands by the Palestinians in Israel in the post-Oslo period.

How are Aspirations Consolidated? Theoretical Frameworks for the Palestinians in Israel

Modernization theory has historically been an analytical framework for explaining the political transformation of traditional societies. Here "modernization" refers to change processes in the direction of increased westernization of various facets of a society (Bendix, 1969; Binder, 1964; Deutsch, 1953; Deutsch and Foltz, 1963; Emerson, 1960). As stated in the Introduction, the term "Modernization Theory" was used by many Israeli scholars to describe the political and social transformations among the Palestinian minority.

The "modernization model" appears in the works of Cohen (1990), Landau (1993), Peres and Yuval Davis (1968, 1969), and Rekhess (1985, 1986, 1989), all of whom believe that the Palestinian minority in Israel underwent rapid modernization. That hypothesis, they explain, is supported by the rise in the standard of living and educational level, which leads in turn to higher expectations. Palestinian society evaluates its status according to the following criteria: the extent of development and the Jewish majority's degree of accomplishment in the state; the existence of gaps between the two groups in various areas, including the under-industrialization of the Palestinian village, the availability of housing for young couples, the disproportionate allocation of water for agriculture, and the lack of assimilation and immersion in the

Israeli economy. These factors and others have led to depression and bitterness among the Palestinians in Israel, and these feelings have pushed them towards radical positions and politics.

Here we present an inclusive approach in order to achieve a comprehensive understanding of the political aspirations of the Palestinians in Israel and of similar minority groups in hegemonic ethnic states. Our main argument is that hegemonic ethnic states allow minorities to experience modernization as individuals but employ group to control to prevent any significant level of collective modernization. The majority and the state employ group control and internal colonialist methods in order to keep the minority in its inferior status. We follow Rueschemeyer's (1976) model of "partial modernization," which he defines as the adoption of some modern norms and values along with the survival of less modern norms and values in the same society (ibid., 757). his is the type of modernization experienced by societies that advance in some aspects and areas while preserving the old character of others. Social and cultural complications can surface as by-products of traditional societies' impulse towards modernity, as well as of the interference in the modernization process by hegemonic factors, such as colonial and other regimes, which want to divert development in a direction that preserves and guarantees their own interests. Some religious and social values, too, may impede full modernization (ibid., 760–765).

In hegemonic states, minorities are allowed to modernize on the individual level but are denied collective modernization, control over their own affairs, and a proper share of power at the state level. This is especially true when the state is a colonial entity that was created against the will of the indigenous group and that employs various techniques of control in order to prevent the minority from achieving collective control over its internal development, thereby ensuring that the minority remains subjugated to the settler majority.

The aspiration and demands of the minority in such hegemonic states derive from their inferior collective status and focus on the basic demand to modify its collective status. The group's demands range from secession to equality and power-sharing. There are several examples of minority groups that preferred the latter option, including the Francophones in Canada, the Catholics in Northern Ireland, the Albanians in Macedonia, the Germans in South Tyrol (Italy), and the Palestinians in Israel.

Table 1.1 *Which of the following best describes your identity? (Percentage of respondents)*

	1994 survey	2001 survey	2008 survey
Arab	7.4	6.4	5.5
Palestinian Arab	9.5	17.5	17.4
Israeli Arab	38.4	21.8	17.6
Israeli	7.8	6.0	3
Israeli Palestinian	8.7	9.7	2
A Palestinian in Israel or a Palestinian Arab in Israel	27.4	36.2	40.4
Palestinian	0.8	2.5	3.2

Individual Demands vs. a Collective Orientation among the Palestinians in Israel

This section is based on an analysis of three surveys that have been conducted among the Palestinian citizens of Israel since 1994 (in 1994, 2001, and 2008) (see Table 1.1).[1] Their main purpose was to determine the current and future political orientation of the Palestinian citizens of Israel. The findings were clear: a large majority of the Palestinian citizens of Israel recognize the State of Israel and its right to exist. In the 1994 survey, an overwhelming majority of the Palestinians in Israel (93.3%) accepted the country's Israel without reservations or with certain reservations. In the 2001 survey, when asked whether they recognized the right of the state to exist, 50.7% of the respondents replied in the affirmative ("yes"), 33.7% replied "yes with reservations," and the rest (15.6%) answered in the negative ("no" or "absolutely not"). That is, a vast majority of the Palestinians in Israel recognize the state's right to exist and accept their status as Israeli citizens.

A well-known fact that does not require corroboration is that most of the Palestinian citizens of Israel support resolving the Palestinian

---

[1] The surveys were a based on a random sample taken from the voter registration lists. In 1994 a total of 768 participants were interviewed, in 2001 a total of 1,202, and in 2008, 500 persons were interviewed. All respondents, aged 18+, were interviewed anonymously, face-to-face, in their own homes.

problem, the core of the Arab–Israeli dispute, by creating a Palestinian state alongside Israel. This is reinforced by the answers to many questions on all the surveys. In the 1994 survey, which investigated support for the establishment of a Palestinian state in the West Bank and Gaza Strip, alongside Israel, 75.1% responded in the affirmative, 18.6% responded affirmatively but with certain conditions, and only 6.2% responded in the negative.

Responses to questions that relate to identity may also be evidence of recognition or non-recognition of Israel and of whether the Palestinians in Israel feel they are its citizens. When Palestinian citizens of Israel were asked to select the option that best describes their individual identity, a majority selected one that includes "Israel" or "Israeli" in some fashion: 82.3% in the 1995 survey, 73.7% in the 2001 survey and 83% in the 2008 survey.

Here we will steer clear of the question of the individual and collective identity of the Palestinian citizens of Israel and the problematic nature of this definition (see Rouhana, 1993, 1997). Nevertheless, the very choice of definitions that combine the two elements, Palestinian and Israeli, and the perception of the term "Israeli" as representing the Arab citizens attest to an acceptance of reality and recognition of Israel's existence. This position is further evidence that the Palestinians in Israel recognize the state and see themselves as its citizens, today and in the future. A comparison of the data from the three surveys indicates that there has been a decline in the number of Palestinians in Israel who see themselves as Israeli without a Palestinian component as well, along with an increase in the percentage of those who emphasize the Palestinian component of their personal identity. This is evidence of a sharp rise in their Palestinian identity and increasing estrangement from Israeli elements that have not given them an appropriate national or civic voice.

Based on the assumption that members of the Palestinian minority will continue to live as Israeli citizens in the future, we continue with data on their level of satisfaction, on both the individual and collective levels.

The Living Conditions of the Palestinian Citizens of Israel, on the Individual Level

The modernization process experienced by the Palestinian citizens of Israel since 1948 has involved every aspect of their lives and has had a far-reaching influence on various domains relevant to their lives as individuals: a drop in the fertility rate; a significant positive change in their attitude about the importance of education for their future prospects; a sharp rise in their educational level (Al-Haj, 1995); a transition from an agrarian economy to one based on modern sectors such as construction and industry (Haider, 1991a, 1991b); a positive change in the type and quality of housing; a change in the status of the individual vis-à-vis the clan as a reference group (Al-Haj, 1986); an improvement in the functioning of the local authorities and the services they provide to citizens (Al-Haj and Rosenfeld, 1990; Ghanem and Mustafa, 2009a); and an improvement in Jewish–Arab relations in the country, with regard to feelings and personal relations (Smooha, 1992, 2005). In general, there is no doubt that there has been a rise in the standard of living, including a decrease in housing density, as a result of the decline in the birthrate.

On a formal level, modernization among the Palestinian citizens of Israel approximates that in Western societies, including the Jewish sector in Israel. Here the important question relates to the state of individual modernization. The 1994 survey sought to illuminate a number of areas associated with this, such as belief in luck, belief in the existence of hidden beneficent or malignant forces, attitudes about allowing children freedom of choice, and so on. The picture on this level proved to be quite different than what might have been expected. A large fraction of the Palestinian citizens of Israel (19.1%) associated an incident that affected them negatively with bad luck rather than with carelessness (29.1% with carelessness, 51.8% with both bad luck and carelessness). A significant number (28.3%) believed in the existence of occult forces that can help or harm them; a majority (54.8%) also believed that prayer and requests to God can help them in their private lives. These figures, which indicate that here the picture is more complex, point to a selective and incomplete change. When it comes to partnership between spouses in running the house or the freedom for children to manage their own affairs the picture is more positive, though not significantly different: about 19.1% of respondents said that in their houses the husband or father made all decisions about the future of the family; 24.8% said that parents should decide their children's future. The picture about belief in a person's ability to shape his or her own future and his or her surroundings is also complex. In that same 1994 survey, respondents were asked a series of questions aimed at investigating belief in their ability to modify or affect certain areas of their lives. Respondents said that many areas were beyond their control or that they had no significant ability to change them.

The surveys focused on the extent to which the Palestinian citizens of Israel are satisfied with their personal situation in four main areas: education, standard of living, employment, and municipal services. Respondents were asked to answer with: very satisfied, satisfied, somewhat satisfied, or dissatisfied, plus the option of noting that the question is not relevant (for example, questions about a spouse's level of education for unmarried or divorced respondents). After accounting for this option, the distribution of the remaining responses indicates that the Palestinian citizens of Israel are generally satisfied with their own situations and those of their families. Only a minority is totally dissatisfied with their children's education (8.1% in 1994 and 15% in 2008). A minority is dissatisfied with their family's standard of living (17.8% in 1994 and 14.5% in 2008) or their employment (11.8% in 1994 and 16.2% in 2008). In general it can be concluded that satisfaction with the areas of life relevant to individual development is high, especially by comparison to satisfaction with the collective situation of Palestinians in Israel, as we shall see below.

The Collective/Group Situation of the Palestinian Citizens in Israel

Here we shall sketch out the Palestinian citizens' satisfaction with their collective attainments: to what extent are they satisfied with their educational level as a group? To what extent are they satisfied with social issues such as the status of women and relations among the religious communities in their society? We will also consider topics such as equality, integration, the behavior of local authorities, the countrywide Arab leadership, the ability to influence the future and decisions at the national level, participation in government, and the like.

Respondents were presented with a series of questions concerning the situation of the Palestinian citizens of Israel and asked to answer with: dissatisfied, dissatisfied and desire improvements, satisfied but desire improvements, and very satisfied. In all categories, most respondents were dissatisfied or dissatisfied and desired improvements (see Table 1.2). In general, the Palestinian citizens of Israel are dissatisfied with the living conditions of their group in every sphere presented, as

Table 1.2 *Palestinians who indicated that they are*
"dissatisfied" and "dissatisfied and want improvements"
in selected areas relating to the collective level
(Percentage of respondents)

	2001 survey	2008 survey
Level of education	66.3	73.7
Status of Arab women in Israel	59.7	65.7
Integration of Palestinians into senior positions in Israel	79.5	80.6
Ability to influence the Israeli government	83.1	88
Jewish–Arab relations	71.0	70.7
Countrywide Arab leadership	60.4	84.3
Arab political organization	68.7	89.6

well as with their collective situation and standing; the dissatisfaction spans all internal arenas crucial to the advancement of the Palestinian citizens of Israel as a whole.

The Palestinian citizens of Israel attach decisive importance to areas such as equality with the Jews, proportional parity with Jews in government employment, increased budgets and improved administration for Arab local authorities in Israel, expansion of the powers granted to these local authorities, the ability to plan their own future, and an improvement in official policy towards them (see Ghanem, 1996, 2001). The Palestinians in Israel are not satisfied with their collective situation in these domains, nor in others presented in Table 1.2. The extremely low level of satisfaction is alarming. This correlates with another distinction drawn by the respondents: when asked to rank the degree of disparity or inequality between Jews and Palestinians in Israel in domains related to the state and influence on its organs, most Palestinians said that there are large and even huge gaps between them and the Jews in these domains (see Table 1.3).

An analysis of the respondents' situation in various domains (defined as important by the respondents themselves) and their perception of gaps in ability, influence, and the benefits extended to citizens – that is, individual perceptions of the extent of the group's collective modernization – indicates that the Palestinians in Israel see their situation as a

Table 1.3 *Perception of the disparity between Jews and Palestinians in Israel in key domains (2001 survey) (Percentage of respondents)*

	Large gap	Moderate gap	Small gap	No gap
Allocation of financial resources	81.8	14.2	2.9	1.1
Definition of the character of the state	76.4	17.2	3.7	2.7
Definition of the objectives of the state	75.7	17.9	4.2	2.2

group as substantially different from that of the Jews in all the areas presented. They see their group status in Israel as generally worse and perceive radical disparities of power and rewards as compared to the Jews. It goes without saying that the Palestinians in Israel are not happy with this situation.

In summary, the survey data indicate that an overwhelming majority of the Palestinian citizens of Israel are satisfied with their level of individual advancement, that is, the individual and personal modernization they have achieved. On the other hand, they are not happy with the progress made by their group with regard to their conditions and achievements, the ability to influence their own future, make decisions, integrate on the countrywide level, and attain an appropriate collective status.

Aspirations at the Collective Level among the Palestinians in Israel

The Palestinians in Israel want equality with the Jewish majority. Most respondents hold that this must be full equality (see Table 1.4). This was emphasized when respondents were presented with categories related to disparities between Jews and Palestinians in Israel: the allocation of financial resources and the definition of the nature and objectives of the state (see Tables 1.5 and 1.6).

The Palestinian citizens of Israel are not satisfied with their collective situation and demand that the state serve them on an equal footing with the Jews, provide them with equal resources, ensure that their group receives equal public services, allocate civil-service jobs fairly to members of their group, permit them full partnership in government and governing coalitions, and grant them parity in determining the

Table 1.4 *Support for "full equality" in key areas*
(2001 and 2008 surveys) (Percentage of respondents)

	2001 survey	2008 survey
Allocation of financial resources	78.7	74.5
Definition of the character of the state	63.9	60
Definition of the objectives of the state	68.2	62.4

nature and objectives of the state. In their eyes the state must serve both groups, the Jews and the Palestinian in Israel, equally. In practice they demand that the state be binational rather than one that favors one group (the Jews) over all others. All of these are reflected in a demand to change the character of the state (see Ghanem, 2001a).

Direct questions about the nature of the state indicate that the Palestinian citizens of Israel are opposed to its Jewish–Zionist character, which is expressed by a clear preference for Jews in all areas related to the state, its future, society, and its citizens in general. Respondents are aware that Israel serves primarily the Jews rather than all its citizens; in the 2001 survey, only 17.3% of the Palestinians in Israel believed that "an Arab can live as an equal citizen in the State in Israel as a Jewish–Zionist state and identify with it." Another 31.1% answered that this is possible; the balance (51.5%) did not believe the statement was true. In 2008, 94.4% of the respondents agreed that "Jewish–Zionist state" means discrimination in favor of the Jews.

What kind of equality are the Palestinians in Israel seeking? In societies that are split on an ethnic, religious, national, or other basis it is possible to distinguish many arrangements (or lack thereof) that provide a legal and institutionalized framework (or sometimes an abstract and non-institutionalized framework) for the status of the various groups, and which guarantee the stability of such societies. Although in practice there is no end to such possibilities, we can distinguish in general three types of arrangements: irredentism and secession, leading to independence or annexation by another country; cultural, political, or territorial autonomy and the institution of a shared binational framework; and integration and assimilation in a civil nation and institution of a liberal civil state.

Table 1.5 *Demands that should be implemented according to the Palestinian citizens of Israel. Each interviewee was asked to state, for each category, whether he/she agrees or disagrees with it and the prospects of its implementation (2008 survey)*

	I agree and work should start immediately to implement this demand	I agree, but this is a demand that can be partially implemented right now	I agree but this is a demand that cannot be implemented right now	I do not agree
Israel should stop being a Jewish state and become a state for two peoples	57.9	21.3	16.3	4.5
Arabic language should be in use just as Hebrew	71.4	19.1	8.3	1.2
Arab citizens should run their cultural, religious, and educational affairs themselves	62.9	20.7	9.7	6.7
The law should ensure the right of the Palestinians in Israel to suitable representation in all state institutions	69.3	21.5	7.5	1.6
The law should ensure the right of the Palestinians in Israel to a proportional share of the state budget	68	22.5	8.3	1.2
The state should give the Palestinians in Israel suitable representation in its symbols, flag, and national anthem	48.5	19.7	21.5	10.3
The state must ask for the consent of the Arab leadership when legislating or crafting any rules related to them	54.6	25.2	13.8	6.5
The state should abrogate the special status given to non-Israeli Jewish organizations such as the Jewish Agency and the Jewish National Fund	40.3	19.4	29.4	10.9

Table 1.6 *Key demands by Palestinian citizens of Israel that are considered to be important to their future (2001 and 2008 surveys) (Percentage of respondents)*

	2001	2008
Direct countrywide elections for the Supreme Monitoring Committee	76.4	78.8
Official recognition of the Supreme Monitoring Committee as representative of the Palestinians in Israel	80.9	80.9
Full and equal integration of Palestinians in Israel in government offices	92.9	91.3

An analysis of their views indicates that the Palestinian citizens of Israel are interested in instituting a model of consociational democracy/power-sharing regime, with clear liberal elements. At first sight this arrangement seems unrealistic, because it combines elements of two different models for solving the problems of minorities. However, recent theoretical literature confirms that it is feasible on both the theoretical level and in daily life (see Gurr, 1993; Horowitz, 1985; Kymlicka, 1995; Lijphart, 1977, 1984, 2002). In practice, any binational option necessarily includes irrevocable liberal elements.

The changes that the Palestinians in Israel desire for their group can be divided into two dimensions: integration into the state and its institutions on an equal footing with the Jews (including the allocation of budgets, jobs, equal capacity to express their views and influence government decision-making and political processes); and institutional autonomy for their group. Their answers emphasize the importance they ascribe to state recognition of their group as a national minority and to areas that reflect their aspiration for autonomy within the state. For example, educational autonomy as reflected by the establishment of an Arab university, independent Arab management of the Arab school system and Arab cultural life (buildings, workers, curricula, and the like), and the establishment of a series of institutions expressly for Palestinians in Israel as a means to express the essence of their institutional autonomy, such as a national body that will represent them as a collective. Respondents also emphasize the importance of direct elections for the Supreme Monitoring Committee, even though most Palestinian citizens of Israel are not happy with its functioning. In 2001, only a minority (42.6%) expressed great or very great satisfaction with its performance; in 2008 the level of satisfaction dropped dramatically, to only 16.1%. Similar findings that confirm the aspirations of the Palestinians in Israel for cultural and educational autonomy were reported by Smooha in his earlier surveys of 1976, 1980, 1985, and 1988 (see Smooha, 1992).

In the 2008 survey, the interviewees were asked whether demands for change should be expressed immediately or if it could be postponed until the time is ripe; in almost every area, the public overwhelmingly preferred that the leadership work to achieve the demands immediately (see Table 1.5).

The data indicate that most Palestinian citizens of Israel are not satisfied with their collective status and aspire to integrate into the state and its institutions. At the same time, however, they also want institutional autonomy – as part of the state and Israeli citizenship – in addition to equality with the Jewish majority. In practice, such autonomy within the state would be a type of binationalism that resolves the co-presence of Jews and Palestinians in Israel.

What Explains the Demand for Collective Equality and Binationalism?

What has caused the awakening of demand for collective equality in general and binationalism in particular among the Palestinians in Israel? We differentiate factors concerning the overall situation and status of the Palestinians in Israel from those that arose or were at least intensified over the past few years because of changes in their status and in the Israeli–Palestinian conflict, as well as developments affecting the entire country.

Groups in situations similar to that of the Palestinians in Israel demand binationalism for several reasons, three of which are discussed below.

First, *the Palestinians in Israel are a distinct group*. The literature defines them as a "national minority," that is, a national group that shares a state with another, dominant national group for various historical reasons: annexation, the disintegration of states, and in certain cases historic agreements between two or more national groups. The national minority group comprises people who have a common past, culture, and language. National minorities are groups that are not alien to the geographic, historical, and cultural space of the countries in which they live. In most cases, they demand integration in the country even if – in certain cases – they aspire to maintain their cultural connection with their mother group, which may be the ruling group in another country. They also continue to perceive themselves as entitled to self-determination within the country in which they live.

Self-determination has two principal forms: *limited*, epitomized in a demand for the right to self-government; and *extensive*, embodied in special representation rights and collective rights. National groups whose ethos resembles that of the Palestinians include the French speakers in Canada and the Kurds in Iraq.

One key result of the status of Palestinians in Israel, as part of the Palestinian people on the one hand and citizens of Israel on the other, is their development as a group that is differentiated in many respects from the two groups that surround it: Palestinians outside Israel and Israeli Jews. All identity studies of this group, published by Smooha, Rouhana, and others, note this special ethos – with varying emphases – and the development of the Palestinians in Israel as a special group at several levels of identity: social, cultural, official, legal, emotional, and the like. Essentially, the group developed a unique consciousness, living conditions, and aspirations for the future that distinguish it from the other groups.

The status of the Palestinians in Israel as a distinct group undermines the basis of the response by many Israelis to the group's demand for binationalism, namely, that the Palestinians are demanding a state and a half: one state in the West Bank and Gaza Strip and half of the State of Israel.

If we accept that the Palestinians in Israel are distinct from other Palestinians, it becomes clear that the Palestinian state is not their country. In this sense, Israel and only Israel is their state and their right to self-determination and to collective self-expression can be realized in Israel but not elsewhere.

Second, *the Palestinians in Israel are an indigenous group.* Indigenous nations are nations that lived in their homeland before the establishment of their state and before the establishment of the political and civil community in that state. Emphasis on indigenous identity is particularly important for nations that are in the minority in a regime controlled by another group that is necessarily an immigrant group.

Such communities have historical continuity in a certain territory despite processes of colonization and despite the conquest of their lands by other nations. These processes rendered them minority groups and essentially positioned them outside the establishment of the state – a development that came at the expense of their sovereignty.

Unlike some national minorities, such as the Scots in the United Kingdom, who were ultimately included in ruling the country where they live, indigenous nations have fallen victim to a deliberate process of exclusion, because establishment of the state was necessarily accomplished at the expense of their sovereignty and resources. Indigenous nations continue to maintain special ties with their geographic space, in which they develop their culture, history, and language (Jamal, 2011).

In general, these communities demand independent states or at least the right to self-determination within the boundaries of a certain territory considered their homeland; alternatively, they demand the right to self-government or to some kind of autonomy, including binationalism, from the immigrant majority group. The conditions accompanying this demand originate in the demographic and national conditions that set the indigenous group apart, as well as in the balance of power it maintains with the majority.

Because indigenous minorities throughout the world suffer from differential manifestations of injustice, the claims they advance differ as well. Repression of indigenous nations does not resemble processes that take place among immigrants, as reflected in the different demands each group raises. Immigrants' demands for collective rights and their opposition to assimilation within the social framework of the majority aim at expressing their cultural uniqueness. Consequently, they may demand rights that are primarily multiethnic in nature and in certain cases special representation rights as well. By contrast, among national minorities and indigenous groups, the demand for collective rights is directed at self-rule in certain aspects of life and at equal ownership of the homeland (which was all theirs in the past).

Third, *discrimination is practiced by the Israeli system.* Israel, as a "Jewish ethnocracy," continues to discriminate against the Palestinians in all aspects of life, without exception, essentially maintaining an entire system that empowers the Jews and is biased against Palestinian citizens, rooted in Israel's status as a Jewish state.

Because Israel is an ethnic state, equality between Jews and Arabs is impossible both practically and theoretically. The chief test for determining affiliation with the state is not citizenship, as is customary, but rather membership in the Jewish people (defined biologically or religiously). The state system is based on an order that violates the condition of equal citizenship and therefore violates democracy. This violation derives from the existential purpose of Israel: Israel is an exclusively Jewish-owned state in theory, ideology, and practice, as it is the state of the Jewish people alone (Yiftachel and Ghanem 2004).

This is the political tool of the Jewish people, that ignores citizenship and yields a state openly and structurally inclined towards one of its two chief ethnic groups. Israel has created the legal infrastructure of an ethnocracy in which the law institutes exclusive rights for the ruling ethnic group (Krezmer, 1992). This is evident in several laws, most prominent of which are the Law of Return and Citizenship and the Basic Law: The Knesset (Article 7A), which define Israel as the state of the Jewish people. As such, Israel is defined as an ethnic state by statute and its order excludes its Palestinian citizens from participation in its national objectives, identity, and mission (Rouhana, 1997)

Moreover, laws that address the most important issues, such as land ownership, education, and distribution of resources, openly accord preferential status to the Jews. There are also numerous regulations that do not mention group affiliation explicitly but grant Jewish citizens preferential treatment nonetheless. Israel thus perpetuates a flawed civil equality within the ruling system. The Jewish ethnic state (as established in Israel) lacks the conditions for egalitarian citizenship and consequently for democracy as well.

The absence of egalitarian citizenship, grounded in law and in the legislative system itself, is supported by broad sectors of the Jewish public and elites. Ethnic citizenship, imposed on the Palestinians by the legal system and public opinion, is inferior and prevents them from constructing a significant collective identity of the type that normally originates in citizenship. In the overt ethnic structure that prefers Jews to Arabs and that sometimes relates to the latter as potential or internal enemies, identification with the state primarily constitutes acceptance of constitutional inferiority and unequal status.

The political structure described violates a basic principle of democratic rule – protection of minorities. Most political thinkers, from Alexis de Tocqueville to Will Kymlicka, have warned against the danger of "legal" tyranny of the majority (Kymlicka, 1995). Consequently, in most democracies, majority rule is limited by mechanisms

that protect individual citizens and minority groups, including a constitution, bill of rights, bicameral legislature or institutionalized ethnic
compromises, such as division of power, large coalitions, regional–
cultural autonomy, or minority veto rights (Lijphart, 1977). Nearly
all these methods and mechanisms are lacking in the Israeli regime.
Israel, as a state and political system, preserves the superiority of the
Jews and the inferiority of the Palestinians in several spheres: ideological, symbolic, structural, political, and constitutional (Rouhana, 1997).

As indicated, in the ideological and symbolic spheres, Israel's objectives, symbols, and policies are based on its status as the state of the
Jewish people. At the same time, the state does not recognize its Palestinian citizens as a national minority. The Jews enjoy their own symbols, values, and state institutions, which are perceived as part of their
heritage and a source for identification, while Palestinian citizens are
alienated by these signs of Jewish–Zionist exclusivity.

At the structural level, the Palestinians are involuntarily excluded from
key Israeli institutions that were often planned to serve ethnic purposes, especially the Judaization of the state. This marginalizes Palestinians in the arenas of political power and decision-making, intensified
by their non-conscription to the armed forces, ineligibility for "security-
sensitive" jobs or senior positions in the Israel Lands Authority, the
establishment of special departments or institutions dealing with Arabs,
and their systematic exclusion from institutions that govern land ownership and use.

In the public policy sphere, the Palestinians encounter various forms
of discrimination and exclusion, whether through informal use of power
or in formal spheres of legislation, enforcement, and participation. The
results are clear: no Arab political party has ever been part of the government coalition; the allocation of state lands and budgets to the Arab
sector is infinitesimal compared with that to Jews, despite several Government decisions calling for greater equality between these sectors.

With regard to legislation, besides the Law of Return and Citizenship
and the Basic Law: The Knesset (as noted above), various provisions
included in significant legislation have exacerbated the Palestinians'
inferior status: (1) Land laws enable further Judaization of land. (2)
Emergency laws enacted by the British Mandatory authorities are still
in force and used against the country's Arab population. (3) Two Basic
Laws enacted in 1992 defined Israel as a "Jewish and democratic"
country and thus reaffirm its ethnic character in the emerging state

constitution. That same year, the Parties Law was amended as well, banning parties that do not recognize Israel as a Jewish and democratic state from Knesset elections. (4) Israel's legal system lacks direct protection of fundamental rights, such as freedom of religion, freedom of expression, and even the right to equality. (5) Laws pertaining to the religious establishment in Israel, especially the Chief Rabbinate Law, openly discriminate against Christianity and Islam. (6) The National Education and Israel Broadcasting Authority Laws establish the Zionist characteristics of these important public institutions. Studies have shown that around 20 Israeli laws discriminate against Arab citizens and that interpretation, enforcement, and court rulings consistently replicate this structural inequality between Jews and Arabs (Krezmer, 1992; Rouhana, 1997).

Because Jewishness is intrinsic and all-encompassing in Israel, the state not only discriminates against the Arab–Palestinian citizens on an everyday basis, it also eliminates the even the theoretical possibility of civic equality that is essential to a state defining itself as democratic. The Israeli system thus embodies problems that retard the minority's progress, including those originating in distorted processes of politicization, partial modernization, and ghettoization of Arab villages and economic shortages. Hence trends among the Palestinian minority conform to what the literature calls a "process of developmental crisis" (Rouhana and Ghanem, 1998), in which the Arab sector in Israel is constantly exposed to problems and crises in the individual and collective spheres, originating in exclusion from resources and rights that prevents its "normal" development. It is clear that the key democratic principles of protection from tyranny of the majority and of guaranteed realization of the development potential and mobility of members of the minority community are constantly violated by the political system in Israel.

The situation described intensifies the minority's opposition to the Jewish ethnocracy. The Palestinians in Israel seek civic, individual, and collective equality, directing their constant and uncompromising demands towards elimination of basic aberrations in the system. A group that is treated in an unequal manner incurs damage not only at the basic levels of human equity, an egalitarian attitude and an open approach to resources defined in abstract terms (such as power, identity, and affiliation) or material resources (such as socioeconomic or employment-related advantages), but also as a result of the threat to its sense of collective worth and human dignity.

The achievement of equality is an essential need for an excluded ethnic group and should be addressed if the state system seeks group consent to its activities, development of affiliation, and connection with the state and prevention of ethnic conflict. Equality is not only a group's basic right but also a basic human need that no ethnic group can forgo. According to Burton (1990), equality and identity are basic needs that cannot be negotiated, ignored, or suppressed. Many claim that if these needs did not exist, the only question would be what political conditions would set off the crisis, rather than whether a crisis will result. Open and legally backed ethnic inequality, as practiced in Israel, is the chief source of tension and conflict.

Why Now?

The rising demand for equality – and for binationalism in particular – and its central position among the issues of concern to Palestinians in Israel may be explained by several developments in Israel and the region, especially over the past two decades.

Israeli–Palestinian peace talks in which the topic of the Palestinians in Israel and the solution of their problems were removed from the agenda: The issue of peace and an end to the Israeli occupation of the West Bank and Gaza Strip – a point of key interest to the Palestinians in Israel and their struggle – was struck from the agenda for several reasons: the achievement of an agreement in principle based on the Oslo Accords and the subsequent contacts intended to mobilize the Palestinian and Israeli partners to fulfill it, as well as direct contacts between representatives of Israel and the Arab states and the interest in resolving the overall conflict. The Palestinians' position was reinforced by a conception that developed over the years and may be summarized as follows: solving the problem of the West Bank and Gaza Strip will promote equality among Palestinians in Israel and help advance their demands in this respect (Ghanem and Ozacky-Lazar, 2003).

As such, an end to the occupation is perceived as conducive to equality for Arabs in Israel. When Israel and the Palestine Liberation Organization signed their agreement in principle in 1993, the content and frequency of public and academic discussion of the appropriate status of the Palestinian citizens of Israel – considering the Jewish–Zionist character of the state – intensified significantly.

Old and new ideas were raised for extended or limited personal autonomy and for annexation of parts of the Little Triangle to the Palestinian entity to be established in the West Bank. Proposals were advanced for more substantive integration of Palestinian citizens within the state, as individuals or as a group. The intensification of political discourse among the Palestinians and certain Jewish elites regarding the Jewish character of the state resulted from the notion that solution of the conflict is liable to perpetuate the Palestinians' inferior status, given that they were left out of the discussion of key issues. The discourse about the nature of the state expressed an understanding that the status of the Arab minority and the issue of equality are connected with the internal nature of the state and not with the external historic conflict.

Changes in the balance of power between Palestinians and Jews in various aspects of life: After the establishment of Israel and the expulsion/departure of most of the Palestinian population, about 150,000 Palestinians remained in the country – a confused remnant of the Arab Palestinian people. This group was characterized by its lack of organization, minimal development, the dominance of traditional values and norms, and an economic, social, and cultural life typical of traditional societies at the beginning of the road towards modernity, including a very low level of education.

Intensive changes took place among the Palestinians in Israel after the establishment of the state, especially over the past few decades, in all aspects of life: economics, education, civic life, geographic location, and the like. Their chief manifestations are a sharp rise in standard of living, life expectancy, living conditions, and ownership of modern amenities such as computers and cars.

The demographic growth of the Palestinians in Israel and changes in the physical structure of Arab localities are decisive processes in this respect. In late 2016, there were approximately 1.5 million Palestinians within the Green Line – nearly 17% of all Israeli citizens. The growing population produced larger Arab town and even cities: Of the 112 localities in Israel with populations of 5,000 or more, 60 are Arab; and 15 of them have more than 10,000 residents. In several places, continuous strips of Arab localities developed; in certain regions (Sakhnin, Wadi Ara, and Majd al-Krum), Palestinians constitute a decisive majority. The number of Palestinians living in cities with mixed Jewish–Arab populations should be taken into account as well.

In terms of age structure, the Palestinians in Israel are far younger than the Jews: About 46% of Palestinians are under 17, as compared with 31% of the Jews. Consequently, even though the Palestinians constitute only 17% of the population, they account for 25% of those under 17. This age structure has considerable potential for development, particularly if the state helps by raising educational levels and encouraging modern development.

As a result of contact with the Jewish sector in the country and emulation of trends in Western Europe and the United States, the Palestinians in Israel are undergoing a process of modernization, reflected in slow and hesitant changes in social and cultural values, the growing importance of the nuclear family, a very gradual change in the status of women, a constant decline in the birth rate, improvement in living conditions and the health services available to members of the group, development of municipal government, establishment of political and social frameworks, and especially a constant rise in the average level of education, including an increase in the number of those with post-secondary education.

The changes in the number of Palestinian citizens and in the physical structure of the village, together with the development of Arab localities since the early 1970s, have reinforced Palestinian self-confidence, creating the infrastructure for development of a separate cultural life and political organization and ascribing increasing importance to joint Arab–Jewish organizations and even to attempts at autonomous economic development in Arab localities.

Changes in the collective consciousness of Palestinians in Israel: During the 1990s, discussion of the collective rights of the Palestinian minority was influenced by changes in Arab society, including extensive political activity and fierce competition among political schools of thought, the efforts by civic organizations to achieve collective rights for the minority, the events of October 2000, and the emergence of a generation of Arab intellectuals who engaged in critical thinking about their society and the state.

The 1990s saw the appearance of new schools of political thought among the Palestinians in Israel and the massive growth of civil-society organizations that dealt with a variety of issues concerning the Palestinian minority, including research, social services, minority rights and status, and feminism (see Chapter 3 in this book). Some of these organizations worked to promote the collective rights of the Palestinian minority.

Furthermore, a new generation of intellectuals arose, with new critical discourse concerning Israeli society and its norms. These intellectuals adopted the discourse of "indigenousness" as a channel for resuming the struggle for their identity and collective rights. They introduced new concepts, such as indigenous minority, collective rights, and cultural autonomy. Relying on critical tools, Palestinian intellectuals created an alternative to the hegemonic academic discourse of the Jewish majority. In particular, they raised doubts about the claim that Israel behaves democratically in its relations with the Palestinian minority. These intellectuals also criticized the Israeli scholars who developed theoretical models to explain how the Jewish character of the state conforms with its democratic nature. Instead, they proposed alternative models to describe the Israeli situation and make it fairer. The Palestinian scholars presented two chief models – a state of all its citizens and a binational state – as alternatives for the present situation.

These changes and others have made a major contribution to the emergence of a separate and consolidated national outlook among the Palestinians in Israel.

Constitutional measures establishing the Jewishness of the state: In Israel, a vigorous process is under way to legislate statutes that enshrine Jewish superiority in the state in an open manner. Effectively, these measures constitute an indirect attempt to intensify the discrimination at the legal level, seeking to transform discrimination based on ethnic classification into a visible and overt component of the law.

This process began in the mid-1980s, with passage of the amendment to Article 7a of the Basic Law: The Knesset, which stipulates that a list[2] cannot run for the Knesset if its objectives include elimination of the character of Israel as the state of the Jewish people. In the early 1990s, this measure was expanded by grounding the principle of the Jewish–democratic state in other Basic Laws, which are supposed to compose part of the future constitution. All Basic Laws, especially the Basic Law: Human Dignity and Freedom, declare that Israel will act as a Jewish and democratic state. Besides the inherent contradiction between these two principles, we note that whenever they do coexist,

---

[2] A list is the representative arm of a political party in the parliament.

"Jewish" will always triumph over "democratic." In practice, this means that in every case in which there is a contradiction between the two principles, preference is overtly accorded to the Jewish aspect.

Over the past two decade, additional efforts have been made to enact a constitution in Israel. Proposed constitutions open with the fundamental declaration that Israel is a Jewish and democratic state, overtly establishing Jewish superiority in Israel at the most explicit formal level. This principle was part of the Kinneret Compact drafted and published in the early 2000s by a group of Jewish intellectuals from all shades of the political spectrum, including the Jewish left. It was cited in the 2006 proposal by the Israel Democracy Institute, *Constitution by Consensus* (Shamgar, 2005),[3] as well as in the official proposal of the Knesset Constitution, Law and Justice Committee for a "constitution by broad consensus" in 2007. None of these documents was approved by any official body representing the Palestinians in Israel; their basic principles were rejected by a decisive majority of the Palestinian public in Israel, including the intellectual and political elites. The result is a push for binationalism by the Palestinians as a counter-demand to the Jews' efforts and desire to make Israel an ethnically exclusive Jewish state.

Summary

The political discourse of Palestinians in Israel has moved from individual achievements to the politics of collective rights and the politics of identity. This discourse is considered of utmost importance in the politics of marginalized groups. Similarly, it represents a change in the evolution of the political discourse of Palestinians in Israel over the last two decades.

Given the state's refusal to recognize its Palestinian citizens as a national group with equal collective rights, two competing political discourses have been emerging among the Palestinians in Israel; the discourse of difference and the discourse of recognition. The politics of difference calls on the majority to respect the minority and its distinctiveness; the politics of recognition demands that members of the Palestinian minority be recognized as equal individuals and not as a collective. The essence of the demand by the Palestinians in Israel is to

---

[3] See https://en.idi.org.il/publications/9127.

transform Israel from a hegemonic ethnic state to a power-sharing and consociational regime – a demand that state officials view as an "attack against the legitimacy of the state."

The situation of the Palestinian minority in Israel is typical of minority groups in hegemonic states (Peleg, 2007), such as the Canadian regime before the Quiet Revolution, Macedonia (1991–2001), and Northern Ireland (1973–1998). The "partial modernization" model presented here can be used as an analytical framework to explain and understand similar cases concerning minority aspirations for integration and equality in deeply divided societies.

2 | Political Leadership among the Palestinians in Israel

This chapter looks at the Palestinian political leadership in Israel and analyzes the patterns and forms that have appeared in the decades since 1948.

Palestinian leadership prior to 1948 was composed of the heads of political factions, clans, and dignitaries in cities and towns. According to al-Hout (1987), these men were able to cooperate under a single political umbrella and coordinate their political activities in the Palestinian community, despite their different backgrounds. Nevertheless, the internal conflicts between the leaders of factions within the national movement played a major role in weakening the Palestinian community and detracted from its political maturity in the days of the British mandate and afterwards (Khalidi, 1997). Nevertheless, the conflicts between the factions had guided the Palestinians' political activity and management of the conflict with the Zionist movement and British authorities. Each faction set its own priorities for the conduct of the struggle and had its own future vision of its resolution.

The *Nakba* left Palestinian towns and villages in ruins; the leadership, both political and religious, was also in ruins. The power vacuum left the Palestinians in Israel weak and leaderless (Kimmerling and Migdal, 2003). Most of those who remained in the new state of Israel were farmers and peasants, severed from its intellectual and political leadership and deprived of the traditional urban elite. In addition, the isolation of Arab towns imposed by the military government weakened material and social ties between different communities. A new brand of leadership emerged to replace the traditional political leadership. In this chapter we will analyze the new patterns of political and social leadership that emerged in Palestinian society in Israel, both local and national.

Traditional and Local Leadership after the *Nakba*

Local leadership played an important political role in the Palestinian community after the *Nakba*. Since then its role has risen and fallen

(Mustafa, 2008). Village mukhtars and later the heads of municipal councils played an essential role in the management of local affairs. At the national level, the local leadership joined the Arab satellite lists affiliated with the Zionist parties and took part in Knesset elections (see Chapter 6).

This situation continued well into the 1980s. By then, however, the satellite lists had disappeared from the scene and the role of local leadership was limited to municipal affairs. Under the military government, from 1948 to 1965, the state supported the traditional leadership, both locally and nationally. Before 1948 that traditional leadership was at the margin of the Palestinian movement, in both urban centers and rural areas. But the distorted modernization process experienced by Palestinian society in the first years of statehood strengthened the local leadership and pushed it from the margins to the center of political activity. The local leadership was pragmatic. The pursuit of personal interests in exchange for political support manifested itself in voting patterns on election day. For three decades, Arab lists headed by local leaders received most of the votes in the Knesset election.

In the 1970s, the power of the local leadership declined, in tandem with the satellite lists on the national level. Several factors were at play. One was the end of the military government, under which the leadership had received its power from a system of privileges and favoritism and through a system of mediation between the state and citizens. In addition, the social, economic, and educational changes experienced by the Palestinians in Israel in the 1970s paved the way for the emergence of a political consciousness, which in turn weakened the local leadership's position on the national level. Other reasons for their decline were the numerous conflicts among those local lists and their competition for the limited number of positions in the Zionist parties. This climaxed in the assassination of Hammad Abu-Rabi'a, murdered as a result of internal conflict among members of his Knesset list (Cohen, 2006). In addition, the Zionist parties, especially Labor, were persuaded to end the sponsorship of satellite lists as a strategy for recruiting Arab voters. They now preferred direct contact with the Arab sector through their own activities there. For the Palestinians in Israel, this in turn opened up the opportunity of joining Zionist parties running on their Knesset lists (Ghanem, 2001a).

In conclusion, the heads of the Arab lists remained in their Arab "leadership" conception and did not really perceive themselves as leaders. They derived their legitimacy from traditional structures that had not been through a process of change or partial modernization. The distorted modernization perpetuated the status of that traditional leadership, turning into a dominant force among Arabs. As mentioned, the military government supported that leadership directly, empowering it, especially on the individual level. Similarly, the local leadership played a major role in municipalities. Local councils colluded with the military government to suppress political protest and activity in the Palestinian sector. In other words, local government was exploited as a tool to control the Arabs (Al-Haj and Rosenfeld, 1990). The local political leadership was a mirror image of the defeated Palestinian community, whose main interest was providing for its basic daily needs and feeling secure in the hands of the triumphant new state (Bishara, 1995: 48).

National Political Leadership

In recent decades, the Palestinian sector in Israel has made significant advances in political strategies and the type of political leaders it has cultivated. Nevertheless, its development has remained heavily influenced by the Israeli context (Jamal, 2006). In the early years after the establishment of the state, most of the national political leadership consisted of holdovers from the old ideologies and political parties affiliated with the Palestine Communist Party and the League of National Liberation, which later merged into the Israel Communist Party, run by Jewish Communists. The Arabs of the Israel Communist Party provided a political alternative to the traditional and local leaders supported by the military government. During this period, the Arab political leadership placed the political and the civil rights of the Palestinians in Israel on its agenda, but it never went beyond the Israeli consensus as defined by the establishment. Alongside the Communist Party, a group of young activists organized al-Ard ("the Land"), which highlighted the national bonds between Palestinians in Israel and the rest of the Arab nation.

During the years of the military government, and despite restrictions imposed by the military government on freedom of movement and freedom of expression, this national political leadership organized protests against the state's practices (Bäuml, 2002, 2007; Cohen, 2006). Tawfik Toubi and Emile Habibi, two leaders of the Communist

Party who had parliamentary immunity as members of the Knesset, enjoyed more freedom of movement and political activity than the leaders of al-Ard. Clearly, the military government, with its restrictions on political organization, had a major impact on the activity of the Arab political leadership. The military government also acted to empower and strengthen the traditional local leadership as an alternative for Palestinians after 1948. Members of the Communist Party and al-Ard were placed under house arrest issued by the military governor and occasionally detained.

Al-Ard was outlawed in the 1960s. At the same time, the Arab leaders in the Communist Party continued their activity within the constraints imposed by the party. This continued until the formation of the New Communist List, which, by adopting a more nationalist platform, created more space for Arab political leadership and gained popularity in the Palestinian sector in Israel (Rekhess, 1993). The Arab political leaders during the military government were very different from their heirs, particularly because the former had lived through the *Nakba* and its trauma, which had a dramatic impact on their consciousness and collective memory. In this regard, the early leaders were no different than the rest of the Palestinian community that been traumatized by the *Nakba* (Rabinowitz and Khawla, 2002).

Although the political leadership continued its activities in the post–military government period without dramatic or radical changes, the end of the military government and the 1967 war created new political, social, and economic conditions for the Palestinian community and its leadership. Tawfik Toubi was re-elected in the Knesset as a representative of the New Communist List, which continued its activity after the end of the military government. Emile Habibi remained a parliamentarian until the Seventh Knesset, when he was replaced by Tawfik Ziyad – new blood that symbolized the transition to a new era of younger politicians.

The 1970s were a turning point in the history of the Palestinians in Israel. That decade saw the creation of national and regional institutions, such as the Arab Students' Committee and the National Union of Arab University and High School Students, the Union of Arab Writers, and the National Committee of the Heads of Arab Local Councils. The institution-building process culminated in 1982 with the establishment of the High Follow-up Committee for Arab Citizens in Israel. By then, young university-graduate leaders with a Palestinian national identification were advancing a new agenda through the Communist Party.

Generally speaking, the educational level of the new leaders was higher that than of their predecessors. Until 1981, most Arab Knesset members, especially those affiliated with Mapai, had little or no formal education. Only seven of the 70 Arab Knesset members from 1947 through 1984 had an undergraduate degree; 19 had never attended school at all (Jamal, 2006: 44). In contrast, 64 of the 74 Arab Knesset members in the period 1984–2006 had at least an undergraduate degree.

Until 1984, most of the parliamentary leaders of the Palestinians in Israel were members of the Communist Party (later called the Democratic Front) or of Arab lists affiliated with Zionist parties. In 1984 the lawyer Muhammad Mi'ari, who had been one of the leaders of al-Ard, was elected to the Knesset on the slate of the Progressive Movement for Peace. Abd al-Wahab Darawshe, who founded the Arab Democratic Party in advance of the elections in 1988,[1] was another new leader. Ever since, parliamentary plurality has been a prominent feature of Israeli Arab politics (Neuberger, 1995). The proliferation of leaders increased the number of Arab Knesset members. Since the mid-1990s new leaders, graduates of the Arab student movement of the 1970s, have reached the Knesset (Mustafa, 2002). They ran in the 1996 Knesset elections, when Palestinian society was in a deep crisis following the Oslo Accords. That crisis manifested itself especially in identity politics (Haider, 1997). Azmi Bishara noted that "the current Arab minority leadership reflects the intensity of the crisis." He added that they manifested the national dimension when they paid condolence calls on bereaved constituents, while their civic dimension was limited to their demands for equality (Bishara, 1995: 47).

The new generation of young political leaders, the second generation after the *Nakba*, appeared in the mid-1990s. Most of their political experience was gained through their activities on university campuses. They generated a new political discourse, which went beyond the discourse of equality that dominated the Palestinian sector in Israel until the mid-1990s, and opposed the Zionist ideology and Jewish character of the state (Mustafa, 2002).

The distinguishing features of Palestinian leaders in Israel in recent years are their high educational level, eloquence and charisma, and sophisticated tactics and strategies. They have a better understanding

---

[1] For more on political organizations among the Palestinians in Israel, see below in this chapter and in Chapter 6 about the Joint List.

of existing institutions and know how to overcome obstacles to achieve the collective interests of the group they represent. Even the young leaders who emerged from the Democratic Front and the Communist party have left the equality discourse of the 1970s behind.

Since its founding, the National Democratic Assembly has promoted the ideas of "a state of its citizens" and "collective rights." Other new movements and parties appeared, led by influential figures that saw the Knesset as the political arena for promoting their agenda.

There are other leaders whose main political activity is extra-parliamentary. Typical of this phenomenon in Palestinian society in Israel are Saleh Baransi, Mansour Kardoush, and Sheikh Ra'ed Salah (although the last-named became prominent in national politics after his election as mayor of Umm al-Fahm). Some claim that a mayor, whether he likes it or not, is an Israeli official. But Salah's leadership was different and distinctive. He made his presence felt among the people, did not depend on parliamentary activity, and leveraged his municipal leadership for national political activity. He continued his national role even after he left the mayor's office. A similar example is provided by the leaders of the Sons of the Village. Their public presence and organizational skills were very limited, despite their ideological influence on an entire generation of young Israeli Palestinians in the 1970s and early 1980s. The comparison between leaders inside and outside parliament demonstrates that leaders' gain strength from being elected. A mayor falls into this category, as does a Knesset member (MK). Despite their disadvantage as members of a national minority, Arab MKs can still provide benefits to their constituents. In sum, the traditional political activism that relied heavily on traditional structures started to disintegrate in the face of new forms of political activism and democratic competition (Jamal, 2006).

The fact that Arab leaders on both the local and the national levels are elected exerts a strong influence on their relations with the community, as well as on their legitimacy (Jamal, 2004). However, local elections have not led to the disintegration of traditional structures, because the election process is not always democratic. In this case, elections are a path to success for those who do well in the local political game and know how to manipulate traditional ties in local elections. In fact, elections have strengthened the clan element, as small clans form coalitions with others to win a place in municipal affairs (Mustafa, 2008).

The new young leadership that emerged in the 1990s has produced a new political discourse and employs new tactics to transform the community from its current conditions into a better status. In recent years concern for people's daily lives and needs has been on the rise. Despite numerous efforts by the political, regional, parliamentary, and extra-parliamentary leadership to invest in this avenue, however, its ability to improve their constituents' living conditions has been very limited.

In conclusion, we can enumerate several factors that have influenced the development of regional political leadership in Palestinian society:

The Traditional Social Structure

Many studies have analyzed the role played by traditional and social institutions in Arab society in general, as well as their impact on political and social life (e.g., Barakat, 2000). These traditional structures are an obstacle in the path of political leaders, and their disintegration or modernization contributes to the latter's influence.

Since the 1970s, when Palestinian society in Israel first developed a middle class, a new culture of political and social criticism of state regulation of Arab society had evolved. The process brought new regional and political leaders to the forefront, albeit in limited number. Nonetheless, the lack of class consciousness in the middle class and its political role makes the disintegration of traditional structures unattainable at present. The majority of this Arab middle class consists of university graduates, professionals, and petty bourgeois, many of whom attempted to overcome those traditional structures; some succeeded and others failed. Another group abandoned politics, while a minority pursued individual interests in local politics.

The Israeli Context

The structure and culture of the Israeli context is itself an obstacle to the emergence of Arab political leaders, especially at the parliamentary level. The Israeli system does not enable Arab parliamentarians to effect significant changes for Arab society. A Mada al-Carmel survey of Arabs who served in the Sixteenth Knesset (2000–2005) found that only 2% of all bills they submitted had been enacted into law (Sa'ahn, 2004). These were of general scope, could benefit all sectors of Israeli society, and did not challenge the current system of governance (*Kul al-Arab*, April 13, 2007). The issue remains that the Israeli Palestinian leaders remain Israeli leaders, because all the institutions in which they function are part of the Israeli system (local government and the Knesset). Even though these Israeli institutions have often replaced the traditional structures, they have become an obstacle to development of local Arab institutions and political movements. These Israeli institutions retain their strong presence in the Palestinian sector, even though its education in Israeli universities has allowed it to develop new means to deal with the Israeli context.

Personalization of Roles and Parties

Max Weber described different types of authority; one of his ideal types was the charismatic, in which the leader's authority derives from the perception that he or she possesses extraordinary qualities that confer legitimacy.

The personalization of leadership plays a major role in Arab political parties and movements (with the exception of the Democratic Front and Communist Party, in which institutions are more significant than leaders' personalities). It reflects a different type of political activity, one that focuses on direct personal ties and reverence for the leader and his or her charismatic person. There is no focus on the ideological aspects or common interests that are the foundation of political parties. Jamal (2006) argues that the personalization of leadership remains based on traditional and cultural factors, as well as public prominence. The last of these is particularly strong at the Knesset level, and is manifested in various ways, especially when candidates switch parties in order to hold on to their seats.

The personalization of leadership and political institutions shrinks the political process to the party leader. It glorifies his or her role instead of the political process. As such, it obstructs the development of alternative leadership, because personality has more influence than the structure. The personalization of political movements can undermine collective activity and prevent cooperation between political movements, because of personality clashes and not ideological differences.

Male Leadership

The Arab political leadership is distinctively male. This is because of the patriarchal structure of Arab society, which hinders women's progress and participation in political activity (Yahia-Younis and Hertzog, 2005). Women are absent from leadership positions, at both the local and regional levels. No Arab woman has ever become a Knesset member through Arab political parties. (Until 2006, only two Arab women, Hussniya Jubarrah and Nadia Al-Helow, had won Knesset seats through Zionist parties.) The patriarchal social structure and male leadership are the main obstacle to the emergence of female political leaders in Arab society. Despite the qualitative and quantitative improvements in Arab women's level of education and the fact that women now compete with men for administrative and professional positions in the private sector, women remain underrepresented in political activity and leadership positions. In the view of a feminist activist, the male dominance of leadership positions in Arab society in Israel, coupled with its patriarchal structure, has excluded women from the political leadership.[2]

Local Government

The 1978 elections were the first in which mayors were elected directly. Voters cast two ballots, one for the municipal council and one for the mayor. Before then, council heads/mayors were elected by the council itself, sometimes on the basis of narrow coalition considerations and interests, which had a negative impact on the municipality's operation (Arian, 1998).

The new situation empowered mayors and gave them more leverage over the council. The idea behind the change was to free the mayor from the political extortion that resulted from his need to satisfy councilors' personal interests. Nonetheless, the new system did not eliminate all pressure and extortion, because the mayors still have their own electoral interests. In a 1998 survey of Arab mayors and councilors, concerning the impact of direct elections, 91% of the former responded that the change had empowered their position. Eighty-six percent said that direct election had improved their image in the public eye. Eighty-one percent said that their position vis-à-vis the Ministry of Interior had improved; 91% said that their standing in their clan or family had risen. Every one of the councilors responded that the change had improved the mayor's position at their expense. In specific cases, 70.4% of municipal council members said that the new arrangement had improved their decision-making capacity; 78.7% reported

[2] An interview with feminist Ghada Ghadban, conducted on March 10, 2008.

that the mayor's ability to hire and fire employees had improved. And 79% said that the new law had given them more freedom to make decisions (Abbas, 1988).

Many studies have analyzed the impact of direct mayoral elections on political parties. Many concluded that the system weakened the national political parties at the expense of local lists. Using two ballots was not a new phenomenon in 1978. In 1955, 1959, 1965, 1969, and 1973 many voters had to cast two ballots – one for the local council and the other for the Knesset (for more see Arian, 1990, 1998). Not only did the new system mandate separate ballots for mayor and council, it also led to a separation of Knesset and local elections. This meant that voters could choose members of their council, generally voting for a clan list, while electing a mayor who might belong to a different list. In the new circumstances, voters and councilors have more opportunities for coalitions. In the past, those negotiations started after election day. The new double-ballot election system enables mayors to function without having to form a coalition, and to make decisions without the need for coalition support (Eisengang-Kna, 2004).

The situation is more complex in Arab society because of the multiplicity of small lists that occasionally win council seats. This fragmentation complicates the process of coalition-making at the local level. To date, the new system has had marginal impact on national and regional parties, as has been evident in elections to Jewish municipal councils (Brichta, 1998, 2001). On occasion, Arab voters do not separate the two ballots in local elections, because of the close ties between the clan and local politics, in which a mayoral candidate represents a clan or a coalition of clans. The differences between clan, economic, and political interests are blurred. The new law was meant to provide mayors with more authority and power vis-à-vis the council, making them accountable to their voters rather than to members of councils. In other words, the intention was administrative and structural, with no thought for the political ramifications that ensued.[3]

To some extent, the new law freed the Arab parties from clan considerations, but only in part. In the old system, voters voted primarily against the Communist list (the only national party that participated

---

[3] The new law was produced by political considerations rather than to improve administrative performance. The political realties created by the law were worse than the situation it sought to change.

in local elections) that competed against the local list. In most cases, agreements were made to ensure that local lists would support the Communists in Knesset elections; in exchange, that party supported the local candidate for mayor (Cohen, 1989). Generally speaking, the national political parties did not take advantage of the direct elections law and actually became more dependent on local traditional forces. That dependency was not due only to the social conditions imposed on the minority; the traditional structures were exploited to increase the power of national parties at both the local and national levels. Local Arab politics can be characterized by competition between local forces (Al-Hajj and Rosenfeld, 1990; Rekhess, 1986) and the marginalization of Arab parties (Ghanem, 1995) that competed for the Arab vote. One of the consequences of the new law was the emergence of new self-styled "educated" politicians. The vast majority were university graduates who returned to their towns and villages, bearing an Israeli diploma, and ran for local office. Even this group did not intend to change the traditional social structures in their towns; instead, they treated those structures as given and attempted to employ them to their advantage. In many cases, the traditional leadership succeeded in co-opting this group and turned them into a tool to gain votes for local and clan lists (Brake, 2005).

In mayoral elections, in many cases it was difficult to determine the candidate's background, because the distinction between clan and candidate overlapped. In the 1978 elections, 30 Arab mayors who ran and won on local lists were partially tied to Zionist parties; 17 were associated with lists linked to the Democratic Front/Communists, and one was linked to the Sons of the Village movement (Harari, 1978). In the 1983 elections, the number of clan-affiliated mayors dropped to 19, while those supported by the Democratic Front rose to 20. There was also a decline in the local clan-based lists for council members.

The rise of the Islamic Movement and its entry into local politics in the late 1980s had many consequences. In the 1989 elections, six Islamic Movement candidates for mayor won. Four years later, however, clan-based lists sprang back and won 16 municipalities; in 1998 they won in 38 municipalities.[4] The Islamic Movement's local political activity declined, and won only in Umm al-Fahm.

---

[4] An interview conducted on April 21, 2007 with Hashem Abed al-Rahman, head of the Umm al-Fahm municipality.

Victory in mayoral elections was influenced mainly by a candidate's clan affiliation. A study of the political role of the clan in local elections found ten mayors won their seats in 1989 due to the support of their clan. This number fell to eight in the 1993 elections. In 1989, 18 elected mayors enjoyed clan support, and 23 in 1993 (Amara, 1998).

In the 2003 elections, the power of local and clan lists rose. Out of 53 localities, eight elected mayors had party support, against 42 with mainly clan support. Interestingly, several victorious candidates were officially affiliated with political parties, but preferred to present themselves as family and clan candidates in local elections. Many university graduates joined the local clan lists and ran for mayor. In other words, the situation of mayors in the Arab sector is complex, with a contradiction between individualism, on the one hand, and the politicization of the clan, on the other hand, coupled with the exclusively male leadership. There has never been a female mayor or council head in Palestinian society in Israel.

The situation is no different for council members. In the 2003 elections, 75% of municipal councilors were clan-affiliated (Mustafa, 2008). Some 66% were between the ages of 30 and 50; the number of women was closer to 1%. Only 41.9% had high school degrees and only 27.7% a university degree. Those 50 and older constituted 30% of municipal councilors; most of them (63%) had graduated from high school (Bashir, 2008: 84). A look at several Palestinian towns and villages in Israel (Umm Al-Fahm, Nazareth, Tur'an, al-Maghar, and Tal'at Arra) suggests that local Arab leadership is drawn from four sources (Mustafa, 2008):

1. The Traditional Clan: The traditional clan structure continues to produce local leaders who compete for the mayorship. These leaders are distinguished from their predecessors of the years after the founding of the state by their more advanced education and younger age. But they still rely on the clan for political advantage.
2. The Political Party: These leaders emerge from the various political parties that compete at the local level. Sometimes they enjoy local support that goes beyond clan and ethnic affiliation. However, we cannot eliminate the clan factor in their selection.
3. The Business Community: This refers to the involvement of businessmen in local politics. Their main concern is to ensure that municipal governments contribute to their economic and personal success. They have no political agenda other than the claim that

they can improve the performance of the municipality. They do not understand that local governments in general, and Arab local councils in particular, are not economic enterprises, but a complex network of social, personal, and formal relationships that require a different form of leadership.

4. University Graduates and Professionals: In the last two decades, university graduates and professionals have become increasingly involved in local politics. Many do not advertise a political or social agenda but insist on their degrees from Israeli universities as a class distinction that makes them different from other members of society. There is a sense of superiority among them, as they aspire to employ techniques learned at Israeli universities not to effect change but to achieve personal benefit.

Local Arab politics do not provide leverage for the emergence of national political leaders, except in extreme cases. Sometimes candidates win local elections as a result of the support of national parties. They also have a future vision and a political agenda for both the local and national levels.

The High Follow-up Committee for Arab Citizens in Israel: A National Leadership Forum?

The High Follow-up Committee for Arab Citizens in Israel was founded in 1982. We will not analyze its history here. The 1970s were a turning point in Arab politics in Israel. In that decade the Arabs in Israel created regional institutions, of which the most significant was the National Committee of the Heads of Arab Local Authorities, founded in 1972. The Committee for Defense of the Land was founded in 1975, as was the National Association of Arab University Students. Before that there were many Arab student organizations at the high school and university levels (Mustafa, 2002). Arab student committees were an example of institutions in which candidates were elected and competition was fair. The National Committee of the Heads of Arab Local Authorities comprised council heads and mayors. One of its main goals was to present its local agenda in the Israeli context. However, its political role was transformed after a group of young activists joined it, coinciding with the election of heads of councils who were members of the Communist Party and the Democratic Front.

National political issues dominated the agenda of the National Committee in the years that followed (Al-Hajj and Rosenfeld, 1990), but it did not become an institution representing all Arabs in Israel as a national group. Its young political leadership behaved much the same way as the traditional leadership, thus ensuring that little progress was made. It was evident that local leadership organized in a regional institution lacked the ability to transform itself into national leadership. Instead, it "brought the mentality of the local to the regional" (Bishara, 1998: 42). The founding of the High Follow-up Committee in 1982 was due mainly to pressing political needs of the 1980s, and the inclusion of new young political leaders in the National Committee of the Heads of Arab Local Authorities. At first, the High Follow-up Committee included mayors as well as Knesset members and members of the Histadrut executive, and even Arab Knesset members affiliated with Zionist parties and representatives of various sectors. But the National Committee of the Heads of Arab Local Authorities remained the main pillar of the High Follow-up Committee.

There are several problems with the performance of the High Follow-up Committee. The first is the unclear relationship between the Committee and Arab citizens. The second deficiency is the lack of a procedure for decision-making and implementation. Shawqi Khatib believes that the reason behind the Committee's creation was the banning of the Equality Convention in 1982:

The Follow-up Committee was founded in response to the Equality Convention. The Arab public wanted to organize such a convention, but the government perceived it as risky. As a result, it banned it using emergency and military laws. This was the context for the founding of the Follow-up Committee, a response to the banning of the Equality Convention. In my view the Follow-up Committee is the most important institution representing the Arab political agenda in Israel. In my view, this form of political activism has become possible due to the distinctive status of the Palestinian public in Israel. The particulars of this case are manifested in the fact that the Arab community lives in a state in which many of its institutions and apparatuses practice daily discrimination against us. Our minority has limited material resources. For that reason, there was a need to create a new form of leadership to include all political factions, organized on the basis of a common denominator, hence the significance of such an institution that allows Arabs to face the political challenges and which clarifies the path for us. The path is clear and the main points have been agreed upon.[5]

---

[5] An interview conducted on April 1, 2008 with Shawqi Khatib, chair of both the High Follow-up Committee and the National Committee of Council Heads.

For Khatib, the Follow-up Committee acts as a coordinator between the various Arab political parties in parliament and outside it. The decision-making process is based on consensus. The Committee cannot tolerate the democratic rule of the majority. Consensus is the secret behind its survival, without it, it would fail to meet the minimum requirements of its activities and struggle. The Committee lacks mechanisms to enforce and follow-up its decisions. In addition, the lack of organizational clarity between the Committee and the Palestinian citizen is the reason for its failure to reorganize itself in recent years.

The High Follow-up Committee is a regional organization and has failed to become a national institution for all Palestinians in Israel. It includes many clashing elements within the Palestinian community. To avoid the risk of falling apart, consensus, rather than majority rule, is its principle for decision-making. The consensus culture of the Committee has exposed its weakness in various cases. In July 2008, it discussed increasing the number of women on the Committee. The goal was to raise the number of representatives on each committee by one, with that second representative being a woman. Most members of the Committee endorsed this suggestion, but not the Islamic Movement. Nevertheless, the Committee announced that the resolution had passed immediately after the Islamic Movement denounced the resolution in a press release, calling it illegal (see *Hadith al-Naas*, September 19, 2008; *Sawt al-Haq wal-Huriyya*, September 19, 2008). The years of heated debate concerning this issue did not produce any reorganization of the Follow-up Committee. Instead, the conflict laid bare the deficiencies of the consensus-based decision-making process as the main factor in the weakening of the Committee's position and its inability to act. There were also different views about the Committee's goals and its agenda, especially with regard to the degree of independence experienced by Palestinians in Israel and the role the Committee is expected to play.

The Follow-up Committee: From Local Leaders to National Politics

To date, four individuals have chaired the High Follow-up Committee. Ibrahim Nimr Hussein headed it until he was defeated in the local elections of 1998. He was followed by Muhammad Zeidan, in a rotation agreement, through 2001. Shawqi Khatib who held the position until 2008, when Zeidan returned to the post. Recently (October 2015), Mohammad Barakeh, the head of the Democratic Front, was elected chair of the Follow-up Committee.

The election of Shawqi Khatib signaled a new era in the Follow-up Committee's activity. He was already the head of the National Committee of the Heads of Arab Local Authorities when elected chair of the Follow-up Committee for a full term from 2003 until 2008. What distinguished Khatib's leadership from his predecessors was his moderate political position within the Palestinian sector (the Democratic Front). For two decades after its founding in 1982, the Committee had a non-political and non-ideological leadership. This certainly shaped the Committee's public image at the time, as compared to the Khatib era. Another point that characterized Khatib's leadership was his success as head of a municipality. The Yaffat al-Nassirah municipality is considered one of the best in the Arab sector. Its success is attributed to Khatib's effective administration. From the moment he won the elections, Khatib promised to reorganize the management of his municipality. At the same time, he succeeded in restoring the role of the Follow-up Committee as well.

Khatib institutionalized the Committee and moved its headquarters to Nazareth, the largest Palestinian city in Israel. In the past, the Committee headquarters migrated to its chair's hometown, from Shfa'amre to Kufr Manda to Yaffat al-Nassirah. He initiated the creation of a group of Arab university graduates to draft a future vision for the Palestinians in Israel.[6] This document attempted to discuss a number of issues, including the minority's relationship with the state, social and cultural issues, and legal aspects and civil society. Khatib also formalized a new relationship between Palestinian Arab society and the Follow-up Committee. He considered civil society to be an active partner with the Follow-up Committee. For example, he looked to Adalah as an advisory organization on legal issues, the Arab Center for Alternative Planning on master plan issues, and the Mossawa Center for equality and discrimination. He also organized several activities involving both the Follow-up Committee and Palestinian civil society organizations. Khatib spearheaded the restructuring of the Follow-up Committee, with a subcommittee based on the political parties, in

---

[6] See Chapter 5.

response to its inability to implement its decisions and also to strengthen its ties with the public.

Years later, the subcommittee failed to restructure the Committee, due to internal factional clashes. Some of the conflicts revolved around the number of committee members, the committee's relationship with civil society, the position of its chair, women's organizations, and the process of decision-making. The failure of the restructuring had many ramifications for the Committee's legitimacy. Concerning this issue, Khatib said:

In 1996 we organized a different convention to discuss equality of Arabs in Israel. One of the convention's recommendations was the restructuring of the Follow-up Committee and the establishment of a subcommittee composed of all political parties. This subcommittee met on a regular basis. When the chair of the Follow-up Committee headed the subcommittee, it in turn, demanded the termination of the subcommittee's activity. There is a clear difference between the following two, restructuring and reorganization. However, despite these differences and my insistent request that the subcommittee terminate its discussions, it managed to draft an agreement. However, there remained several disputed points, one of which was the disagreement over the principles of elections and actual elections.[7]

Khatib added:

The central point of disagreement was the principle of elections. A few members of the subcommittee wanted the election discussions documented and enumerated. In contrast, another group rejected the inclusion of those principles in the restructuring. This was a source of disputes. Much was agreed upon, but the central disagreement was on the basic principles of elections. Some members wanted to include direct elections, while others believed that the Follow-up Committee as it stood was already an elected committee. Members of the Committee are elected heads of municipalities. Members of the Follow-up Committee are elected members of the Knesset who were directly elected by their parties and their public. For that reason, one cannot say that the current committee has not been elected. Whoever wishes to see a different structure of the committee must name it by another name. Since this issue has yet to be resolved, members of the subcommittee were in disagreement and they believed that the issue required further discussions and debates, a point which was agreed upon.[8]

---

[7] From interview, April 1, 2008.   [8] Ibid.

Elsewhere, Khatib stated that the restructuring subcommittee brought to the discussion two proposals regarding the restructuring of the Follow-up Committee. Neither proposal included any new points regarding direct elections; rather, both proposals asserted either support of the elections or their rejection (*Sawt al-Haq wal-Huriyya*, May 18, 2007).

Media and political criticism of Khatib by journalists, politicians, and academics increased during his chairmanship of the Follow-up Committee. The criticism focused on the role of the Follow-up Committee and its current condition. On several occasions, the criticism resurged each time the Follow-up Committee failed to successfully organize annual commemorations of Palestinian national events, such as Land Day or the al-Aqsa Intifada. On both occasions the failure was attributed to the Committee's chair. Shawqi's responses to these attacks emphasized the symbolic role of the Follow-up Committee: it should not be criticized because it is the sum of its parts. He asserted that criticism should instead be directed at Committee members. In an interview Khatib criticized those who criticized him: "The Follow-up Committee does not have clerks, nor does it have professionals or any decision-making mechanism. One would assume that the responsibility falls on the shoulders of the participants of the Committee and those participants should be held accountable for executing its decisions" (*Sawt al-Haq wal-Huriyya*, May 18, 2007, p. 31). There is some truth to Khatib's statement. Political activity in recent years has shown that political parties have far more power to mobilize the public to participate in political activities than does the Follow-up Committee. In addition, we must not ignore the historical context in which Khatib was elected chair of the Follow-up Committee. Those were the days following the al-Aqsa Intifada, which had significant ramifications for public participation in political and national activities.

The Current Head of the Follow-up Committee, Mohammad Barakeh: Facing the Challenges Ahead

In October 2015, Mohammad Barakeh, the head of the Democratic Front for Peace and Equality (DFPE) and a leading member in the Communist Party, who had served in the Knesset for 15 years (1999–2015), was elected the new head of the Follow-up Committee. Right after his election he stated that the Follow-up Committee under his leadership aimed to re-evaluate its status and activities and reorganize the committee in a way that will help achieve the interests and demands of the Palestinians in Israel. Having been a member of the general council of the Follow-up Committee for many years, he seems to be well aware of the need to enhance the consensus about its political platform and activities, something that is very difficult in light of the internal division. He declared, however, that he is totally committed to acting within this consensus. "The High Follow-up Committee of the Arab Citizens of Israel is the official representative of the Palestinian citizens in Israel. It includes representation of all political parties and Arab Members of the Knesset, all Arab mayors and heads of Arab local councils, and the majority of civil society organizations".[9] In a special interview we conducted with him for the purpose of this book, he stated:

Since its establishment, the Follow-up Committee was founded on the basis of persuasion and consensus ... we seek broader agreement on our core and important issues. I agree with this approach. Our basic strategic nowadays weights a consensus on major issues and not a normal majority. The function of the Follow-up Committee is based on two elements: Political representation and the principle of volunteerism or voluntary work. It's a representation committee and at the same time a form of a resistance committee, the delicate combination between the two aspects is essential to preserve.

The topic of "Institutionalization" of the Follow-up committee is broadly debated. Some are proponents of a gradual abandonment of different Israeli citizenship circles, which I find extremely dangerous. The Follow-up Committee is a leadership body that combines combinations of all the components of our society, including any civil work components ranging from community activity to affirmative pilgrim issues. We are a guidance and an address to many issues the community faces.[10]

With regard to co-opting professionals to join the Follow-up Committee, he told us: "The institutions of the Follow-up Committee are open to Arabs professionals for their plans, views and professional opinions. We are all sharing the same process and action in order to serve the need of our society." He claims that he has a specific and clear program that will:

---

[9] From the introduction of the letter that Barakeh sent to the secretary general of the United Nations, Mr. António Guterres, in advance of the second International Day for Solidarity with the struggle of the Palestinian Citizens in Israel, January 2017.

[10] Interview with Barakeh, May 24, 2017.

gather the political elites and the public for a comprehensive, professional and well planned program. The need to organize Arab human capital under the umbrella of the Follow-up Committee will be added to several projects that I'm pushing, such as: the International Day in support of the Palestinians in Israel; the re-establishment of the Arab Parents' Committee; the publication of the alternative curriculum for civic education; the re-establishment of the National Committee off Arab Secondary School Pupils; the establishment of the Follow-up Committee for Public Health in Arab society; the establishment of the Committee to Fight Violence in Arab society; the Committee to Support Political Prisoners; the establishment of local public committees in each locality; the forum for international advocacy in support of the struggle of Arabs in Israel for equal rights; the forum of Arab local councils members in the mixed cities; and the forum of Arab entrepreneurs and businessmen.[11]

The internationalization of the struggle by the Palestinians in Israel to attain equality, through International Day for Solidarity with the Struggle of the Palestinian Citizens in Israel, is a core idea that is presented by Barakeh:

In the wake of accumulating repressive campaigns and the increase of governmental and public racism, the narrowing of the democratic margins – which were narrow to begin with – and in the wake of continuous waves of demolition of Arab houses and continuing land confiscation and the increase of restraints on the lives and the free movement of Palestinian citizens in Israel on the one hand, and the shrinking democratic nature and actions of the Israeli government and its policies, on the other hand we aim to internationalize the struggle for equality for the Palestinian minority.

On the issue of direct elections for the Follow-up Committee, Barakeh's position is very clear. He prefers gradual change rather than a revolution:

In my opinion, the election of the Follow-up Committee at this stage may lead to several negative results. First, by virtue of its structure based on voluntary and representative work, it may lose its representation if one party feels that it is outside the equation. Second, any election to the Follow-up Committee will promote fragmentation and tribalism. Thirdly, it is not unlikely that this will be exploited by the state to evade its duties towards the Arab citizen. Fourthly, there is the technical issue of how to manage it, but let us say that it can be overcome at a certain stage. I want the Follow-up Committee to be a gathering of elected personalities and not an elected committee.[12]

[11] Ibid.   [12] Ibid.

Barakeh's political program to reorganize and restructure the Follow-up Committee seems to be a new phase in the annals of the collective leadership of the Palestinians in Israel. The reorganization of the committee and the vision to include the political leadership alongside professionals is a new way of thinking and action of the collective leadership. We need to wait and see the results on the ground of this vision, as well as the ability to handle the challenges ahead, on which we elaborate below.

Challenges Ahead

The idea of electing members of the Follow-up Committee has been presented on numerous occasions. Many activists, the Islamic Movement, the Progressive List, the Sons of the Village movement, as well as the National Assembly (al-Tajamu) have proposed it in the last three decades, in pursuit of the creation of a sort of Arab parliament in Israel. The idea has been thoroughly discussed by Palestinian intellectuals from various perspectives. Later, the Islamic Movement reintroduced it as part of the restructuring attempt. There is no doubt that the idea of electing members of the Follow-up Committee contradicts the basic ideas of the DFPE, which believes that the Follow-up Committee, in its current form, plays merely a representative role. The DFPE perceives this role as disengagement from Israeli citizenship and the way that the Palestinians in Israel enforce their rights and participation within Jewish society. In our interview with Barakeh, he said that the idea of electing Committee members was not practical at the present time and would not change the Committee's status. These ideas challenge the political parties and those who support the election of the Follow-up Committee.

This division reflects two competing views of how the Follow-up Committee should be reformed. The first camp contends that the Follow-up Committee needs to be restructured; the second camp argues that only reorganization is required. The difference between restructuring and reorganizing is that the latter demands reforms within the committee, while the former demands external changes, starting with the dissolution of the Committee. Restructuring requires a constitution that will guide the Follow-up Committee and stipulate the form it should follow.

Most restructuring plans revolve around a change from the consensus culture, which has been the connecting thread of the Follow-up

Committee's activities over the years, to democratic majority rule. In other words, a change from nomination to election and from decisions based on consensus to majority control. The common proposal is the direct election of members of the Follow-up Committee by Palestinians themselves; the groups that favor this include the extra-parliamentary Islamic Movement, the Democratic National Assembly, and the Sons of the Village. The opponents include the DFPE; the parliamentary wing of the Islamic Movement also has some reservations on the subject. In spite of the differences between these two views, restructuring has some advantages:

1. It is important that all political parties agree on the restructuring plan, because any opposition, especially by a major stream in Palestinian society, such as the DFPE, will undermine this process and make it illegitimate. It is the responsibility of the other parties that endorse this plan to convince the Front to support elections and make sure that those elections do not set a precedent for disengagement from citizenship. It should not be seen as a process of secession by the Palestinians in Israel. Instead, it must be viewed and presented as part of the legitimate rights of Israeli citizens. Those who consider this idea under anything but the umbrella of citizenship see the project as doomed to failure and a prescription for a confrontation with the authorities.

2. It is important to educate the general Palestinian public about this plan. The idea in itself is revolutionary and creates fear among various sectors within Palestinian society, who might consider it a step towards separation. Hence we believe that consensus on the issue of elections must be reached, with the collective support of the public.

3. In conjunction with the above-mentioned suggestions, it is important to inform the Jewish public about this process as well. It is important to present the Palestinian move as part of the basic minority right to build its own national institutions. In this way we avoid presenting that process as a move to break away from the state.

4. There is a need to create a professional team of experts to lay the foundations for the elections and their procedures, based on democratic values compatible with the structure of Palestinian society in Israel.

5. A constitution must be drafted for the Follow-up Committee, specifying its name, goals, authority, structure, nomination and electoral processes, and subcommittees.

Several stages that must be considered before a final restructuring plan is achieved. The most important step is the transition from consensus to majority rule in decision-making.

This issue is not included in future structural reform proposals, but it could be part of a new political culture. Majority rule enforces the culture of the majority with all its positive and negative consequences. The majority rule principle requires the adoption of a different political culture by the members of the Follow-up Committee. We are confident that, thanks to their political experience, members of the Follow-up Committee are capable of ensuring the success of such a new culture. This transition is essential for those who call for reforms, among whom we are numbered. We call for direct elections to be the center of the restructuring committee's agenda. The principle of elections changes the culture from that of consensus to majority rule. It would be non-viable to reject the majority rule principle in decision-making, because its rejection will raise questions about our ability to endorse majority rule in direct elections to the committee.

In summary, the question of leadership is one of the central points in the development of the Palestinians minority in Israel. One of the challenges facing this minority is the election of a national leadership to organize its common political activities. Despite the qualitative improvement in the Arab political leadership over the last two decades, there is still a long way to travel.

3 | The Empowerment of Civil Society: Palestinian Non-Governmental Organizations in Israel

Introduction

The concept of "civil society" began to draw the attention of scholars interested in democratic development, to describe action by citizens opposed to Communist rule in Eastern Europe, such as the workers' organization Solidarity in Poland. This organization was supposed to be a substitute for the Communist regime, which "does not represent its citizens" (Muslih, 1993: 258). Though this concept has been used for a civil society in confrontation with the regime, and despite its definition and use by scholars in various disciplines (see Shils, 1991), the modern use of the term is to denote the community action and organizations that seek to define the public agenda, including non-governmental or Third Sector organizations that exist alongside the regime and its institutions (Kumar, 1993). Civil society is a realm of associational and voluntary activity conducted by both domestic and foreign non-governmental organizations. Its various manifestations include trade unions, domestic and international non-governmental organizations (NGOs), professional guilds, welfare organizations, educational institutions, and sports associations.

NGOs are voluntary forms of association that fall between the organized establishment of state and regime and the primordial groups of family and clan. Organization in civil society is thus less than membership in the state and more than affiliation based on blood ties; it is founded on a personal or group choice to join together with others in order to serve the members of the organization or the wider public in other ways than the government does and independently of it.

In many Western countries, the last few decades of social policy, characterized by increasing liberalization and privatization, have led to the growing involvement of civil society organizations (Savas, 2000). The dynamic between these organizations and the state have been the focus of many studies that suggest different typologies for analyzing their relationship (Anheier 2001a, 2001b; Anheier *et al.*, 2003; Coston, 1998; Keane, 2004; Najam, 2000; Yishai, 1991, 1998). For example, in Najam's typology (2000), this relationship can take four forms: (a) cooperation, when the state and the civil society organization agree on goals and strategies; (b) complementarity, which refers to agreement regarding goals but not strategies; (c) co-optation, when civil society and the state disagree on goals but employ similar strategies; and (d) confrontation, or disagreement about both goals and strategies.

In general, NGOs constitute a mechanism and tool for the self-empowerment of a group of individuals who aim to contribute to the public weal through one (or more) of the following mechanisms:[1]

- **Empowerment.** NGOs are considered to be a tool for the empowerment of weak and marginal social and political groups. Individuals and groups from marginal sectors get together and form an NGO with an agenda and programs that serve the aims that they consider as important. The NGO gives its members the opportunity to act as a group and not only as individuals, with an organizational structure and ability to act as a legal entity in the public sphere and enhance their ability for collective action at the local, national, and international levels.
- **Autonomy.** The ability to act as an NGO promotes its members' ability to promote an autonomous agenda, different from those of international actors, the state, or its local and regional branches. On the other hand, NGOs founded by activists in weak societies can function as a tool for group empowerment and autonomy to express limited self-determination in certain levels and spheres.
- **Philanthropy.** Social activists use NGOs as a channel for social and material support for weak sectors and groups with special needs. In many cases these philanthropic NGOs extend their support to other societies, especially in times of emergency.
- **Advocacy.** For marginal groups and sectors of society, NGOs can serve to advocate for their needs and views. Minority groups, persons with special need, and social groups like women and LGBTs may set up an NGO to allow them to raise their voice and express

---

[1] For a broad discussion of the concept and its connotations, see Bell, 1989; Bishwapriya, 1997; Fernando, 1997; Hanafi and Tabar, 2005; Keane, 1988; Mehra, 1997; Shils, 1991; Walzer, 1991.

their needs and concerns in the public sphere, demanding changes in its agenda and priorities in order to meet what they consider to be important.

- **Social change.** NGOs function as a mechanism for social change on two levels: for their members, who use their activity to achieve social mobility, and for the entire community they serve. Each NGO's projects, initiatives, and activities may be used for collective social change for their target group. For example, NGOs that are active among women in traditional societies usually aim to empower traditional women and enhance their social status.
- **Serving needs.** NGOs that are active in weak and marginal societies provide services through collective action. For example, in rural areas in the Third World, NGOs build water and sewage systems or educational institution and religious services. The need for NGOs to provide services is most important for marginal groups and areas that are not treated equally by the state. The existence of discrimination between citizens, on the basis of ethnic, geographic, or other parameters – that is, the state's intervening for the benefit of one specific ethnic group or geographic area – becomes an obstacle to the formation and establishment of civil society, though the discrimination may actually encourage the victimized group or individuals to establish civil society institutions in order to meet the needs the regime does not and to narrow the gap between themselves and the preferred group or groups.

Doron (1996) claims that there are two separate civil societies in Israel, which operate in different circles and have no meaningful relationship between them. That is, civil society in Israel is divided along national lines. Following Payes (2005), and given that Palestinian civil society was not recognized or included in the Jewish–Zionist project, we would like discuss Palestinian civil society as an "ethnic civil society" that is continuously and systematically excluded by the state (Yishai, 1998).

According to Agbaria and Mustafa (2014), there are two separate civil societies among the Palestinian in Israel – organizations motivated by state-centered politics of difference, and organizations that represent community-centered politics. The first type is the quintessence of the politics of contention: opposing the Jewish hegemony, calling for the establishment of a broad secular Palestinian identity, and demanding national recognition and group rights for the Palestinian minority in Israel. These organizations pursue these goals with whatever the hegemonic discourse allows; they seek change from within, using the tools and opportunities provided by democracy – protest, litigation, and lobbying – against the exclusive Jewish nature of the state. In other words, these organizations, characterized by a "within and against" approach, place the state at the center of their sociopolitical efforts in order to improve the quality of life and obtain equal allocation of material and symbolic resources, substantive recognition in historic and social narratives, and inclusion in decision-making.

The second type of Palestinian civil society in Israel, which also uses the politics of difference, is characteristic of the Islamic organizations that operate primarily through a network of institutions (for community development, welfare, and education) in areas and communities that are neglected by the state. These organizations constitute a new breed that places Palestinian society, or key parts of it, at the focus of their activity. They promote a politics of difference that resists the hegemonic discourse of the Jewish state from the outside, rather than from within. In other words, these "without and against" organizations endeavor to empower Palestinian society from the inside and construct an integrated Islamic–Palestinian identity that is sectoral and specifically Muslim. It is important to note that these organizations often operate in complete isolation from state policy and government practices towards Palestinian society.

Palestinian civil society organizations operate in every sector of Palestinian society, including education, culture, health, welfare, entertainment and leisure, religion, law, and the status of women (Evan Chorev, 2008). The data of the Israeli Center for Third-Sector Research highlights the number of non-profit organizations in the field of education. In 2007, the largest single category of NPOs were those in education (28%), following by culture (19%) and housing and development (10%) (Balbetchan, 2008). There was roughly one organization for every thousand Palestinian citizens, or only a quarter of the rate in the Jewish sector (Gidron and Elon, 2007). As for religious organizations, Evan Chorev (2008: 43) found that:

the sector of Palestinian NGOs includes many religious organizations. These organizations perform religious services yet they engage in welfare, development, and education activities as well. Their methods and courses of action characterize civil society organizations. However, religious goals and motives have precedence in these organizations' activity and they do not necessarily adhere to the underlying idea of civic equality. . . . In addition, they tend not to register officially. For these reasons, religious organizations were not included in the current survey.

An example of such contentious and ethno-national politics is the "Future Vision" document published in 2006 by major Palestinian civil society organizations in Israel (Agbaria and Mustafa, 2011).[2] It calls for a deeper, but negotiated and transformative, engagement with the state, with an end to the Jewish hegemony over the state's resources and identity. The document's vocabulary and perspective are secular, drawing on conceptual frameworks such as liberal democracy, consensual democracy, constitutional democracy, liberalism, and collective rights. Its vision of democratizing the state is perceived as controversial, if not indeed hostile, by Jewish Israeli society, but in Palestinian society as well. Specifically, it is rejected by the Islamic Movement (Agbaria and Mustafa, 2012), which developed its own and divergent vision. As mentioned above, this Islamic vision seeks to Islamize Palestinian society rather than democratize the state, and advocates strengthening the Palestinian society in Israel as self-reliant and self-empowered.

Oded Haklai (2011) argues that Israeli politics, specifically internal Jewish politics, molds that of the Palestinians in Israel. Changes in the character and scope of Palestinian political mobilization are largely a result of the sector's political fragmentation and the state's withdrawal from key areas in public life. For Haklai, the impermeable boundaries of exclusion, which sustain the inequality and subordination of the Palestinian minority, do not provide an adequate explanation of the recent ethnonational turn in the politics of the Palestinian minority. He contends that as politics has become more divided, the economy more privatized, and civil society more diverse, the central government's ability to constrain minority organizations has diminished appreciably. Consequently, the minority's ethnonationalist political activism has become more parochial and vociferous. The Achilles' heel of Haklai's analysis is that it leaves Palestinian politics expressing limited agency and autonomy, because it ignores not only its anti-colonial nature but also the religious and theological aspects of faith-based organizations.

---

[2] On the Future Vision document, see Chapter 5.

Although the functions of different types of NGOs are much broader than those mentioned above (for more details, see Berthoud, 2001; Brinkerhoff et al., 2007; Hilhorst, 2003; Keck and Sikkink, 1998; Witt, 2006), we think that the main functions are those listed in the previous section and will limit our discussion to these dimensions.

In what follows, we present a general overview of the Palestinian NGOs in Israel and their fields of activity. We will examine their ability to function as a tool for empowerment, autonomy, and social change within their target group, the Palestinian community in Israel.

Historical Background

The first attempts to create Palestinian NGOs to serve various social functions predate 1948 and the establishment of Israel. During the Mandate era, many sectors established organizations to provide their members and the general public with services, however. But the *Nakba* of 1948 and the expulsion of hundreds of thousands of Palestinians destroyed most of those organizations and halted attempts to create new ones.

There were several attempts to create NGOs after the establishment of Israel, but state policy and the firm grip of the military government prevented the revival or creation of voluntary organizations. Almost none were founded until the 1970s, after the end of the military government (see Table 3.1).

Without dismissing the importance of older organizations,[3] we note that the last three decades have witnessed considerable momentum in the emergence of Palestinian civil society organizations that promote democratization, empowerment, and community development (Jamal, 2008; Payes, 2005). Most importantly, ever since the Oslo Accords these organization have been major players not only in the struggle for civil equality, stronger political awareness, and increased socioeconomic mobility in Palestinian society (Jamal, 2008; Payes, 2005), but also in igniting the recent ethnonational turn in the Palestinian political activism in Israel to end the Jewish ethnic hegemony (Haklai, 2011). This transformation of the political discourse among the Palestinians in Israel has been marked by a transition from the politics of inequality

---

[3] See Payes, 2005.

Table 3.1 *Palestinian NGOs in*
Israel, by decade of establishment[4]

Year of establishment	Percentage of organizations (%)
Through 1948	5.4
1949–1959	2.2
1960–1969	0.5
1970–1979	16.7
1980–1990	75.2

Source: Yaffa Research Institute (Yaffa, 1990: 10).

and grievances to the politics of recognition and belonging. Haklai characterizes this transition as ethnonational, pointing to the politicization of the Palestinian minority's indigenous identity as a platform on which the demands for collective rights, including in education, as well as more power-sharing, recognition, and equality, are raised. All in all, these demands seek to end the Jewish ethnic hegemony and to transform Israel into a bi-national state.

Since the 1980s we have witnessed continued efforts to initiate and build new NGOs that address different aspects of life in Palestinian society in Israel. Drawing on data about Palestinian NGOs in Israel, collected from primary and secondary sources, including 38 interviews we conducted with Palestinian activists and political leaders, we will now consider these organizations' ability to serve as a means for the collective empowerment of their community.

Palestinians NGOs in Israel: A Profile

According to a study conducted by Nakhleh and the Yaffa Institute, there were 180 Palestinian NGOs in Israel in 1990, which provided

---

[4] According to statistics provided by the Yaffa Research Institute, there were 186 foundations among Palestinians in Israel in 1990. The 1990s witnessed a leap in the establishment of Palestinian foundations, both quantitatively and qualitatively. Since then, specialized organizations have been established in various fields.

Table 3.2 *Number of NGOs and their field of activity, 2004*

Field of activity	Registered	Active
Not specified	19	12
Culture and entertainment	638	365
Education	337	212
Health	52	34
Welfare	308	168
Environment	18	11
Building and development	196	67
Social change	135	89
Voluntarism	27	26
International	5	1
Religion	340	135
Vocational institutes	26	10
Commemoration	8	5
Total	2199	1135

Source: Evan Chorev (2008: 12).

services to their members and to the general public. Given the reality of the daily lives of Palestinians in Israel, many organizations had to abandon their specialty areas and provide general services.

According to the Center for the Study of the Third Sector, at Ben-Gurion University, at the end of 2004 there were 2,200 registered NGOs in the Palestinian sector in Israel, of which 1,135 were active. Most of these organizations are in the north and work mainly in the fields of culture and entertainment, religion, and welfare (see Table 3.2).

A plurality of these organizations were created between 2000 and 2004 – 698. Only 598 organizations were founded between 1995 and 1999, 471 between 1990 and 1994, and 301 between 1985 and 1989. In 1984, there were only 117 NGOs all told. These numbers demonstrate that the NGO concept has gained steam among Palestinians in Israel over the last two decades (Evan Chorev, 2008: 12). This development can be attributed to the influence of globalization, the spread of market forces, the decline of the welfare state, and growing discrimination against Palestinians in Israel. This phenomenon is not limited to Palestinian society. Between 2000 and 2004, 8,443 NGOs were established in Israel, of which only 8% were by Palestinians.

The preoccupation of Palestinians in Israel with issues of discrimination and their relationship with the state has increased the number of NGOs set up to meet specific needs. These organizations spread rapidly in Palestinian society between 1986 and 2006. Only 3% of the Palestinian NGOs founded through 1986 were established to meet specific needs. This figure statistic increased to 13% for 1987–1991 and peaked at 21% in 2002–2006. The average percentage of active NGOs founded to provide specific services is 11% of all organizations (Alon, 2007: 7).

Nakhleh has classified NGOs into four groups. The first consists of those founded to provide a specialized service – in healthcare, culture, the arts, or education. The second group consists of NGOs limited to a geographical area; they have no specialty and provide a variety of services. The third group consists of NGOs that focus on specific problem throughout the country, such as social issues or matters concerning religious groups. The fourth and final group consists of national NGOs founded by political parties, such as the Islamic Movement, and other organizations affiliated with political parties (Nakhleh 1990).

A different classification distinguishes Islamic from non-Islamic NGOs. Here the former means those affiliated with the Islamic Movement, while non-Islamic means those not affiliated with it, even if they do not have a secular ideology. This classification can provide a better handle on the NGO phenomenon in Palestinian society. Dozens of organizations are affiliated with both Islamic Movements (parliamentary and extra-parliamentary) and active in various fields, including education, culture, social action, missionizing, public relations, legal matters, and student affairs.

The significance of this system relates to the fundamental differences between Islamic and non-Islamic institutions, in three major dimensions. The first is political independence: formally and publicly, the majority of the non-Islamic NGOs are independent, even if their members have close ties with political parties. In contrast, the Islamic institutions and organizations are closely linked to the Islamic Movement, from their founding and definition of their goals through the recruitment of employees and choice of a name. Although they are registered in compliance with the law, they are structurally and emotionally bound to the Islamic Movement, which views them as its own.

The second dimension encompasses support and funding. The majority of the non-Islamic organizations depend on foreign, non-Palestinian, and non-Islamic sources. In contrast, funding for Islamic institutions comes exclusively from the Islamic Movement, which acts as an umbrella fundraiser, raising money from Palestinian–Islamic sources or from contributions by Palestinians in Israel or Muslims throughout the world. As a result, Islamic institutions do not devise projects and request funding; instead, their agenda is determined by the Islamic Movement, which bankrolls them.

The third dimension is the pattern of activities. Most non-Islamic organizations work to influence state policies. They also emphasize the relationship between the minority and the majority in the state. That is not to say that these non-Islamic organizations neglect internal social problems. For example, women's NGOs work on women's issues internal to Palestinian society in Israel. Simultaneously, these organizations attempt to influence the status of women by pressuring the state to change its policies concerning women through legislation. These women's organizations endeavor to close the gap between Jewish and Palestinian women and to put an end to discrimination against the latter.

The parallels between the religious and secular approaches in modern Arab thought have resulted in a new conceptualization of civil society and its role. The secular approach refers to voluntary organizations as civil society; the Islamic approach sees them as communitarian social organizations. The former seeks to influence the policy of the state, while the latter focuses on changing the character of the community. Another characteristic of these two models is that the civil is found mainly in towns and in cities, the communal in villages and rural districts. The former expresses modern power and production relations; the latter, the traditional relations (tribe, clan, ethnicity) (Mahmad, 2006, quoted by Abu-Zaher, 2008: 204). We believe that this division is too simplistic and does not account for the fact that the supporters of the Islamic Movement are usually middle class, and their power sources are usually located in Palestinian cities and not rural areas (Ibrahim, 2004).

Islamic organizations and institutions focus on internal matters within the Palestinian community and neglect the relationship between the internal domain and the state. In other words, the Islamic Movement does not attempt to change state policy (except for several lawsuits filed by the Islamic Movement when the state violated Islamic and Waqf institutions). The Islamic Movement and its organizations do not call for changing the structure of the state, closing the gap between Jews and Palestinians, or putting an end to discrimination. By contrast, non-Islamic organizations make use of citizenship to empower Palestinians at the individual and collective levels. They utilize this discourse of citizenship in their relations with the state and demand change. Citizenship as a political tactic does not play a role for the Islamic institutions and organizations.

Additionally, over the years the Islamic Movement has cultivated the building of an independent community, predicated on the establishment of Palestinian institutions that do not draw on state resources, including education. Sheikh Raed Salah, the head of the Islamic movement, called this concept *al-Muj'tama' al-A'sami* or the "self-reliant society" (Salah, 2001: 5). Note that the idea has become popular among members of the northern faction of the Islamic Movement, which is an extra-parliamentary movement that refuses to take part in Israeli politics at the countrywide level. It believes that the construction of a Palestinian Muslim community is the only solution for the Palestinian–Muslim minority in Israel. Indeed, the movement rejects all other proposed political solutions for regulating the majority–minority relationship, such as a state of all its citizens, a binational state, or various forms of proposals (Ghanem and Mustafa, 2009a). In this context, the words of Dan Rabinowitz (2001: 350, 359–360) are particularly pertinent:

The Islamic Movement ... is completely alienated from the state, and will likely remain as such. It is likely that the alienation of Palestinian Israeli citizens from state institutions, dominant market forces and accessibility to the media, will continue to strengthen their recognition of the potential of this triple power to produce evil. Such recognition may make them a group that strives to strengthen the elements of civil activity within it. If so, the organizational example of the Islamic movement may act as inspiration for other movements and inspire other more equal, tolerant, and essential movements. ... The issue of education, including non-religious institutions, ... signaled to the public that the association was allocating its role in initiating advancements in a broad expanse of areas. This expansion of the meaning of the term "Islamic movement" and applying it to matters unrelated to religion has increased the political relevance of the association.

Salah's "self-reliant society is based on three principles that he detected as already existing in Palestinian society: capital, the land, and the economy (Ali, 2007). In particular, Salah emphasizes the "purity of capital," which should originate from strictly Islamic sources, including charities, the Waqf, and donations from Muslim organizations and individuals (Ali, 2006). Haklai (2004a) argues that Palestinian organizations that accept donations from foreign, particularly Jewish, sources are designed to strengthen the civil dimension of the struggle of the Palestinians in Israel in the framework of a democratic Jewish state. Haklai perceives the agenda of Jewish foundations as maintaining the Jewish character of the state by improving the status and condition of Palestinians on the civil level (ibid.). The lack of independent funding for Palestinian organizations is considered to be a significant challenge for Palestinian civil society, because dependence of foreign funds may prove dangerous should there be an economic crisis or a conflict arise between the agenda of the funding bodies and that of the organization (Jabareen, 2007).

The overall Palestinian–Islamic dimension plays an important role in the autonomous "self-reliant society" project. Salah argues that the establishment of such a society (or community) requires that the relationship between the Palestinian world and Muslim nation at large be further cemented. This may indicate that the extra-parliamentary Islamic Movement sees itself as part of the Muslim nation not only in symbolic and cultural terms but also in the practical sense. The connection between the establishment of an independent Muslim community in Israel and the deepening of the relationship with the Islamic world highlights the ideological orientation of the extra-parliamentary movement, which denies the uniqueness of the condition and status of Muslims in Israel. On the other hand, the parliamentary movement believes that the situation of the Muslims in Israel is unique.

NGOs as an Empowerment Mechanism for the Palestinians in Israel

NGOs are an integral part of the process of institution-building within Palestinian society in Israel. Shawqi Khatib,[5] former chair of the High Follow-up Committee for Arab Citizens in Israel and the National Committee of Arab Local Council Heads, believes that civil society organizations have had a positive impact on political activity:

[5] Interview with Shawqi Khatib, April 1, 2008.

In my view, these organizations have made our work more professional, more original. These organizations help us receive and disseminate information using advanced technologies and scientific methods, even when we are out in the field. This is a positive development in itself as it reflects on our performance as a society. All that I have mentioned has proven our need to maintain civil society's activities in the legal scientific and practical aspects.

The Palestinian NGOs in Israel are active in the process of institution-building and group organization and take upon themselves responsibility for providing cultural, economic, social, and political services. These services can supplement or be an alternative to those provided by the state – especially when state institutions fall short in providing the necessary services to Palestinians in Israel. Some within the Israeli establishment and among Palestinians view the development of non-governmental organizations in Palestinian society as part and parcel of the process of institution-building and autonomy, without dependence on the state. In his book, *Strangers in Their Homeland*, Ra'anan Cohen considers this phenomenon to be one of the most threatening to the Jewish majority (Cohen, 2006: 260).[6]

By contrast, the Palestinian elite in Israel considers the creation of civil society organizations to be an integral part of the process of community building and self-empowerment. Many studies have discussed the phenomenon of NGOs among Palestinians in Israel and considered these phenomena to make an important contribution to the empowerment of Palestinian society in Israel (Haklai, 2004a, 2004b, 2009; Jamal, 2017; Payes, 2003, 2005). Payes' comprehensive study of Palestinian NGOs focuses on the relationship between these organizations and the state. It argues that Palestinian NGOs play a significant role in promoting equality and the civil rights of Palestinians in Israel. They have also contributed to expanding political activism and political–economic consciousness among Palestinians (Payes, 2003, 2005). Jamal mentions two factors behind the increase in the number of non-governmental organizations Palestinian society in 1990s, internal and external. He explains that each factor includes two patterns, one positive and the other negative (Jamal, 2008: 291).

[6] The others are the demographic growth among Palestinians in Israel, the rise of the Islamic Movement, the strengthening of the Palestinian national identity, the concept of a state of all its citizens, the concept of dual nationality, and the migration of Palestinians to live in Jewish neighborhoods (Cohen, 2006: 259–261).

Among the internal factors, Jamal mentions on the negative side of the ledger the decline in classical political activity in Palestinian society, the weakness of political Palestinian parties, and the inadequate social services provided by Arab local councils. The positive elements include the rise of individualism in Palestinian society, an increase in the number of Palestinian university graduates and professionals, a rise in political consciousness and deeper understanding of the meaning of citizenship, an increase in social initiatives among young Palestinians, and, finally, the successes of non-governmental organizations that provide a model for social involvement.

As for the external factors, there are several key reasons for the establishment of new NGOs: the decline in Palestinians' political participation in the Knesset, the inadequacy of the social and economic services provided by the state, and the barriers to Palestinian participation, particularly against educated Palestinians in the Israeli labor market. Here the positive factors are the globalization of the indigenous minority and human rights discourse, the growing role of civil society and social organizations across the globe, the emergence of Israeli civil society and its impact on the Israeli public space, and the many external actors that support the creation of non-governmental organizations.

Palestinians NGOs in Israel: Community Needs vs. Essential Dilemmas

Because many NGOs in Palestinian society – research institutes, cultural and educational institutions, and legal defense groups – focus on human rights and the protection of the Palestinian minority's rights in Israel, there is a general feeling that they contribute to the empowerment of their society. Although their activity has expanded in recent years, they remain dependent on international funders and are limited by Israeli politics and laws. These organizations are often harassed and interrogated by various organs of the state. Below we will present and analyze the internal shortages and dilemmas facing Palestinian NGOs in Israel.

Conflicts and competitions among organizations detract from their ability to serve the needs of the community. Some of those differences derive from their ideological and partisan political affiliation. Such factors can limit the effectiveness and scope of organizations' activities and prevent them from becoming a force that can influence the Palestinian public arena.

Knesset Member Haneen Zuabi, who was formerly executive director of an NGO, appraised these organizations and institutions as follows: "The first observable phenomenon about these organizations is their chaotic rapid growth and proliferation, not due to lack of social supervision or mentoring – for these are abundant – but due to the non-homogeneous manner in which these organizations grow, compared with the development in other political, cultural and economic institutions."[7] In addition, their rate of growth is not compatible with the frequent lack of the human skills needed to operate these institutions or the development of the internal social economy that is supposed to support these institutions.

In like manner, these organizations have not expressly applied the principles of the creation of national institutions and their influence on the creation of collective identity that which would help democratize and modernize society. These organizations came into being after a group of the educated elite was rejected by the Israeli labor market and academia. For its members, Third Sector jobs in the Palestinian society were a source of livelihood, even though there was slight opportunity to effect political and social change. Thus the expansion of grassroots organizations and non-governmental organizations was driven by the desire to expand the Palestinian labor market. For that reason, "working for these organizations remains more attractive than the values they espouse."[8]

Many of these organizations have run up against organizational hurdles. Over the years, they suffered financial instability due to their dependence on external funding sources. In addition, they lacked skilled workers capable of embarking on initiatives or participating in general activities. In principle, these organizations suffered from constant fear and suspicion of the state (Nakhleh, 1990: 9–17).

Three major challenges face Palestinians NGOs in Israel. The first is finding alternative sources of financing. Their dependence on foreign funders places their very existence at risk.[9] NGOs receive millions of sheqels from foreign donors, particularly the European Union.

---

[7] Interview with Haneen Zuabi, former director of the *I'alam* Center, which advocates for the media rights of Palestinians in Israel, March 2008.
[8] Ibid.
[9] Interview with Hassan Jabareen, director of the Adalah Center, January 2007.

According to the EU representative in Israel, Palestinian organizations received a ground total of nearly 18 million sheqels from the European Union in fiscal 2004/2005 (Jabareen, 2007: 95).

Finding alternative funding sources requires the cultivation of local Palestinian donors and the strengthening of the relations among these organizations, local society, and the Arab world. In recent years, Jewish and Zionist organizations have offered them financial assistance, in the belief that an improvement in the Palestinians' living conditions would help maintain the Jewish nature of Israel and facilitate the assimilation of Palestinians (Haklai, 2008). In 2005, these Jewish organizations gave close to $3,000,000 to Palestinian NGOs. This support represents a challenge to Palestinian institutions because they which must tailor their agenda to the foundations' priorities, which often contradict the fundamental needs of Palestinian society in Israel.

The second challenge relates to the issues of public legitimacy and representation. Even though all these organizations are focused on improving the collective rights of Palestinians in Israel, their links with political parties means that their legitimacy on the Palestinian street and their work on behalf of collective rights become questionable (Jabareen, 2007). Even though the issue of collective rights is dealt with through professional legal and lobbying systems, politics remains a significant present in the work of civil organizations.

As Haneen Zuabi noted, "this dichotomy between political parties and NGOs raises questions unrelated to logical or foundational differences between the two."[10] Theoretically, the difference between the two is manifested in their activity models and not in the degree of politicization or level of nationalism. The difference between grassroots organizations and political parties ought to be, broadly speaking, in their actions and goals, as well as in the level of public representation.

The boundaries between political parties and NGOs are inherent in the difference between the political and ideological belief system of a political party and an NGO's practical agenda. Political parties enjoy (and need) public legitimacy, while many view Palestinian NGOs in Israel as remote from society and an agent for foreign political agendas, mainly due to the American and European sources of their funding. Many Palestinian NGOs form a closed club of the middle class, with

[10] Interview with Haneen Zuabi, March 2008.

its own interests that diverge from the real needs of the majority of the Palestinians in Israel.

Islamic forces view the donors as foreign agents with a Western agenda that distances these organizations from the national agenda. In fact, NGOs often find themselves under pressure by their constituencies, who see an inherent conflict between the organization's financial sources and their national obligations.

There are practical reasons that tie NGOs to political parties. The NGOs need the legitimacy the parties provide and need to maintain good relations with them as a target audience for their services and activities.

One cannot ignore the conflict between NGOs and political parties. Civil society organizations have become more prominent in the last decade and even overshadow the political parties, due to the weakening of the latter and decline of collective political activity by the Palestinians in Israel.

This leads to the third challenge facing Palestinian civil society, namely the ties and relationships between the organizations and the Palestinian public at large. Most NGOs do not have close ties with the latter. Their conferences are often attended by the same people and their activities are limited to a select group. This challenge is closely related to the first two. These organizations' ability to develop internal sources is related to their perceived legitimacy and grassroots activities.

This situation is similar to attempts by political parties to gain their voters' trust. According to Ameer Makhoul, "one of the weaknesses of these organizations on the local level is their relationship with their target audiences."[11] Part of this problem is related to the problem of foreign financial support for these NGOs.

Foreign donors do not wish to see these NGOs expand and turn into advocates for collective sociopolitical rights. In fact, they seek to detach them from their popular base, in the hope of containing them and creating a schism between the elites and their society. This explains some of the hostility that foreign organizations and institutions have shown to the heads of organizations and institutions that took part in the composition of the "Future Vision" document, including the demand for the abrogation of the current Israeli regime and its core foundations (Ghanem and Mustafa, 2009a).

---

[11] Case Foundation magazine, No. 1 (September 2007).

In the last two decades, the development of civil society activity has pushed educated groups and political activists to abandon their political activism and join them. This has weakened the political parties, especially those with a national agenda.

Criticism of Palestinian NGOs in Israel

Israeli Palestinian NGOs have become part of the general social and political structure and believe that they can contribute to a change in the relations between the state and its Palestinian citizens. On the other hand, some of the organizations, especially those funded by foreign donors, play a limited role in the Palestinian community and do not feel obligated to seek legitimacy. They are bankrolled by sources that pay less attention to the collective national interest and often work to destroy any collective national strategy. Some of those organizations flourish thanks to their public relations and media presence, which makes them popular in the community (but this means that a large chunk of their financial resources are spent on maintaining an image, instead of being invested where needed). This phenomenon is common in the Third World, and particularly among Palestinians in the West Bank and Gaza Strip (Hanafi and Tabar, 2005).

On the other hand, many large Palestinian organizations that have received financial support focus on the relationship between the state and the Palestinian minority. They have abandoned their role of bringing about social change within Palestinian society in Israel and focus instead on working a change in the relationship between the minority and the state – an issue that is part of the national consensus and does not require endless labor to effect social change.

In addition, many of these NGOs were created by political parties, foreign investors (American and European funds), activists who failed to acquire prominent positions in political parties, or academics who organized and created their agenda without giving adequate consideration to the needs of society or the public at large. In these circumstances, any political and social changes they initiate seem to be remote from what society needs.

The fact that many civil society organizations have adopted an agenda that does not empower society, increase its opportunities, or fulfill its political needs is not a coincidence. Unlike the case in many Western democratic societies, they did not grow from the bottom, with a wide base of popular support. Instead, they were created from the top, by a select group that claims to understand the needs of society and asserts it has reinvented itself whenever it is scrutinized.

Many of these organizations were established by political parties in order to exploit the organizations to raise funds and provide jobs for their activists. Others were created by foundations and foreign groups in order to influence processes within Palestinian society and co-opt some of the political and academic capabilities of Palestinians in Israel. In other cases, the donors wanted to use them as intermediaries between society and political institutions.

Summary

Palestinian NGOs in Israel have been influenced by global changes, especially in the 1990s. Since then, these organizations have incorporated concepts such as human rights and recognition of the Palestinians in Israel as a national minority into their platforms. They have also drawn on the experiences of other ethnic groups throughout the world (Payes, 2005: 711).

Palestinian NGOs have not yet created an organized civil society that is legitimate and able to contribute to the empowerment of this group and to strength its autonomy and internal sources of funds. They have not reached the stage of political struggle where they can address the needs of Palestinian society, for four main reasons. The first is the Palestinians' minority status and the discrimination against them in Israel. Israel is governed by an ethnic regime that grants preference to one group (the Jews) over all others (especially the Palestinians). It employs various policies and legal arrangements to ensure the superiority of the dominant group (see Ghanem, 1998; Kretzmer, 2002; Rouhana 1997; Rouhana and Ghanem, 1998; Smooha, 1990, 2002; Yiftachel, 2006b), and maintain control of the minority and its institutions. It allows the development of only a limited civil society among the subordinate dominant group, the Palestinians.

The second reason is related to the complex and conflicting structures within civil society, and the characteristics of the main actors there, including their personal interests, level of proficiency, and ability to maneuver at the local, national, and international levels.

The third reason has to do with the factors that prevent Palestinians in Israel from creating collective institutions. This has impacted on agenda, performance, and strategies of civil society institutions, which occasionally use contradictory tactics. Competition among organizations has had negative consequences, as well.

Finally, there is the external factor of foreign funding. Institutions have little room to maneuver against the foundation-supported and financed organizations. And they have even less room to maneuver in their relationship with the state, which deploys political and legal powers to limit their these institutions and impose restrictions on their funding.

On the other hand, one cannot deny the positive role that Palestinian NGOs have played in raising awareness of public issues. These organizations have also helped train specialists. So despite the many criticisms of these organizations, we cannot deny their role in this emerging culture of institution-building.[12] Haneen Zuabi adds that many of these institutions often came under two opposing influences. On the one hand, they have raised the bar of political public activity for many marginalized groups. On the other hand, these organizations have limited and constricted the intellectual, political, and national activity of several people who could have overcome such influences. They promote an "average level" of activism and political work. That is to say, the institutions and organizations have produced political and national mediocrity. They further diluted the political and national discourse and caused members of the organizations to be afraid of political activities (the crystallization of thought, party platforms, participation in demonstrations, political rallies, and party work).[13]

According to Ameer Makhoul, "Palestinian organizations have the capability and experience to use international institutions and charters. This is indicated by the participation of these organizations in international institutions, membership in them, and cooperation with them."[14]

---

[12] Interview with Haneen Zuabi, March 2008.   [13] Ibid.
[14] Cases Foundation magazine, No. 1 (September 2007).

4 | *Politicization of Islamic Activism in Israel*

"Political Islam" began organizing in Mandatory Palestine before 1948. The Muslim Brotherhood, founded in Egypt in the 1920s, did not begin to take an interest in events in Palestine until the mid-1930s. After the eruption of the Palestinian revolt against the British and to protest Jewish immigration, in 1936, movement representatives came from Egypt to encourage the Palestinians in their struggle. The first local branch of the Muslim Brotherhood was founded in Jerusalem in 1946. During the 1948 war, three battalions of volunteers from the Brotherhood enlisted in the Egyptian army (Shabi and Shaked, 1994). However, the results of the 1948 war, the dispersal of Palestinians, and the establishment of Israel, which imposed a military rule on the Palestinian communities, limited the activity of political Islam. In fact, one cannot point to any such organization by Palestinian citizens of Israel during the 1950s, 1960s, or 1970s. After 1967, the situation changed as a result of renewed contact between the Palestinians in Israel and Palestinians in the occupied West Bank and Gaza Strip and the existence of fundamentalist organizations and religious seminaries there. New conditions were created for the development of political Islam among the Palestinians in Israel (Mayer, 1988).

A number of young people who completed high school and were attracted to an Islamic environment continued their studies in the Islamic colleges and institutes that prepared them for the title of "sheikh." These young men began unorganized activity to preach religion in their home communities and elsewhere in Muslim communities, including sermons in the mosques and at meetings held on Muslim festivals (Mayer, 1988). Their activity paved the way for the Islamic stream to organize in the form of political and social associations.

The younger generation began to organize in almost every community where there were Muslims, establishing voluntary associations both to promote social activity and to gather funds for them. They also began to organize on a countrywide basis, enrolling new members and preaching for a return to their religious roots.

The Islamic Movement focused on providing the services associated with the institutions of civil society and on propaganda. Ever since its founding, the Islamic Movement has provided essential services to the local population in every community where it is active (see the list in Abu-Raiya, 1989). These services include an educational network to supplement the state system, libraries, computer centers, community centers, preschools, rehabilitation centers for ex-convicts and addicts, medical and dental clinics, and so on. These can be found all over the country, including towns where the Islamic Movement is not part of the local coalition (e.g., Umm al-Fahm, Kufr Qassem, Kufr Bara, Kufr Kanna, Nazareth, Kabul, Nahaf, and others).

The Islamic Movement employed various means to manage and fund these institutions. It focused on volunteer activity and on mobilizing its members for projects that address community needs. The mosques, found in every locality where Muslims live, hosted these projects. The movement also took over the collection of the *zakat*, the tax that every Muslim must pay to support the poor. These funds underwrote a large portion of the movement's activities. In localities where the movement could draw on other financial sources, including governmental sources – especially in towns where it controlled the local council – it did so.

The history of Islamic religious organization in Israel can be divided into three periods. The first period (1979–1981) featured a semi-military underground organization composed of a small core of people who believed in armed struggle against the Jews and the State of Israel; they called themselves "Asrat al-Jihad" (the Family of Jihad). This group was apprehended by the Israeli security forces in 1981 and its leaders imprisoned, putting an end to this period. The second period, from 1983 through the 1996, began with the emergence of Sheikh Abdallah Nimr Darwish of Kufr Qassem (in the Triangle) as the leader of a new organization that called itself the "Young Muslims." The third period, from 1996 through the present, began when the Islamic Movement split in two, with two different political organizations and political orientations and goals, as we will see below.

Until 1996, the Islamic Movement did not participate officially in Knesset elections, even though it did not formally boycott them. Before Election Day it would call on its members to act in accordance with their conscience. Before the elections in 1996, however, the Islamic Movement set up a joint list with the Democratic Arab Party. Two of its representatives then won seats to the 14th Knesset (out of four seats for the joint list); it also placed two representatives in the 15th Knesset (out of five seats for the joint list). Some members of the Young Muslims seceded in protest against the group's participation in these elections and established an alternative movement, led by Raed Salah, the mayor of Umm al-Fahm (Ozacky-Lazar and Ghanem, 1996).

Numbering close to 1,200,000 in 2009, or 18% of Israel's population, Palestinian Arab citizens in Israel are 80% Muslims, 10% Christians, and 10% Druze.[1] The Muslims are Sunnis, enjoying the status of the largest group among the Arabs and part of the Muslim majority in the region. On the other hand, they are split by region (the Galilee, Triangle, and northern Negev), socioeconomic level (poor, working, middle, and upper class), and political orientation (supporters of Jewish parties, supporters of predominantly Arab parties, and independents).

The present chapter offers a comprehensive model for understanding the Islamic fundamentalist orientation and political activity, with special reference to the Islamic Movement(s) in Israel. The split within the Islamic Movement in 1996 and the creation of the two different movements with two different orientations will be used as the case study.

The Politics of Islamic Organizations in Israel: Theoretical Context

Explaining the development of Islamic fundamentalism in general, and of Palestinian political Islam (inside and outside Israel) in particular, has been a popular academic activity in the last few decades. The theoretical explanations for the phenomenon of "political Islam" among the Palestinians are similar to the explanations for the general phenomenon of political Islam and Islamic fundamentalism (see, for example, Hroub, 2004; Tamimi, 2007). At both levels we may identify two different and alternative theoretical explanations for the phenomenon and the aims of Islamic fundamentalism. First, Islamic fundamentalism may be seen as a reflection of the desire to implement religious doctrine

---

[1] These figures exclude more than 250,000 Arabs in East Jerusalem and 15,000 Arabs in the Golan Heights who are by and large not Israeli citizens (but they are included in the official statistics because these areas were incorporated by Israeli law).

in daily life, including politics, culture, the economy, and society. According to this approach, political Islam in modern times is a political phenomenon that aims to implement the commands found in Islamic *shari'a* (laws), which are based on the Quran (Islam's holy book), the *sunnah* (the Prophet Muhammad's "trodden path," "custom," or "tradition"), and the *hadith* (the Prophet Muhammad's sayings), as well as in later religious regulations created or developed by the *ulema* (leading religious scholars and clerics). In other words, political Islam's mission is to implement the *shari'a* in the lives of contemporary Muslims (see, for example, Juergensmeyer, 2000: 21; Lewis, 1988; 1993a; and the analysis by Moaddel, 2002).

This is how G. H. Jansen, in his book *Militant Islam* (published in 1979, at the peak of the rise of Islam, following the Islamic revolution in Iran), begins his summary:

There are many and varied aspects to militant Islam. Under Ayatollah Khomeini it appears harsh and stern, the variety presented by Allal al-Fassi or Mohammad Nasir is open-minded and flexible; with Sadeq al-Mahdi it is flexible but impatient; the Jamaat's version in Pakistan is at once detailed and equivocal, while with the Muslim Brotherhood it appears well thought out and menacing. But beneath these variations there is always the same steely core. Partly this is explained by the fact that these movements have been hammered into hardness by repression. A more valid explanation is that these groupings, even though some of them may call themselves "parties," are much more than mere political parties trying to implement a party program. They are, rather, deliberately and self-consciously, engaged in the high and holy task of infusing the principles of a higher religion into workday politics, economics and social affairs. (Jansen, 1979: 188)

The literature refers to Islamic fundamentalism as a reflection of rigid beliefs and a specific way of life. According to this image, the radical fundamentalists are extremists and fanatics *(muta'assibun)*, who suffer from an inferiority complex that is reflected in their aggressiveness, authoritarianism, intolerance, paranoia, and conspiratorial tendencies. Fundamentalists are further described as idealistic, highly devoted, ready to live an austere lifestyle filled with struggle and sacrifice, and pledging absolute obedience to Allah and to the leader of the fundamentalist movement (Dekmejian, 1995).

In accordance with this approach, Lewis (1993b: 133–154) stresses that the Islamic movements active during the second half of the twentieth century were rooted in the universal belief in the unity of "church and state" and that Islam was the central element in Muslim identity. Lewis adds that various Islamic movements in the modem period, including the pan-Islamism of Ottoman Sultan Abdulaziz in the 1870s, the rise of Egyptian Muslim Brotherhood in the 1930s, and the Iranian Revolution of 1977–1979, were manifestations of this universality and centrality.

Many students of the Palestinian Islamic movements have used this model in order to explain this phenomenon; these scholars do not distinguish between different groups and orientations within political Islam. Israeli (2008) maintains that all Islamic movements are identical in their goals and political objectives, and that any differences between the movements are very minor and superficial. Regarding political Islam in Israel, he claims that the two Islamic movements work to achieve the same goals, with no substantive difference, and that these goals are also identical to the goals of other Islamic fundamental movements: they all aim to destroy Israel and establish an Islamic entity in Palestine, but employ different tactics in pursuit of this goal.

Bukay (2004) argues that there is only one Islamic culture and that there is no difference between different streams among Islamists, including in their interpretations of the religious texts. Bukay agrees with Israeli that all Islamic movements aspire to destroy Israel and establish an Islamic state in its place (Bukay 2008).

Rekhess (1998) asserts that there are strong ties between different Islamic movements, including those that are active among the Arabs in Israel and their brothers in the occupied Palestinian territories. He claims that political Islam in Israel is simply a branch of Palestinian Islamic fundamentalism, which means that the common characteristics of Islamic movements in the two communities, in Israel and in the Palestinian Authority, are one and the same.

The alternative explanation understands political Islam as a political phenomenon of the modern state and society and part of their political, social and economic development. In this approach, Islamic fundamentalist movements are first and foremost "social and political movements engaged in mobilization, organization, and possibly the seizure of the political authority" (Dessouki, 1982). Therefore, these movements are guided by a political cost–benefit calculus, at least in the short run. In addition, like other sociopolitical forces, these movements are riven by factionalism, personal conflicts, and controversies about the strategies and tactics to achieve their common goals. This is because political Islamic movements are populist movements. Their populist nature is expressed at the symbolic level in their self-perception and presentation to the public as "fronts" *(jabahat)* open to all Muslims, and not as conventional political parties that represent particular interests. Another reflection of this populist nature is the political Islamic movements' heterogeneous social base, which includes the poor and the rich, the rural and the urban, and the educated and uneducated, and allows Islamic fundamentalism to appear in different forms and to adopt different targets and strategies.

In this view, the structural dimension of Islamic activism is conditioned by local and global contexts. Islamic activism reflects a desperate search for a stabilizing anchor in a disrupted traditional social order that has been displaced by haphazard modernization projects and failed nationalisms (Haddad, 1992; Salla, 1997: 734; Voll, 1982), and is very much affected by global forces (Beckford, 2000: 69; Roy, 2001; Wuthnow, 1980; see discussion by Hashem, 2006). Hashem (2006) claims that the ecology of Islamic activism is always in flux, combining fixity with pragmatism as it responds to environmental challenges. Like other social movements, Islamic activism develops through the "interplay of aims, resources, and obstacles" (Melucci, 1985: 92), which results in adaptations that are justified by an Islamic ideology. The Islamic past is appropriated to justify courses of actions deemed necessary for effective efforts by Islamic social movement in today's environment (Mamdani, 2002: 67).

Several scholars have used this model in order to understand Palestinian Islamic fundamentalism in general and Islamic fundamentalism in Israel in particular. According to them, although political Islam in Israel is part of the general awakening of Islamic fundamentalism that began in the 1970s, it has special characteristics rooted in the Israeli experience of the Arab minority, including the emergence of the Islamic Movement in a Jewish state with a clear Jewish political and cultural hegemony (Ali, 2004; Malik, 1990; Mayer, 1988; Rekhess, 1993). These scholars stress the fact that the Sunni Muslim minority in Israel is the only Muslim minority that lives in a territory considered to be Arab–Muslim in the historical and contemporary Muslim consciousness as well as sacred Muslim land. Islamic fundamentalism in Israel is a complex phenomenon that takes account of the Israeli reality, as well as the general context of the Muslims, including the holy text. The two parallel contexts affect the content of the different Islamic fundamentalist movements and their orientation in Israel.

Political Islam in Israel was strongly influenced by the Israeli reality, but also by the Islamic religious doctrine and culture outside Israel. It must strike a balance between preserving the Muslim identity in all its aspects and obeying Israeli law.

Issam Abu-Raiya (2004) uses these two approaches to present a third explanation that fits within the two explanations presented earlier. He maintains that, on one level, the different political strategies can be explained by the abstract or concrete nature of the interpretation of the religious texts. A more concrete interpretation holds that Islamic precepts must be translated into a specific, and generally rigid, political program. Moreover, for a concrete interpretation of the religious texts, participation in electoral politics is likely to provoke charges of deviating from *shari'a*. A more abstract interpretation of religious principles allows for greater flexibility and improvisation in the approach to non-Islamic politics, without considering this a deviation from holy writ and the "straight path." One of the Islamic concepts used to abstract Islamic doctrine is *ijtihad*. Ijtihad and other Islamic concepts enable political Islamic movements to "combine religious fundamentalism with political realism," to balance "between final goals and immediate interests and needs; a rhetoric of religious fanaticism with an interpretation that justifies compromise and pragmatism" (Abu-Raiya, 2004: 440–441).

With regard to the split in the Islamic Movement in Israel in 1996 into two rival groups, Abu-Raiya (2005) states that disagreement about participation in Knesset elections, based on the difference between the abstract and concrete interpretations, was one factor behind the schism.

One stream, led by Sheikh Raed Salah (the mayor of Umm al-Fahm at the time), asserted that participation in the Knesset elections endangers the values of the Islamic Movement as a religious movement and would lead to the Israelization of the Muslim society. The other stream, led by Sheikh Nimr Darwish, believed that representation in the Knesset could advance the goals of the Islamic Movement and of Arab society (Ghanem and Mustafa, 2009a).

Sheikh Ibrahim Sarsur (2005), who became the leader of the parliamentary Islamic Movement after Darwish, admits that the pre-1996 united Islamic Movement did not successfully accommodate divergent views; the schism was inevitable, given the divergent and incompatible viewpoints within the Islamic Movement. The split was essential in order to preserve the movement's purity. Sheikh Salah concurs with him on one point: that what happened in 1996 was not the "result of an isolated incident, but the cumulative result of numerous incidents over many years" (*Sawt al-Haq wal-Huriyya*, April 4, 1997, 5).

In our view, these alternative explanations suffer from an excessive focus on the Islamic movements themselves and on their platforms and methods, and from an attempt to explain the phenomenon as one that dictates development in accordance with religious doctrine or, at best, in accordance with the political situation these movements aspire to change. We would like to offer an alternative, comprehensive, and representative explanation of the development of political Islam in general and its Palestinian expression in particular, focusing on the different orientations of the two Islamic movements in Israel. The fact that the two movements (which began and developed as a single move-ment from its inception in the early 1980s until 1996) split due to the decision to contest Knesset elections and became separate movements that are substantially different in their platforms, work plans, orienta-tion, and methods of political involvement can teach us a great deal about the nature of religious fundamentalism, both in general and in Israel. It will serve as a test case for building a broad explanatory model that goes beyond the Islamic Movement itself to address the human and political environment in which the supporters and leaders of political Islam operate.

The Development of Political Islam: Towards a General Model for Understanding the Phenomenon

Our basic working assumption is that the models presented above to explain the phenomenon of political Islam and the activity of the Islamic movements do not provide a comprehensive explanation; addi-tional effort is needed to come up with a better explanation of the phenomenon in all of its nuances. We will outline a suitable model that addresses the internal and external environment of political Islam and accounts for each component of this environment.

Our explanation is built on four levels of factors that, taken together, compose the overall explanation: (1) the political context (the broadest factor); (2) the political orientation of the general public as the Islamic

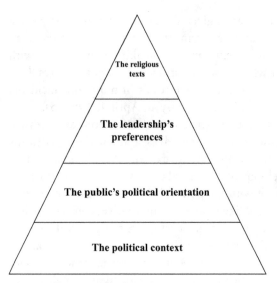

Figure 4.1 The four levels of related variables

Movement's target community; (3) the nature, orientation, and prefer-ences of the political leadership of the Islamic movements themselves; and (4) the meanings this leadership ascribes to religious texts (see Figure 4.1).

The Political Context

Like secular or semi-secular political organizations, political Islam operates within a political, social, cultural, and economic environment at every level that affects life in the modern state (local, national, regional, and international). Every political party, including the Islamic movements, tries to advance its objectives and develop work methods based on an assessment of the influence of environmental factors. Political Islam in Israel, like other political organizations that operate among the Arabs in the country, has developed in light of the internal situation of the Arabs in Israel, including social, cultural, economic, and political issues affecting them. The developments are also affected by the national and civic status of the Arabs in the Israeli polity, especially the fact that Israel is an ethnic state that gives preference to Jews over Arabs and discriminates against the latter in every domain (see Ghanem and Mustafa, 2009a; Yiftachel, 2004.)

Political Islam is also affected by the general situation of the Palestinian issue and the Palestinian aspiration for self-determination, and by internal political developments, including power struggles between the religious and secular currents of the Palestinian national movement. This conflict is found throughout Arab and Islamic arena in the region, in various forms, including violent struggles and less violent confrontations (for example, the Islamic stream has fought elections in Egypt, Jordan, the Palestinian Authority, and Turkey). The West's war against political Islam, lumped together with "Islamic terror," constitutes another set of environmental factors that influence the activity, objectives, and basic orientation of the Islamic movements in Israel, as well as their political choices regarding issues of concern to their society.

The Public's Political Orientation

The basic orientation of the group in which political Islam operates is a key element for explaining the Islamic Movement's orientation and methods. The Islamic movements, like all political parties and movements, seek public support and operate on the assumption that their ideology, objectives, and methods resonate with a community of supporters who constitute their reservoir of members, activists, and voters.

Research on the political orientation of the Arabs in Israel has attracted considerable attention in the past three decades (Al-Haj, 1988, 1993; Ghanem, 2001a, 2001b; Ghanem and Mustafa, 2009a, 2009b; Rekhess, 1989; Rouhana, 1997; Rouhana and Ghanem, 1998; Smooha, 1983, 1984, 1989a, 1989b, 1992, 2005). In many aspects, they all reach the same conclusions: most Palestinians in Israel have accepted their status as a minority and anticipate a different future than the rest of the Palestinians, Arabs, and Muslims in the region. On the other hand, they oppose the Jewish character of Israel and demand the establishment of a state in which Arabs and Jews are equal.

An in-depth study of the political orientation of the supporters of political Islam in Israel indicates that there are significant differences with regard to many areas and issues (Smooha and Ghanem, 1998, 2000). These differences can explain the decision to split into separate movements and constitute the human, political, and social basis for the continued existence of two movements.

The Leadership's Preferences and Interests

The personal preferences and interests of the leaders themselves and, in many aspects, the elites who support them are part of the explanation of political behavior in general and of political Islam in particular. The leaders of political Islam in the Arab and Islamic world make decisions about their attitude vis-à-vis the state and other groups in the society (including non-Muslims) as part of their own profit-loss calculations.

In the Israeli context, the Islamic Movement formed in the 1970s remained united as long as its founder controlled the organization and no rivals contested his position. But a new generation of leaders came on the scene in the early 1990s, consisting primarily of charismatic mayors, regional leaders, and activists.

The new generation included some who saw themselves as potential leaders of political Islam and challenged the founding leader, Sheikh Abdallah Nimr Darwish. Notable among this group were the former head of the Kufr Qassem local council (and later the head of the parliamentary branch of the movement, Sheikh Ibrahim Sarsur); the former head of the Kufr Bara local council, Sheikh Kamal Rian; and the former mayor of Umm al-Fahm, Sheikh Raed Salah (now the head of the banned extra-parliamentary Islamic Movement), and his deputy, Sheikh Kamal Khatib. Salah suspected Darwish of planning to pass on the leadership to a relative, Sarsur, and of steering the Islamic Movement in a way that served his own interests, including his close relations with the Jewish establishment. These suspicions played a central role in the schism in 1996.

The Interpretation of the Religious Texts

The religious texts occupy an important place in any explanation of the phenomenon of political Islam (see, for example, Juergensmeyer, 2000: 21; Lewis, 1988, 1993a; Moaddel, 2002). Our argument is that political texts do not have any substantial or decisive significance on the phenomenon of political Islam in the modern era. Only the interpretation attributed to the text is important for the leaders, activists, members, and supporters of the Islamic movements, based on the general political context, the orientation of the particular public and the interests of the leadership. What is important is the profound meanings of each religious text in the context of Islamic activity – and there are yawning contradictions in how they are interpreted by the different Islamic movements.

In the Israeli context, as we will see below, the leaders of the competing Islamic movements translate the religious texts in completely different ways at the political and practical levels. The divergent and contradictory meanings assigned to the same text support our assertion that the text itself is not important. What is crucial is the interpretation of the text.

To illustrate our assertions, we present them in the form of a pyramid, starting with the broad political context and culminating in the "meanings of the text" (see Figure 4.1).

Political Islam in Israel: Two Movements and Two Orientations

The substantial differences between the two Islamic movements within Israel proper can exemplify the model we presented, including the different meanings of implementing Islam. We will examine the political and ideological differences between the two Islamic movements in Israel, focusing on the fundamental issues that divide them (Table 4.1). We will survey their divergent views about participation Knesset elections and

Table 4.1 *The differences between the two branches of Political Islam in Israel*

	The parliamentary branch	The extra-parliamentary branch
Type of politics	Politics of recognition	Politics of difference
Participation in Knesset elections	Has participated in elections since the split in 1996	Boycotts the elections; its stance has become more rigid over time
The future of the Muslim minority in Israel	Achieving equality via negotiation or pressure on the state to persuade it to allocate resources for improving the status and situation of the Muslims in Israel	Build institutions that are independent of the state on the road to realizing the aspiration of establishing a Muslim (Arab) community that is independent of the state
Various political and social issues	Moderate	Conservative and radical

of the future of the Muslim and Arab minority in Israel, as well as their attitude towards the Future Vision document (published in 2006).

The Future of the Muslims (and Arabs) in Israel

The two Islamic movements in Israel share the goal of strengthening religion as a major component of the collective identity of the Arabs in Israel. They pursue this goal through religious preaching and diverse religious and social activities that have produced a wave of Islamization among the Arabs in Israel (Ali, 2006). But a close look at the activity of the two movements indicates that they are not partners for the future of the Muslims in Israel, particularly in regard to the relations between the state and the Muslim minority. From a theoretical perspective, we can distinguish two types of politics in the two movements: (1) the parliamentary Islamic Movement employs the tools and pursues the objectives of general Arab politics in Israel, which always focuses on the "politics of recognition" (Taylor, 1992: 25–73) and (2) the extra-parliamentary Islamic Movement remain aloof from general Arab politics and parliamentary politics, especially in its intensive use of the tools of the "politics of difference."

The difference between the politics of recognition and the politics of difference is related to the question of citizenship and the relations between the majority and the minority in the state. The politics of recognition attempts to improve the status and situation of the Arabs in Israel through negotiation, influence, and pressure on the state and on the majority, in order to compel them to adopt a policy and corresponding measures of equality, affirmative action, and recognition of the Arabs' identity and status as an indigenous minority entitled to collective rights recognized and supported by the state. The politics of difference, on the other hand, focuses on activity conducted within the community and attempts to cut itself off from any support by the state. It is not interested in the issue of recognition by the majority or by the state. The extra-parliamentary Islamic Movement's politics of difference is aimed at building an independent society that can survive and manage itself in isolation from the state. Sheikh Salah called this project *al-muj'tama' al-a'sami* (the independent or self-reliant community) (Salah, 2001: 5).

On the community level, religious fundamentalism is expressed by forging a community with separate and distinct institutions, whose members conduct most of their lives within it and feel great loyalty towards it (Ali, 2004). The project of the extra-parliamentary Islamic Movement is not integrative. Hence it faces constant persecution by the security and political establishment in Israel, more than the parliamentary Islamic Movement. The latter's activity sees Israeli citizenship as an important political tool and is considered to be integrative. This view is not shared by the extra-parliamentary movement, whose activity is regarded by the Israeli establishment as endangering the fragile relations between the Arab minority and the Jewish state (Smooha and Ghanem, 1998). The political and ideological dimension of the extra-parliamentary Islamic Movement's activity excites the state's fear more than the security dimension of this activity. The state is afraid that the extra-parliamentary movement is gradually coalescing into a mass social movement with broad popular support and strong ability to mobilize it (Abu-Raiya, 2005).

Sheikh Salah's idea of an independent or self-reliant community is also linked to the extra-parliamentary movement's rejection of the other solutions offered by both the Arabs in Israel and by the Jewish majority. Salah asserts that the creation of an autonomous Arab–Muslim community is the only solution for the Arab–Muslim minority in Israel. He rejects the other solutions, such as a state of all its citizens (Bishara, 1998), a binational state (Ghanem, 2009), and various autonomy proposals (Smooha, 1999).

Sheikh Salah's concept of the independent community is based on three fundamental principles: capital, land, and the economy (Ali, 2007; Ghanem and Mustafa, 2009a). He demands the rejection of contributions from non-Muslim entities, due to the concern that the foreign entities will demand something in exchange for this money and thereby threaten the independence of the Muslim community. The extra-parliamentary Islamic Movement asserts that the non-Muslim donations are not "pure" and seek to change the character and identity of the Muslim community (Ali, 2006).

The pan Arab–Islamic dimension plays an important role in the project of the independent community. Salah argues that the establishment of an independent community requires closer ties with the Arab world and the Islamic nation, not only in the symbolic and cultural domain but also in the practical sense. The link between the establishment of an independent Muslim community in Israel and stronger ties with the Islamic world reflects the ideological orientation of the extra-parliamentary movement, which denies the uniqueness of the situation and status of the Muslims in Israel and sees itself as an integral part of pan Arab–Muslim political Islam. Conversely, the parliamentary movement believes that the Muslims in Israel are in a special situation and that political Islam in Israel exists in a unique political context that demands special treatment of the issues on the agenda of the Muslims in Israel (Sarsur, 2005).

The independent community is a significant component in the politics of difference practiced by the extra-parliamentary Islamic Movement, as opposed to the politics of recognition practiced by the parliamentary Islamic Movement. The latter employs all the means provided by Israeli politics to strengthen Muslim society in Israel. For example, while the extra-parliamentary Islamic Movement works to protect Muslim sacred sites and Waqf property via community activity such as preserving the holy places, organizing volunteer days when Muslims tend graves in abandoned Palestinian villages, etc., the parliamentary branch tries to pass legislation to require the state to preserve Muslim holy places in Israel and allocate resources for this purpose. This is a good example of the difference between the two movements: the first tends to focus on activity within the community and to mobilize the Muslim community to attain its goals, while the second tries to convince the state to institute measures that will improve the status of the Muslims in Israel.

There are other differences between the two branches of political Islam in Israel. They employ different political terminology that reflects the differences in their political discourse. For example, the extra-parliamentary Islamic Movement calls itself "the Islamic Movement in the Palestinian Interior." This ignores the Israeli context and emphasizes the Palestinian aspect of the movement's identity. The parliamentary branch, on the other hand, generally goes by the name of "the Islamic Movement in the country" or, infrequently, "the Islamic Movement in Israel." In another example of terminological variance, the extra-parliamentary Islamic Movement uses "the Israeli establishment" for the various authorities of the State of Israel, while the parliamentary branch uses "the government of Israel" or "the State of Israel." This is not merely a matter of semantics. Rather, it is ideological and indicative of the user's political and ideological orientation.

In addition to the terminology, there are also political disagreements between the two branches. The principal one is related to the peace process between the Palestinians and Israel. The parliamentary branch supports a peace process that would ultimately lead to the establishment of a Palestinian state. In fact, its former leader, Sheikh Darwish, supported the Oslo accords and even participated in several assemblies and rallies in support of the Oslo Accords and the peace process. On the other hand, Sheikh Salah, the head of the extra-parliamentary movement, opposed the accords and called them "an act of treason." Similarly, Salah's deputy, Sheikh Kamal Khatib, called the accords "a betrayal of the rights of the Palestinian people" (Mustafa, 2013).

Participation in Knesset Elections

Participation in Knesset elections is one of the issues that separate the two Islamic movements in Israel. As noted, it was this dispute that led to the split between them. The branch that boycotts elections is led by Sheikh Salah. Before every election campaign, he publishes a series of articles in support of the extra-parliamentary movement's opposition to contesting them. The main point is that the Knesset is merely a forum for protest and cannot change the situation of the Muslims in Israel. Salah also contends that the Knesset represents the Zionist movement, which is responsible for the *Nakba* of the Palestinians. Any participation in the elections grants legitimacy to this institution, which symbolizes "the Zionist project" and enacts laws that discriminate against the Arabs and Muslims in Israel and creates only hardship for the Palestinian people in the occupied territories. On the eve of the 2003 Knesset elections, he wrote a series of articles in the movement's newspaper, *Sawt al-Haq wal-Huriyya* (the Voice of Justice and Freedom), under the title "The Elections and Us." He wrote:

The role of the Arab members of Knesset, from the first day an Arab Knesset member entered the Knesset and until today, continues to lead to one conclusion: the Knesset is a forum for protest and nothing more. I say this knowing that Arab members of Knesset have made an effort to perform a successful role, but the ground on which the Knesset is based does not allow any Arab member of Knesset to fulfill a successful role. ... The status of Knesset has thwarted them and continues to thwart them because this is the supreme establishment of a state that defines itself as the state of the Jewish people, in a way that completely disregards our existence, and because the Knesset is the supreme establishment of the Zionist project, which does not recognize us as a national minority or as citizens entitled to receive equal rights. Therefore, the Knesset has never been a supreme establishment for us, the Palestinian Arab minority in this land. (Salah, 2002: 4).

In an article Sheikh Salah wrote on the eve of the 2006 Knesset elections, he continues along the same lines in calling for a boycott of the Knesset elections:

I am more and more convinced that the mechanism of the Knesset is one of the expressions of the Zionist enterprise and is only designed to serve the Zionist enterprise – both on the local level and on the global level. ... If there are accomplishments by some of the Arab members of Knesset, they are very modest achievements in relation to the amount of time all of the Arab members of Knesset spend within the Knesset mechanism. (Salah, 2006: 4)

Salah bases his call to boycott the Knesset elections on two main contentions: (1) the Knesset is a symbol of the state's Jewishness and part of "the Zionist project"; and (2) the Muslims and Arabs in Israel cannot better their status and situation through representation in the Knesset.[2]

This boycott is ideological rather than political. A political boycott, which is the dominant form among the Arabs in Israel, is linked to the boycotters' dissatisfaction with the performance of the Arab political parties and protests their inferior status in the state. An ideological boycott, on the other hand, rejects the current political system and aspires to change it (Ghanem and Mustafa, 2007).

Unlike the extra-parliamentary stream, the parliamentary Islamic Movement believes that participation in the Knesset elections is an inseparable part of the overall outlook of political Islam that "Islam is the solution." Sheikh Ibrahim Sarsur, the head of the parliamentary Islamic Movement, in an interview for the movement's newspaper *Al-Mithaq* (the Covenant), said:

Religious preaching is the main thing and politics is part of it, and the parliament is a branch of the religious activity. The political activity is part of the broader whole of activities aimed at bringing the people back to religion and building the individual and society, and preserving the identity and the land. Therefore, there is no contradiction between our participation in the parliament and the rest of our activity. (*Al-Mithaq*, November 21, 2008)

---

[2] Interview with Sheikh Salah, April, 13, 2008.

The parliamentary movement argues that participation in the Knesset elections is aimed at improving the Arabs' everyday life. Another argument it uses is the need to counter the rise of the extreme right in Israel, which calls for the political exclusion and even the physical transfer of the Arab minority. That is, the Arabs must increase their representation in the Knesset in order to neutralize the aspirations of the extreme right:

There are already those who deal with the Palestinian issue abroad – in the West Bank, Gaza and the exile – but no one deals with our problem in Israel: ... unification and understanding of our public and leadership. The Islamic Movement does not suffer from an ideological crisis because I am completely certain that participation in elections has already become a duty aimed at serving the Arab public, and it constitutes a realization of the need for active participation by the Arabs in the Israeli arena in order to deter the extreme right in Israel that is seeking to strip the Arab vote of any influence. ... In regard to those calling for a boycott as an expression of protest, the discussion with them is legitimate and needs to continue. What we can say at this juncture is that participation in the elections, particularly on the level of the Islamic Movement, will decisively help in determining the political format of the character of relations the state and its citizenry. If there were no benefit in the elections – and despite the fact that there are many benefits – the very fact that the participation is occurring in the face of the calls to return the Arab sector to the period of the military government, constitutes a sufficient reason for us to support this.[3]

Similarly, Sheikh Abdallah Nimr Darwish, the founder of the Islamic Movement in Israel and its leader until 2003, attacked the stream that boycotts the Knesset elections. Sheikh Darwish is considered a moderate. He pushed the movement to participate in the Knesset elections in 1996 and has always believed that there is a strong basis in Islamic law justifying the Islamic Movement's participation in the parliament of the Jewish state (Ghanem and Mustafa, 2009a). He also asserts:

There is no alternative to having the Arab lists represented in the parliament, even if their influence is weak at this stage, when the extreme right is dominant. Therefore, I call on all of the politicians to accept each other and unite in frameworks that are sure to succeed and cross the threshold percent. ... I know that the intentions of the brothers who call for boycotting are good and honorable intentions, but good intentions cannot justify flawed behavior

---

[3] Interview with Sheikh Sarsur, September 20, 2008.

in light of our Arab public, which is frustrated by the current situation and by the inability of the Arab MKs to generate the desired change. I understand this frustration, but there is a difference between frustration whose results are negative and frustration that leads to renewed activity and determination. Thus a decline in the Arab voting rate would directly hurt Arab representation, but would not hurt the extreme right or the ruling establishment. (*Panorama*, December 13, 2002)

Participation in Knesset elections is one of the main obstacles to unifying the Islamic Movement in Israel and constitutes the essence of the dispute between the two branches of political Islam in Israel. Over the years, each branch has become more entrenched in its position and has become more rigid in its rejection of the position of the other branch. All the attempts at rapprochement b have run aground on this issue, with each side backing its stance with interpretations of Islamic law – indicating that the two branches draw from the same religious texts but interpret it in different ways. The dispute reached a new peak in the 2009 Israeli elections. The extra-parliamentary movement called for a boycott and launched a fierce campaign against participation in the elections, with the war in Gaza in the background; the other branch strongly opposed the boycott campaign – also by referencing the war in Gaza. The former called on people to boycott the elections as an act of protest, while the latter called on them to come out en masse to vote for the Arab parties in order to punish the Zionist parties for their support of the war.

The "Future Vision" Document

In 2006, a large group of Arab activists and intellectuals, led by the chairman of the High Follow-up Committee for Arab Citizens in Israel, published *Future Vision of the Palestinian-Arabs in Israel* (2006), a document that in many ways is considered to embody the demands of the Arabs in Israel, including their attitude towards a future accord between the Palestinian national movement and Israel (see Chapter 5).

The differences between the two branches of political Islam are exemplified by their stand regarding the Future Vision document. The document stirred up strong opposition by Israeli Jewish society and the Israeli establishment, but also by the extra-parliamentary branch of the Islamic Movement, which regarded it as a secular vision that does not reflect Arab society in Israel (Ghanem and Mustafa, 2008, 2009a).

Sheikh Salah's movement was fiercely opposed to the document. At first it simply denied its legitimacy, because it was not published by the High Follow-up Committee for Arab Citizens in Israel (which includes representatives of all the Arab political parties). According to Salah, "it is clear that all of the ideas expressed in this publication do not represent the Follow-up Committee, and it is clear that this publication represents only those who are responsible for it, whether they be individuals of groups" (*Sawt al-Haq wal-Huriyya*, February 2, 2007).

Sheikh Salah's movement criticized the method and means of the Future Vision document without delving into its content and without denying the existence of fundamental disagreements, as he stated in another article:

I must first emphasize that I am not addressing in this discussion the various ideas that appear in the document, even if I have much to say about them. Nonetheless, I would like to point out, clearly and uncompromisingly, the measures that accompanied the publication of this document and the fact that some have insisted on showing that the Follow-up Committee stands behind it, and that the document represents the committee, whether they like it or not, and I felt compelled to point out these measures. (*Sawt al-Haq wal-Huriyya*, February 3, 2007)

The parliamentary Islamic Movement, through its leader Sheikh Sarsur, expressed its esteem for the Future Vision document, but preferred to adopt "constructive ambiguity." That is, Sarsur noted that it is not in the Arabs' interest to clearly define their position on every matter and that it is best to maintain some ambiguity. In addition, he noted that the Future Vision document was produced by the elites and that the Arab society needs a more grassroots presentation of its problems (Ghanem and Mustafa, 2009a).

The Future Vision document expresses the differences between the two branches. The extra-parliamentary branch presents a radical and uncompromising view in its opposition to the document, while the parliamentary branch does not strongly oppose the document, agrees with much of its content, and does not reject the right of people to express and write a document that expresses the narrative and vision of the Palestinians in Israel as perceived by a group of Arab intellectuals in Israel.

There are additional differences between the streams of political Islam in Israel. One important issue is the political involvement of women. The extra-parliamentary branch opposes granting women permanent representation on the Follow-up Committee, seen as the supreme political body of the Arabs in Israel. The parliamentary branch supports the proposal and voted for it together with secular Arab parties. It cites precedents from various periods of Islamic history. Another issue that demonstrates the divergence between the two streams has to do with cooperation with Arab civil society organizations in Israel. The extra-parliamentary stream opposes any collaboration with such organizations, sometimes even denying their legitimacy, because they receive funds from non-Muslim entities, which could lead them to adopt a non-Islamic political and social agenda. The parliamentary stream collaborates with civil society organizations and regards them as an integral part of the political and social development of the Arab society in Israel. Thus, it participates in these organizations' events and supports their activity.

Summary

The differences between the two streams of political Islamic in Israel derive from several interrelated factors. First of all is the general political context of the State of Israel as a Jewish and democratic state that allows members of the minority group some degree of political involvement and influence on policy. In practice, one Islamic stream advocates integration into the Israeli political game and tries to influence it from within, while the other sees Israeli politics as a foreign environment and does not believe that the Arabs and Muslims in Israel can improve their religious and civic status in its framework. The extra-parliamentary stream views the Israeli–Jewish context as part of the overall Zionist project that excludes the Arabs and, by definition, discriminates against them, while the parliamentary stream tries to exert influence from the inside. Although aware of the limitations of the Israeli context, it attempts to advance issues and concrete matters that could improve the status of the Muslims in Israel.

The political orientation of the Arab public in general and of the supporters of political Islam in particular also explains the differences and the disparate orientations of the two movements. The leadership is aware of the disagreement among the public regarding the issues on the agenda and adapts its positions in accordance with its assessment of how the ideas it proposes will be accepted by the Arab public and by its supporters. The disagreement about the Arabs' status as a minority, the nature of relations with the state and the majority, and the differences of opinion on social and cultural issues (such as the political status of women and the attitude towards the holy places, and especially the al-Aqsa Mosque) constitutes the arena in which the leaders of the two streams devise their strategies.

Of course, the leaders' own preferences and interests are another factor explaining the split into two competing movements. The younger generation's aspirations to reach positions of leadership sharpened the differences and were another factor leading to the split. What is more, the leadership has become more entrenched in their positions and bear ultimate responsibility for the failures of all the efforts to unify the two branches. The conflicting interests of the leaders at the national, regional, and local levels have foiled all unity proposals. Unity would detract from their status and erode their authority. So the leaders tend to preserve the status quo and transform personal disagreement into ideological disputes, emphasizing the differences between the two streams rather than what they have in common.

The interpretation of religious texts, too, explains the differences between the two Islamic movements. The fact that the two sets of leaders understand the same religious texts in opposite ways demonstrates the importance of the interpretation of the text rather than the text itself. Participation in Knesset elections is an example of this: the extra-parliamentary stream sees it as a deviation from religious doctrine, while the parliamentary movement employs a different interpretation of the same texts to accord legitimacy to participating in the Jewish state's parliament.

5 | The "Future Vision": The Consolidation of Collective Identity Politics

In December 2006, a group of Palestinian politicians and intellectuals published *Future Vision of the Palestinian-Arabs in Israel*, a document that attracted national and international interest and elicited a wide variety of responses across the political spectrum of Jews, Palestinians, and others, both inside and outside Israel (Committee of Arab Local Authority Heads in Israel, 2006). This project was chaired by the head of the High Follow-up Committee for Arab Citizens in Israel, their most authentic representative body, and by the National Committee of the Heads of Arab Local Councils.

The document's publication was a historic event in the annals of the Palestinians in Israel and in their relationship with the Jewish majority and the State of Israel on one hand, and their interaction with the Palestinian national movement on the other hand. It was the first time a representative national body of the Palestinians in Israel had drafted and published a comprehensive paper that describes both the existing situation and the changes that are needed in a broad spectrum of domains: relations with the Jewish majority, the legal status of the Palestinian minority, land allocations, social and economic issues, the Arab education system, the status of Arab civil and political institutions, etc. The document, which was written by activists from all political currents among the Palestinians in Israel, delineates what is necessary to ensure a positive future relationship between the majority and the minority in the State of Israel, including the definition of the character of the state. In this chapter, we analyze the document's background and argue that the Future Vision provides a path for the Palestinians in Israel to cope with their exclusion from the Palestinian National Movement on one hand and their exclusion from the peace talks between the PLO and Israel after the signing of the Oslo Accords in 1993, on the other hand. We also publish and discuss poll data on the support for the document and its concepts among Palestinians in Israel.

After the Future Vision, two additional documents were published by Palestinian civil society organizations in Israel. The *Haifa Declaration* was the product of collective thinking by Palestinian intellectuals in Israel, who met at Mada al-Carmel, the Arab Center for Applied Social Research (see Mada al-Carmel, 2007). Adalah, the Arab Center for Palestinian Minority Rights in Israel, published its *Democratic Constitution* (see Adalah, 2007). The main points of these three documents are delineated and discussed in this chapter, with the focus on the Future Vision.[1]

The publication of these documents ignited heated public debate about their ramifications, including whether they represent radicalization of or reconciliation by Palestinians in Israel. The academic literature has focused on analyzing the sociopolitical background against which the documents were authored, reflecting on the responses to the documents in Jewish and Arab societies, understanding their contribution to the creation of a consensual collective political agenda for the Palestinian in Israel, and assessing their influence on the relationship between the Jewish majority and the Palestinian minority (Agbaria and Mustafa, 2012; Ghanem and Mustafa, 2009a; Jamal, 2008, Ozacky-Lazar and Kabha, 2008; Rekhess, 2007; Schueftan, 2007).

The Background of the Future Vision

At the end of 2006, the National Committee of the Heads of Arab Local Authorities, which constitutes more than 80% of the membership of the High Follow-up Committee, took a serious step by publishing the Future Vision. This historic document presented the committee's collective vision for the future of the Palestinians in Israel (see, for example, Abulof, 2008; Jamal, 2008; Waxman and Peleg, 2008), setting it as a guide for accomplishing the committee's agenda and opening its contents for public discussion. According to the document's introduction,

It is clear that we, the Arab Palestinians in Israel, need to synthesize our various self-definitions in order to produce a lucid, integrated, and homogenous vision of our self-identity, the relations with our Palestinian people and with the state, a clear self-definition that relates to all existential areas – political,

---

[1] For convenience, in the rest of this chapter we will refer to these three documents as Future Vision, Haifa Declaration, and Democratic Constitution.

cultural, economic, educational and social, developed by all streams of our political, cultural and research professionals. (Future Vision)

The background for the publication of the Future Vision is rooted in the political situation during the preceding years. Ghanem (1997a) and Rouhana and Ghanem (1998) theorized that Palestinian society in Israel has not developed naturally and is rather the product of a crisis. The political situation that resulted from the crisis reflects the Israeli state's policies towards the Palestinian minority. The Nakba and the distorted modernization process obviously influenced the development of Palestinian society in Israel. Moreover, Al-Haj (1997) argues that the peace process aggravated the already difficult marginal status of Palestinians, both in the State of Israel and in the Palestinian national movement (Ghanem and Ozacky-Lazar, 1996).

The crisis state in which Palestinians live in Israel formed the backdrop for political programs that appeared in the 1990s and sought to liberate the Palestinians from their distress. This was clearly represented by the establishment of the National Democratic Alliance (the NDA; Arabic *al-Tajamu al-Watani al-Dimuqrati*; also known by the Hebrew acronym Balad); its slogan was "Israel as the state of all its citizens" and it demanded cultural autonomy for the Palestinians (Bishara, 1998). It was also visible in the independent community project of the Islamic Movement, under the leadership of Raed Salah (Ghanem and Mustafa, 2014) and in the prominent role of civil society institutions that attempted to compensate for the Jewish political parties' neglect of the Palestinians' rights. The al-Aqsa Intifada in 2000 intensified the debate about national identity. The inability of Arab civil society to effect the necessary political change became more obvious, despite changes in the political debate initiated by both sides and the realization of some of the rights through a legal struggle, that nevertheless appeared to be more and more restricted (Ghanem and Mustafa, 2009a).

Research on the relations between the Palestinians in Israel and the Palestinian national liberation movement indicates that the latter views the former as a marginal entity (Al Haj, 1993, 1997; Ghanem, 1996). The movement does not see them as part of the Palestinian issue and has not included them in the Palestinian national agenda or envisaged them as participants in the Palestinian political future. This is why they have never been given a seat at the negotiating table (Ghanem, 1996).

In general, the Palestinians in Israel believe that a solution to the Jewish–Palestinian dispute will improve their civil status (Barzilai, 2003). There is a strong correlation between the civil status of the Palestinian minority in Israel and the extent to which they express the Israeli component of their identity in their consciousness, behavior, activities, and political thinking (Ghanem, 1996; Haider, 1997). In other words, the political discourse of the Palestinians in Israel links their civil status with their desire to maintain their national identity; their willingness to accept the status of Israeli citizens is linked to the solution of their national dilemma or their desire for national autonomy.

In the mid-1990s, opinion polls indicated that 60% of the Palestinians in Israel supported the peace process, in contrast to 20% of Jews (Tami Steinmetz Centre for Peace Studies, 1995). Palestinians in Israel supported this process without any clarification of the eventual solution for Palestinian national status, because discussion of this issue was postponed to the final stage of the Oslo process. They supported the peace process because they thought it would lead to substantial improvement in their civil status in Israel. In 1992, this belief led many Palestinians in Israel to vote for the Labor Party under Yitzhak Rabin, despite their disagreements with the party itself. The disconnection between their awareness and action, and between their political aims and actual civil status, motivated Palestinians to vote for a Zionist party at that stage, when the political expression of their national aspirations was focused on pushing through legislation that could improve aspects of their daily lives (Ghanem, 2001a).

The Declaration of Principles signed by Israel and the Palestinian Authority recognized the PLO as the representative body for negotiations with Israel. This signaled the start of a track that was supposed to lead to the solution of the "Palestinian issue." But missing from the various proposals for solution of the Palestinian issue was consideration of the status and fate of the Palestinian citizens of Israel (Ghanem, 1996; Haider, 1997). The PLO did not discuss or seek to negotiate on this issue with the Israelis; even today the Israeli authorities consider this to be an internal affair, not open for negotiation with any outsider. The result was a rather odd situation in which efforts were being made to reach a comprehensive solution for the outstanding issues between Israel and the Palestinians, but the problems of the Palestinian minority inside Israel were ignored. The increased strength of the Israeli right wing since the mid-1990s, paralleled by the Palestinian Authority's inactivity, brought the political process to a standstill. This has escalated tensions about the existence of a Palestinian minority in Israel and sharpened the need for a solution. The publication of documents or basic texts by the Palestinians in Israel, and notably the Future Vision, represents this minority's attempt to articulate its rights and requirements, and establish its status as a national minority, and overcome its marginal status for the Palestinian problem.

Thus the stalemate in the peace process since the late 1990s has weakened the political discourse among the Palestinians in Israel that might have linked the issue of their Palestinian national identity with their status as Israeli citizens. It became obvious that any solution to the issue of the Palestinian nation would not have implications for the Palestinian minority in Israel. Instead, scholarly discourse has explored arguments and scientific theory about how the character of the Jewish state affects the status of the Palestinian minority. This discourse exposes the duality in the definition of the Israeli political regime as democratic, despite its undemocratic nature (Ghanem and Yiftachel, 2005), as expressed in its failure to grant personal and collective equality to its Palestinian citizens (Ghanem, 2001a). The civil status of the Palestinians in Israel is tied to the issue of the Palestinian nation as well as to their connection with the State of Israel and the substance of this connection. This realization has led to deliberations about patriotism in the context of the Israeli state and its Jewish identity.

The crystallization of a sophisticated statement in the Future Vision, as a result of internal Palestinian political discourse, exposed the crisis situation in which the Palestinians in Israel live. This situation is partly due to the Jewish character of the state and its hegemony over symbols and historical narrative, which tend to distance the Palestinians from the state. This crisis is also connected, though less directly, to the Palestinian national movement and its lack of clarity on the matter, the effort to maintain the Jewish character of the state, and the dispute about the type and substance of its political regime.

One result has been the efforts to enshrine the Jewish character of the state in legislation, culminating in the Israel Democracy Institute's proposal for a consensus constitution that would emphasize the Jewish character of the state, with its symbols and narrative (Shamgar, 2006).

The issue of the Jewish nature of the state is the substance of the dispute and argument between Palestinians and Jews in Israel. The

Palestinians believe that the Jewish character of the state has implications for their status as a national minority, while the Jews hold that the Jewish character of the state and their right to live in the country is legitimized by their right to self-determination. Given this dispute, the issue of Palestinian nationality has become a repetitive theme that amplifies the problems of the Palestinian's minority status. Some scholars have begun to see a change in the Jewish character of the state and institution of a binational state on the territory of the Palestine Mandate as the appropriate solution (Ghanem, 1999, 2005).

The eruption of the al-Aqsa Intifada in October 2000 can be seen as coming at a time of Jewish ethnic radicalization, when the Jewish nature of the state was emphasized in an unprecedented manner (Ghanem, 2001b). Although the state claims to be Jewish and democratic, Palestinian citizens and many scholars see a contradiction between these two terms and may even perceive it as an apartheid, ethnocratic, and anti-democratic state (Gavison, 2000). In contrast, there is a current in right-wing Zionism that seems to understand democracy as fighting "enemies at home" and "preventing them from exploiting the state and acting against the Jewish character of the state." They counter this supposed trend through legislation that curtails democratic freedoms and bolsters the Jewish nature of the state.

But the democratic and Jewish facets of Israel's identity cannot be separated, because they appear in the country's Basic Laws, such as the "Basic Law: Human Dignity and Liberties," passed in 1992.[2] It stipulates, in part:

8(a) The purpose of this Basic Law is to protect human dignity and liberty, in order to establish in a Basic Law the values of the State of Israel as a Jewish and democratic state.

The "Basic Law: Freedom of Occupation," passed that same year, defines its purpose as follows:

2: The purpose of this Basic Law is to protect freedom of occupation, in order to establish in a Basic Law the values of the State of Israel as a Jewish and democratic state.

[2] See "Basic Law: Human Dignity and Liberties" on the Knesset website: http://main.knesset.gov.il/Activity/Legislation/Documents/yesod3.pdf (in Hebrew).

Both statutes emphasized the Jewish nature of the state and enshrined Jewish hegemony over Arabs. In the whirlpool of this debate regarding the Jewish nature of the state, the ruling Jewish elite attempted to create a wall-to-wall Jewish–Zionist consensus on this point, rooted in the country's Proclamation of Independence. These efforts peaked in the 2002 Kinneret Declaration, authored by a group of politicians organized as the Forum for National Responsibility. It reflected Jewish national consensus regarding the Jewish nature of the state but also stated:

> 5: The State of Israel respects the rights of the Arab minority. The State of Israel is obligated to treat all of its citizens equally and impartially. In areas in which Israeli citizens who are not Jews suffer from injustice and neglect, vigorous and immediate action is called for in order to bring about the fulfillment of the principle of civil equality in practice. Israel will ensure the right of the Arab minority to maintain its linguistic, cultural, and national identity. Jewish history and Jewish tradition have taught us the terrible consequences of discrimination against minorities. Israel cannot ignore these lessons.

But the Jewish elite produced the Kinneret Declaration on its own, without the participation of Arab citizens.

The Kinneret Declaration was preceded by other attempts to draft academic theoretical alternatives for the status of the Palestinian citizens of Israel. The Peace Institute at Givat Haviva summarized these alternatives in *Seven Roads: Theoretical Options for the Status of Arabs in Israel* (Ghanem, Pappe, and Ozacky-Lazar, 1999):

1. Perpetuation of the present situation of Israel as an ethnic democracy – the "Jewish and democratic state" (Smooha, 1999)
2. The boundaries of the Zionist paradigm (Saban, 1999)
3. A more severe situation than at present, with retreat from and weakening of the democratic framework (Amara, 1999)
4. A binational Jewish–Palestinian state on the territory of the Palestine mandate (Ghanem, 1999)
5. An Israeli state (Kaufman, 1999)
6. A binational state within Israel (Rouhana, 1999)
7. The option of separation: irredentism, independence or transfer (Khamaisi, 1999).

To promote a new debate, a group of Arabs and Jews, mostly academics, worked to draft a common proposal under the aegis of the Israel

Democracy Institute (IDI). Its members held ten sessions in 1999–2001 and met with dozens of Arab and Jewish intellectuals. The participants reached a consensus regarding civil equality for all citizens, but disagreed about the Jewish character of the state. The two sides expressed willingness to discuss or agree on this matter, but for one reason or another the Arab participants rejected the proposed document that envisioned a constitution by consensus. Uzi Benziman chronicled the discussions in *Whose Land Is It? A Quest for a Jewish–Arab Compact in Israel* (Benziman, 2006).

The IDI also offered a draft of a constitution by consensus in which the Jewish nature of the state was emphasized in terms of its symbols, legal definitions, and semantics. The document was meant to serve as a foundation for deliberations by the Knesset Constitution, Law, and Justice Committee about a constitution.

The constitution proposed by the IDI defines Israel as a "Jewish and democratic state." Article I states that "Israel" is the name of the state. Article II begins: "Israel is a Jewish and democratic state" (Shamgar, 2005: 91–93). It emphasizes the Jewish character of the state with regard to the "right of return," citizenship, and state symbols (ibid.).

It has been maintained, based on surveys and polls conducted by the IDI, that most Arabs in Israel support this version of the constitution and its definition of the state; but other surveys and polls have found otherwise.[3]

In any case, the activity to produce a constitution that emphasizes the Jewish character of the state has been accompanied by major efforts to enact laws with the same tendency, so as to buttress the advantages enjoyed by the Jewish majority in different domains.

The amended Citizenship Law (2003) is a glaring example. Security considerations were given as the official reason for its enactment, but the practical reason was to protect the Jewish demographic majority.

---

[3] According to the IDI, 77.4% of the Arab population would support a constitution that recognizes Israel as a Jewish and democratic state. Many scholars have criticized the way in which this question was presented, linking the matter of identification with the issue of equality, without the interviewee understanding the statutory and legal implications of this identity. The question should have been asked in the following way: Would you support the identity of the state as a Jewish and democratic state in which equality is realized for Arabs? In 2004, the annual survey by Mada al-Carmel found that 62% of the Arab population believe that Israel cannot simultaneously be a Jewish and democratic state.

Some Knesset members even voiced this publicly, including Yuval Steinitz of the Likud: "I am not interested in talking about the security axes added to the law. . . . The state has full rights to protect itself from a demographic aspect" (Soltany, 2004: 21). Professor Ruth Gavison, one of the leaders of the constitution initiative, expressed her opinion that the amendment of the Law of Return was "anchored in part by the effort to continue to maintain Israel as a state in which the Jewish people maintain their right to self-determination. . . . Whoever believes in justice, that it is the Jewish state, must also agree that it is its right and that it must maintain the conditions which will allow the continuation of its existence" (Gavison, 2000).

Alongside the intellectual and conceptual efforts that constituted the background for the Future Vision, we must also note political developments that influenced its content. In the period after the events of October 2000, there was growing talk of revoking citizenship and even transferring the entire Arab population out of the country. This trickled from the political margins into Israeli society and politics; at its height, the slogan of a large political party advocated the cession of Arab villages and towns in the Triangle to the Palestinian Authority and revocation of Arabs' Israeli citizenship (Ariele et al., 2006). These proposals enjoyed broad public support[4] and were enthusiastically adopted by several leading politicians.

In September 2003, the report by the Orr Committee, which had investigated the clashes between Arab citizens and the Israeli security forces, added another layer to the former's sense of alienation. The committee did not identify or blame those responsible for the deaths of 12 Arab citizens in October 2000. Despite its recognition of discrimination against the Arab minority, it tried to balance and divide the responsibility for the events between the police and the Arabs (Orr Committee, 2003: Vol. B). Even today those responsible for the killings have not been brought to trial. It is no surprise that Arab citizens' trust in the state institutions has deteriorated over time.

Palestinian citizens' political behavior before the elections for the Seventeenth Knesset in 2006 and voting patterns during the 2006 election then testified to their alienation from the state, as expressed in a

---

[4] A survey by the Center to Combat Racism, published in March 2006, showed that 40% of the public was in favor of encouraging of Arabs to emigrate (Ha'aretz, March 23, 2006).

trend to boycott the election. Through this boycott, the Palestinian population expressed its sense of marginality in the Israeli system and its belief that it has no ability to influence decision-making in the Knesset and Government. It discovered the possibilities of action outside the parliamentary arena and realized that there was no benefit to participation in Israeli parliamentary politics.

In summary, the marginality of the Arab minority in Israel for the Palestinian issue and lack of influence on this issue increased. The Arabs find themselves in a double periphery, with regard to their citizenship in the State of Israel and with regard to their affiliation with their own nation and the Palestinian liberation movement (Al-Haj, 1997; Ghanem, 1996). In the first of these domains, the sense of marginality has grown because of their continued exclusion from all areas of state activity (Ghanem and Mustafa, 2011). In the second domain, their influence on a solution for the Palestinian issue has been stifled by the Israeli decision to manage the dispute and its resolution in a one-sided manner for the foreseeable future. It does not seem likely that the blocking majority in the Knesset, in which Arab parties collaborated with Jewish parties to support the Rabin government and pass the Oslo Accords will ever be revived (Ghanem, 2001a).

The Importance and Content of the Future Vision

The political and media weight accorded the Future Vision almost certainly stemmed from the fact that it was the first attempt by Palestinian citizens of Israel to produce a collective declaration of their demands and challenge the country's sociopolitical system. This public attention was also stimulated by the fact that the document was produced by leading scholars and activists representing the full political spectrum of Palestinians in Israel and had the support of Shawqi Khatib, the then-chair of the Follow-up Committee. The document had added significance because it had been endorsed by the National Committee of Arab Local Authority Heads, which adopted it as its official program. Some public opinion polls found that the document's demands represent the views of a vast majority of the Palestinians in Israel.

Here we discuss the contents of the three sections of the Future Vision, with the focus on the historical narrative, the challenge of symbols, and the political framework proposed for the status of

Palestinians and Jews in Israel. Agbaria and Mustafa (2012: 718) argue that the publication of the Future Vision:

[c]hallenges both the political inclusiveness of the identity of Israel as a "Jewish and democratic" state and the political continuity of collective identity of the Palestinian people. With these documents, the Arab civil society organizations reclaim responsibility over their political future by adhering to the Israeli citizenship framework, but at the same time attempting to change its nature from within, by re-associating the Palestinians in Israel with the core issues of the stumbling peace process, especially in regard to the "Right of Return."

According to the director of the Mossawa Center, Jafar Farah (2007: 39): "We submit the result [the Future Vision document] as a topic for discussion and debate within the Arab society, and also within the Jewish–Israeli society."

Hussam Abu Bakr explains:

The Jewish public should see the document as an invitation to a profound and imperative public discussion between equals, a discussion that demands a considerable amount of tolerance and ideological pluralism. I believe this is possible. (Quoted in Rekhess, 2007: 14–15)

For Abulof (2008: 62), "This is not much ado about nothing: These documents pose a moral and practical challenge to both the Jewish majority and the Arab minority in Israel."

For Jamal (2008: 27–28),

The documents reflect the development of a unique collective political consciousness that aspires to speak on its own behalf and to express its needs. ... This is political consciousness that is fed by the differences between it and the rest of the Palestinian people. ... Thus, the Vision documents locate themselves outside of the Oslo Accord between the PLO and the Israeli government in 1993. At the same time, they also locate themselves outside the boundaries of the Israeli Declaration of Independence. ... Despite the differences in language between the various documents, and even though they speak in the language of the indigenous minority and collective rights, their futuristic aim is towards the potential creation of a new collective.

The Historical Narrative

The Future Vision and earlier documents by Arabs in Israel sought to consolidate a historical narrative that highlights their cultural uniqueness

and fend off the challenge of another narrative, as part of their collective identity. The Future Vision expresses the historical narrative that
best represents the Palestinians in Israel and their conception of the
dispute between Jews and Palestinians and of the Palestinian issue. This
historical narrative of the Palestinian–Jewish dispute appears in the
introduction to the chapter on relations with the state and expresses
how the Palestinians perceive Jewish settlement in their homeland and
the war of 1948 (Future Vision, p. 9). The placement of this section as
an introduction to the chapter entitled "The Palestinian Arabs in Israel
and their relation to the State of Israel" is not coincidental (ibid.).

The Future Vision asserts that Israel is a colonialist product based on
the attempt to find a solution to the "Jewish question" in Europe. The
Zionist founders devised a national project grounded on Jewish religious and ethnic foundations and linked to the Jews' presence in the
"Land of Israel" 2000 years ago. Like most national movements, the
Zionists expanded this story and linked it to the modern phenomenon
of nationalism. Essentially, they asked for legitimation of the construction of a "national home" justified by the past existence of Jews in the
"Land of Israel." The project of settling and colonizing Palestine was
catalyzed by the decline of the Ottoman Empire, the Balfour Declaration, and the British Mandate, all of which contributed to the establishment of the State of Israel and the devastation of Palestinian Arab
society in 1948.

After the 1948 war and the Palestinian Nakba, Israel emerged as
formally democratic, while conducting a focused program to Judaize
the land and country by perpetuating colonial control of the native
Arab population. In parallel, it promoted and continues to promote
an ethnocratic policy. Although Israel has projected the image of an
"open" democracy in principle, with free elections and relatively free
media, it is effectively devoted to the spread and control of a single
ethnic group at the expense of the Palestinians. Judaization remains the
real basis of the Israeli ethnocratic regime, with continued immigration
by Jews, Jewish control of the armed forces, ongoing Jewish settlement,
a power structure that distinguishes between Jews and Palestinian
Arabs, open access to foreign Jewry and the barring of the return of
Palestinian refugees, and military control of the territories of the Palestinian Authority. The historical narrative in the Haifa Declaration,
which resembles that in the Future Vision, describes its authors as the
"sons and daughters of the Palestinian Arab people who remained in

our homeland despite the Nakba, who were forcibly made a minority in the State of Israel after its establishment in 1948 on the greater part of the Palestinian homeland" (Haifa Declaration, 7). It continues:

Towards the end of the nineteenth century, the Zionist movement initiated its colonial-settler project in Palestine. Subsequently, in concert with world imperialism and with the collusion of Arab reactionary powers, it succeeded in carrying out its project, which aimed at occupying our homeland and transforming it into a state for the Jews. In 1948, the year of the Nakba of the Palestinian people, the Zionist movement committed massacres against our people, turned most of us into refugees, totally erased hundreds of our villages, and drove out most inhabitants of our cities. (ibid., 11–12)

The historical narrative in the preamble of Adalah's Democratic Constitution is not substantially different from those in the Future Vision and the Haifa Declaration:

The Palestinian Arab citizens of the State of Israel have lived in their homeland for innumerable generations. Here they were born, here their historic roots have grown, and here their national and cultural life has developed and flourished. They are active contributors to human history and culture as part of the Arab nation and the Islamic culture and as an inseparable part of the Palestinian people. (Democratic Constitution, 4)

Agbaria and Mustafa argue that this the narrative, which opposes the Zionist narrative, is not presented only as the story of the confrontation between the Zionist movement and the Palestinian national movement, but as that of the conflict between the Zionist state and its Arab citizens (Agbaria and Mustafa, 2012).

Jewish Symbols

The Future Vision challenges the Zionist symbols of the state, such as the national anthem, the national flag, and the Law of the Return, which grants automatic admission to Jews only. The Future Vision demands the alteration of the state's ethnic symbols and the creation of new symbols that represent all its citizens. It also notes the issue of historic rights and stresses that the Palestinians in Israel are "native residents of their homeland," implying that most Jews are immigrants to the Palestinians' homeland. The Future Vision blames Israel for the Palestinian Nakba and the history of discrimination against the Palestinians in Israel:

The State should acknowledge responsibility for the Palestinian Nakba (tragedy of 1948) and its disastrous consequences for the Palestinians in general and the Palestinian Arab citizens of Israel in particular. Israel should start by rectifying the damage that it has caused and should consider paying compensation to its Palestinian citizens as individuals and groups for the damages that resulted from the Nakba and the continuous discriminating policies derived from viewing them as enemies and not as citizens who have a right to oppose the state and challenge its rules. (Future Vision, p. 10)

The main challenge posed by the Future Vision is the demand that Israel recognize the Palestinians as an indigenous cultural national group:

Israel should acknowledge the right of minorities in line with international conventions. It should admit that the Palestinian Arabs in Israel have a special status within the institutions of the international community and are acknowledged as an indigenous cultural national group enjoying total citizenship in Israel. It should also acknowledge that the Arab minority in Israel has international protection, care and support according to international conventions and treaties. (ibid., p. 11)

Like the Future Vision, the Haifa Declaration challenges the country's symbols, stressing that the Palestinians are a minority living in their homeland and demanding redress of the historical injustice against them:

As we are a homeland minority, whose people was driven out of their homeland, and which has suffered historical injustice, the principle of equality – the bedrock of democratic citizenship – must be based on justice and the righting of wrongs, and on the recognition of our narrative and our history in this homeland. This democratic citizenship that we seek is the only arrangement that guarantees individual and collective equality for the Palestinians in Israel. (Haifa Declaration, p. 14)

This symbolic challenge demanding the recognition of the Palestinians as a minority in their homeland, entitled to cultural rights, was also stated as a legal challenge to be included in the proposed democratic constitution:

Since their political status has been changed against their will, making them a minority in their homeland; since they have not relinquished their national identity; and since the rights of a homeland minority must include, inter alia, those rights which should have been preserved and developed as much as possible had they not become a minority in their homeland, thus, the legal starting point of this constitutional proposal is: The Arab citizens in the State of Israel are a homeland minority. (Future Vision, p. 4)

The Future Vision calls for a consensual democracy to replace the current ethnocratic regime in Israel, so as to ensure equality and recognition of the Palestinian minority as a partner in policy- and decision-making. It demands that the state recognize the Palestinian Arabs in Israel as an indigenous national group entitled to collective rights, including an elected national political body representing the Palestinians in Israel, cultural autonomy, and control of its own cultural, educational, and religious issues. The Future Vision challenges the hegemony of existing Zionist symbols, such as the national anthem, the flag, and the Law of Return, and demands the creation of new symbols that can be shared by all citizens. The Future Vision demands that the state "ensure suitable representation on a collective basis in the system of the state's symbols" (ibid., p. 14). The same demand appears in the Haifa Declaration (pp. 15–16), and Adalah's Democratic Constitution (p. 8).

Political Alternatives

The three documents present an almost identical vision of the future of the Palestinians in Israel and the status of Palestinians and Jews within the Green Line (the 1949 armistice line). Although each document uses its own terminology and perspectives, the theoretical substance of their political proposals is identical. The documents constitute a revolution in Palestinian political thinking, in that all three recognize the Jewish–Israeli right to self-determination.

The Future Vision sees Israel as the shared homeland of Jews and Palestinians, who should live together in a consensual democratic framework.

The State should acknowledge that Israel is the homeland for both Palestinians and Jews. Relations between the Palestinians and Jews in Israel should be based on attainment of equal human and citizenship rights based on international conventions and the relevant international treaties and declarations. The two groups should have mutual relations based on a consensual democratic system. (Future Vision, p. 11).

The future envisages here is one in which Israel is no longer a Jewish state, but one that grants equal national and citizenship rights to Jews and Palestinians. Instead of the current situation, in which the state recognizes the existence of only one national group, the Jews, the Future Vision proposes a new political framework in which the country redresses the historical injustice caused to its Palestinian citizens:

Israel should refrain from adopting policies and schemes that favor the majority. Israel must remove all forms of ethnic superiority, whether they be executive, structural, legal or symbolic. Israel should adopt policies of corrective justice in all aspects of life in order to compensate for the damage inflicted on the Palestinian Arabs due to the policies of ethnic favoritism for the Jews. The State should cooperate with representatives of the Palestinian Arabs to search for a possibility to restore parts of their lands that Israel confiscated not for public use. Israel should also dedicate an equal part of its resources for the direct needs of Palestinian Arabs. (ibid.)

The Haifa Declaration, too, recognizes the right of Israeli Jews to self-determination, alongside the right of the Palestinians in Israel to self-determination. This reciprocal recognition is seen as part of a reconciliation process between Palestinians and Jews:

This historical reconciliation also requires that we, Palestinians and Arabs, recognize the right of the Israeli Jewish people to self-determination and to life in peace, dignity, and security with the Palestinian and the other peoples of the region. (Haifa Declaration, p. 15)

The political framework proposed by the Haifa Declaration, one based on historical reconciliation as well as the right to self-determination for both peoples, is not dissimilar from that of the Future Vision:

Our vision for future relations between Palestinian Arabs and Israeli Jews in this country is to create a democratic state founded on equality between the two national groups. This solution would guarantee the rights of the two groups in a just and equitable manner. This would require a change in the constitutional structure and a change in the definition of the State of Israel from a Jewish state to a democratic state established on national and civil equality between the two national groups, and enshrining the principles of banning discrimination while ensuring equality between all of its citizens and residents. (ibid., p. 16)

Adalah's document defines Israel as a "democratic state," which implies the abrogation of its Jewish character: "The State of Israel is a democratic state, based on the values of human dignity, liberty and equality" (Democratic Constitution, p. 6). The Democratic Constitution envisages a binational state that is more or less the same as the consensual democracy of the Future Vision and the democratic state of the Haifa Declaration. It phrases this, however, in terms of bilingualism: "Hebrew and Arabic are the official languages of the State of Israel and enjoy equal status in all of the functions and activities of the legislative and executive branches" (ibid., p. 8).

The Controversy over the Future Vision

Reactions to the Future Vision came from representatives of four main groups: Palestinians in Israel, Jews in Israel, Jews from the Diaspora, and Palestinians living outside Israel. We will look at the first two groups below.

The Palestinians in Israel

Palestinians in Israel expressed contradictory attitudes about the Future Vision. Some welcomed the document and saw it as an important step and a conceptual challenge to previous Arab political discourse. But others rejected it, accusing the authors of "Israelization." The NDA was pleased with the Future Vision, which it saw as expressing ideas very close to its own platform. According to Jamal Zahalka, "When Arab intellectuals consolidate and draft plans and viewpoints relating to their fate and the status of Palestinians in Israel they find themselves relating to main principles expressed in the NDA platform and these obviously predominate here" (*Fasel Almakal*, December 22, 2006, p. 30). But he criticized the document for omitting several issues: "There is no consideration of the occupation and of Palestinian sovereignty as a substantive problem in our struggle with the state. It does not relate to the occupation, not the border of 1967, not Jerusalem, not the Right of Return, not the fence, not settlements, not international decisions" (ibid.).

The leaders of the Democratic Front for Peace and Equality (DFPE; Arabic *al-Jabhah al-Dimuqratiyyah lil-Salam wa'l-Musawah*; also known by the Hebrew acronym Hadash) and the Communist Party had different reactions to the Future Vision. Then-MK Muhammad Barakeh of the DFPE was positive.[5] He saw the document as an

---

[5] Barakeh's words and attitudes are based on a lecture he gave at a symposium on the Future Vision in Umm-al-Fahm on May 11, 2007.

unprecedented and praiseworthy effort. Nevertheless, he criticized what he saw as an exaggerated aspiration to reach a consensus when there were still disputes about the character of the proposed society. He felt that a single collective stance was not necessarily the natural or correct situation for a modern society. Barakeh added that no consolidated approach could ignore two facts: the affiliation of Palestinians in Israel with the Palestinian Arab people and the fact of their Israeli citizenship. In his opinion, the true fundamental declaration by the Arab public was created at the Congress of the Arab Masses in 1981. He criticized the avoidance of the status issue and especially that of personal status and asserted that the narrative of the Nakba was not presented adequately. Raja Za'atra, one of the leaders of the Communist Party, criticized the Future Vision, repeating Barakeh's idea that there was a lack of continuity between it and the documents that had emerged from the banned Congress of the Arab Masses in 1981. He felt that the Future Vision was something positive and that its contents merited discussion.

Other Communist leaders were more critical, however, because the Future Vision does not support their thinking and the documents and concepts that the party has developed. Perhaps they wanted the Future Vision to give more emphasis to the role they played in the Palestinian struggle by referring to the documents it had published at various times periods in the past (*al-Ittihad*, January 5, 2007).

The fiercest opposition to the Future Vision came from the Islamic Movement of Sheikh Raed Salah. It began by rejecting the document's legitimacy, in that it was published by the Committee of Local Authority Heads rather than the Follow-up Committee. According to Salah, "it is clear that all the ideas expressed in this publication do not represent the Follow-up Committee and it is also clear that this publication represents only those responsible for it, whether people or public bodies" (*Sawt al-Haq wal-Huriyya*, February 2, 2007).

This means that the Islamic Movement began with procedural reservations and only later objected to the content. When it did begin a limited discussion of some of the content of the Future Vision, it did not develop into a comprehensive debate about everything there. For example, in the first of a series of articles entitled "Where is the Follow-Up Committee Headed?" Salah wrote that "the Future Vision does not relate to the issue of the Islamic Holy Places and in fact closes this file" (ibid., January 26, 2007).

The Islamic Movement and its leaders criticized the Committee of Local Authority Heads for publishing the Future Vision without the consent of the other parties represented on the Follow-up Committee, without conducting further discussion of its contents and the issues it raised, and without recognizing the existence of substantive disagreement. As Salah wrote in another article:

Firstly I wish to emphasize, that I am not discussing the different ideas that appeared in the document, even if I have much to say about them. Nevertheless, I do wish to clearly and uncompromisingly protest the steps that accompanied the publishing of this document and the insistence of some of the people to show that the Follow-up Committee was behind it and that it represented it, whether or not this was so, and I felt it imperative to relate to these steps. (ibid., February 3, 2007)

Sheikh Ibrahim Sarsur, who at the time was the leader of the parliamentary Islamic Movement, praised the Future Vision, but added that he would have preferred for it to have adopted a "constructive vagueness." Sarsur insisted that it was not in Arabs' interest to define their stance in a clear manner with regard to each and every matter and that there was room for a certain lack of clarity regarding their attitudes. Moreover, he noted that the Future Vision was the product of the elite; Arab society needed a more popular vision to represent the problems that occupied the masses.

The Islamic Movement's opposition is understandable, because the Future Vision expresses a secular and liberal discourse that runs counter to its religious worldview.

Jewish Society

Reactions by the Jewish public ranged from support and understanding to rejection and opposition (Cohen, 2007). Some saw it as another strategic stage in the Arab campaign to change the character of the state (Smooha, 2008); others viewed it as an attempt to strip the State of Israel of its Jewish national character and destroy it (Schueftan, 2007), as an abandonment of the idea of "two states for two peoples" (Rubinstein, 2007), and as a blow to relations between Jews and Arabs (Rekhess, 2007: 16–17). In any case, a majority of Israeli officials, academics, and periodicals were strongly negative about the Future Vision (Ghanem and Mustafa, 2008), even though its demands are quite similar to those made by other indigenous minorities.

The Israeli–Jewish reactions can be placed into three main categories:

Understanding of and Support for the Future Vision

A marginal slice of Israeli Jewish society expressed understanding of the Future Vision and supported it. They believed that the document was "moderate, since it did not demand the destruction of Israel, and the distance between the writers of this document and Ahmadinejad was as far as East from West" (Petter, 2007). Danny Petter, a radical left-wing journalist, noted the document's failure to mention the class aspect, especially with regard to the economic context. He also noted its failure to address the occupation and the Palestinian issue. He opposed the idea of establishing an Arab parliament or similar elected body in Israel, because that would only deepen the split between Arabs and Jews in the state.

The Israeli historian Miron Benvenisti, writing in *Ha'aretz* on December 17, 2006, was optimistic about the Future Vision:

It appears that the Palestinian-Israeli collective's process of consolidation has reached a point of maturity. Its leaders succeeded in forming a consensus demanding equal collective rights. ... There is a basis and a possibility for the unification of moderate and logical Jewish powers, to support the just struggle of the Palestinian public in Israel, with the intention of realizing the program detailed in this document.

For Uzi Burstein, a Jewish member of the Communist Party, "the document highlights the existence of two camps in Israel: the war camp and the peace camp. In order to realize the true and just Future Vision of the Palestinians collaboration should be emphasized and the document does not at all contradict being part of the Jewish Arab front for peace, peace and not war" (*al-Ittihad*, December 27, 2006).

Understanding but Rejection of the Future Vision

The prominent reactions in this category were those of Israeli intellectuals and authors who supported the motive and understood the circumstances that led to the Future Vision but did not support its content.

A good example is Yitzhak Reiter, who has written extensively on the Israeli–Palestinian dispute: "The series of documents published in recent days by the Arab leadership is a positive phenomenon from the aspect that it sets the dream of its demands on our doorstep in a most overt manner" (*Ha'aretz*, December 27, 2006). But he enumerated points in the Future Vision that he read as matching the Palestinian historical narrative and ignoring the Jewish narrative. He believed that the substance of the Future Vision was rejection of the Jews' right to demographic hegemony (repeal of the Law of Return), spatial control (the territories and settlements), and cultural dominance (alteration of the state symbols). These three dimensions, according to Reiter, are the essential foundations of the Jewish character of the state. He proposed actions that the Jewish majority should take in response to the Future Vision, such as creating a joint vision for Jews and Arabs, and dialog between the Arab leadership and the state to get agreement about specific issues (ibid.).

Outright Rejection of the Future Vision

Opposition to the Future Vision cut across the political camps in Israeli Jewish society. Journalist Nahum Barnea, generally seen as a leftist, described the Future Vision as a major catastrophe, showing that "the Palestinian Arabs in Israel believe that they can dance [simultaneously] at two weddings" in order to achieve everything that the Western welfare state grants and at the same time attain autonomy within Israel under international patronage. In his reading of the Future Vision, the Arab elites related to Jews as enemies and not as partners (*Yedioth Ahronoth*, December 1, 2006).

In *Maariv*, journalist Ben-Dror Yemini wrote that "the different programs recently suggested by the Arabs in Israel ... renewed the unceasing dispute regarding their status." He stressed that the documents represent a double demand – the abolition of the Jewish and democratic character of the State of Israel and the granting of collective rights to the Arab minority in a manner that would transform Israel into a binational state.

The demand for equality is a just demand and cannot be disputed, but the demand to abrogate the Jews' right of self-determination is a racist, fascist and harsh demand. ... National realization for the Palestinians must be achieved within the frame of a Palestinian national state. This is the concept of two states for two peoples and the interpretation of the UN decision concerning the establishment of two states, whereby one is defined as the Jewish state. (*Maariv*, April 9, 2007)

Alexander Yakobson, an Israeli scholar, uncompromisingly attacked the authors of the Future Vision for daring to advance ideas that challenged the existing regime. In his opinion, they were not advancing the just demands of minorities (*Ha'aretz*, January 16, 2007).

Under the headline, "They Shot themselves in the Foot," Zeev Schiff, the military affairs correspondent of *Ha'aretz*, wrote that the publication of the document resembled a person who lights a fire under his own feet and feared that response to their demands of the Arabs would have terrible results (*Ha'aretz*, January 25, 2007).

The historian Shimon Shamir, who had been a member of the Orr Committee, published an article in the Arabic-language *a-Sinara*, in which he attacked the document and said it constituted a threat to every Jewish citizen of Israel:

It is difficult to free oneself of the feeling that the purpose of their tendentious definition is to negate the identity of the Jews of this land. Even for the friendly Jewish reader the document arouses a sense of threat. The only way to achieve their rights passes through Jewish society. The document that you have drafted does not advance that process, but causes it to regress. (*a-Sinara*, January 26, 2007)

The Israel Democracy Institute adopted a similar stance and rejected the document's contents. The IDI had sponsored the "constitution by consensus" that emphasized the Jewish character of the state. The core of its press release about the Future Vision was that "a large gap is left by these documents, which deny the Jewish character and substance of the State of Israel as a Jewish and democratic state." "We note the separatist intentions of the document's authors and the attempt to annul the right of the Jewish people to self-determination."[6]

The Future Vision as a Collective Agenda for the Palestinians in Israel

The future of the Palestinians in Israel depends on several variables; some of which are related to their ability to capitalize on developments on the international or state level, within the Jewish majority, or in the context of the Palestinian issue. More important than all these is their ability to seize the initiative and advance from a stage of dependence on external events and reaction to various developments and become proactive. The vision documents embody this stage. This change in strategy requires serious preparations for the future, on several levels,

[6] See "A Call to the Arabs in Israel" at the IDI website, www.idi.org.il.

Table 5.1 *To what extent do you agree or disagree with the following statements? (Percentage of respondents)*

	I do not agree	I tend not to agree	I tend to agree	I agree
There is a need to improve the structure, performance, and approach of the High Follow Up Committee	6.9	7.7	31.1	54.3
Like the Arabs, Jews have rights in this country	21.6	17.1	25.5	35.7
Israel has the right to exist, within the Green line borders, as an independent state where Jews and Arabs live	19.6	16.5	27.9	36.0
Israel is a colonial (settlement) phenomenon that was illegally established on Arab land	9.1	12.9	23.4	54.5

of which the most important is the drafting of a collective national program that reflects their needs.

A comprehensive public opinion poll conducted in June and July 2008 among a representative sample of the Palestinians in Israel[7] found that an overwhelming majority supports the basic principles of the Future Vision (see Table 5.1). This affirms that the Palestinians in Israel support the leadership's view of these demands as the core of their collective political aspirations in the future.

The survey probed whether the vision reflects the community's needs and interest in changing its situation. Most respondents tended to agree (29.4%) or agreed (50%) that "changing the Arabs' situation is their own responsibility as well." There was clear support for the publication of the Future Vision, with 47.2% agreeing and 35.2% tending to agree that "the publication of the Future Vision as a collective action program is a positive thing that should have a continuation." Additionally, the vast majority (88.4%) supported the very fact that the Follow-up Committee had published the Future Vision.

[7] The study, conducted by As'ad Ghanem and Nuhad Ali of the University of Haifa, involved a sample of 500 persons interviewed in their homes by trained interviewers (with a 4% error margin).

Most respondents agreed (54.3%) or tended to agree (31.1%) that "there is a need to improve the performance, structure and approach of the Follow-Up Committee," precisely as stated by the document.

A majority of the respondents supported the basic principles of the Future Vision, notably the perception of Israel as a colonial phenomenon while also recognizing the Jews' right to self-determination as an inherent right based on the political existence of the Jews during the twentieth century and the development of their social affiliation and acquired identity, which qualify them to determine their own fate in a binational entity, along with other indigenous peoples in the same territory.[8]

Irrespective of respondents' concrete knowledge of the Future Vision, the poll results indicate sweeping public support for its principles, from the initial basic demands through the internal social ones. Support for the document encompassed more than 90% of the sample (see Table 5.2).

When asked to evaluate the priority of each of the demands in the Future Vision and whether they thought they could be achieved immediately or if their implementation should be postponed until the time is fit, respondents called on the leadership to work to meet almost all the demands immediately (see Table 5.2). This indicates that the demands stated in the Future Vision and its principles represent political demands that are not merely the result of an ideological or intellectual exercise.

Although the Future Vision can be put forward as the official collective program of the Palestinians in Israel, an essential element for its implementation is missing: the Arab political parties' failure to reach a consensus about the document has meant that they never brought it up for a democratic vote and authorization by the Follow-up Committee.

---

[8] Contrary to the views of many critics of the Future Vision, who allege that it negates the Jews' right to self-determination, we believe that this allegation is an intentional or unintentional mistake about the meaning of self-determination. The consensus in the relevant political literature is that self-determination is a relative matter relating to the existence of one or more national groups. If nationality is a civil status and related to citizenship, as in France and the United States, it is clear that the French or American people have the right to self-determination. But if nationality is determined by ethnicity, as in Canada, Belgium, Iraq, and Switzerland, the right to self-determination must be the same right for all ethnic groups; granting that right to only one group would establish a system of "tyranny of the majority," as was the case in the United States before there was equality for (the same principle currently applies in Estonia).

Table 5.2 Do you agree with these demands and should they be implemented immediately? (Percentage of respondents)

	I agree and work should start immediately to implement this demand	I agree, but this is a demand that can be only partially implemented right now	I agree but this is a demand that cannot be implemented right now	I do not agree
Israel should cease to be a Jewish state and become a state for two peoples	57.9	21.3	16.3	4.5
Arabic language should be in use just like Hebrew	71.4	19.1	8.3	1.2
Arab citizens should manage their cultural, religious and education affairs by themselves	62.9	20.7	9.7	6.7
The law should ensure the right of the Arabs to suitable representation in all state institutions	69.3	21.5	7.5	1.6
The law should ensure the Arabs' right to their proportional share of the State budget	68	22.5	8.3	1.2
The state should give the Arabs suitable representation in its symbols, flag, and national anthem	48.5	19.7	21.5	10.3
Arab leadership must agree to any legislation or rules relating to Arab citizens	54.6	25.2	13.8	6.5
The right of all Palestinians to return to Israel should be ensured	41.3	17.1	32.9	8.7

The state should acknowledge its responsibility for the Nakba (Catastrophe) that befell the Palestinians during the 1948 war	53.9	15.3	24.9	5.9
The state should compensate Arab citizens for land confiscated from them	62.8	19.2	14.4	3.6
The state must recognize the Arab citizens as Palestinians and ensure their right to maintain relations with the Palestinian people and the Arab nation	50.1	25.3	19	5.7
The state should cancel the special status given to non-Israeli Jewish organizations such as the Jewish Agency and the Jewish National Fund	40.3	19.4	29.4	10.9

A cursory survey of the reactions to the document by the various ideological and political streams indicated that it does constitute a solid a basis for internal discourse within the Palestinian Arab community in Israel (Ghanem and Mustafa, 2008). The parties have yet to devote adequate attention to the vision. We believe this is due to the weakness of Arab political activity and to the inability of existing political structures to delve into an ideological discussion that would lead to clear stands on the future of the people they represent. This matter requires serious action and the organization of the collective Palestinian leadership in Israel. A prompt start is needed before it becomes more difficult to act in this regard.

Summary

The future of the Palestinians in Israel depends on their ability to place their problems, status, and the question of their future existence in the State of Israel at the center of their political activity. This should be their national project, not merely a weak and marginal substitute for "more important" issues, which depends on the experiences of other national groups. Their future project and its basic features should be clarified as a project that differs from those of other national, religious, or ethnic groups in the region, and perhaps rescue the Palestinian national movement and the Palestinians in Israel from their ideological crises. It is very clear that one factor that weakens the cause of the Palestinians in Israel, ultimately stemming from the choices of some of their leaders, is that they follow and attempt to find their place within the projects of others: the vision of Islamic, Israeli, or pan-Palestinian movements that do not see them as partners but only as secondary actors in projects that do not include them. This has hindered their collective achievement and further exacerbated their already difficult situation.

Considering the factors that govern the possibility of change in divided societies and the stages needed to implement that change, it is important to point out that the success of the struggle of the Palestinians in Israel is contingent on one basic condition and another complementary one: the organization of the Palestinians in Israel as a national group with united goals, and the use of well-conceived means to attain the defined goals. The Future Vision is a major step towards this goal.

6 The "Joint List" of Arab Parties in the 2015 Knesset Elections: The National Consensus from Concept to Practice

The creation of the Joint List was an important political event in the history of the Palestinians in Israel. It followed decades of popular debate as to whether the Arab parties should form a single list for Knesset elections, representing the collective national and civic demands of Palestinians in Israel. The Joint List was also a political experiment that expressed hope amidst the divisions and fragmentation in the Arab and Palestinian arena. The Joint List comprised of many political movements active in Arab society: the left, Communists, nationalists, and Islamists. As such, it was a step forward in Arab political action and helped subdue the quarrels, rivalries, distrust, and lack of cooperation in the political culture of the Arab community.

The creation of the Joint List responded to the internal demands of the Arab sector, which actually outweighed the external demands posed by the Israeli regime and government. This was particularly true with respect to organizing the Arab community, building its national institutions, and developing leadership for community work and the popular struggle; traditional parliamentary activity was not enough. The Joint List also constituted a model of unity for Palestinians in the West Bank and diaspora, a model that can be emulated to end the split between Hamas and Fatah. As will be shown in this chapter, the Joint List gave hope to all Palestinians, and not only those living in Israel.

The public expectations of the List extended to its political approach and practice. They included maintaining the unity of the List within the Knesset and not splitting into factions, improving its parliamentary performance as compared to that of its component parties in the past, and demonstrating an ability to lead the popular struggle, build regional and national Arab institutions, and increase people's confidence in political action. The political parties and their leaders (or at least many of them) considered the Joint List to be the best route to electoral success. The Arab public, however, saw it as a far broader political framework and not just a way to win a parliamentary seat.

In early December 2014, after a date was set for Knesset elections (March 17, 2015) the Palestinian parties in Israel decided to establish a joint slate. Four parties enlisted in the project: the Democratic Front for Peace and Equality (Hadash), which had won four seats in the 2013 elections; the southern branch of the Islamic Movement, which has run for the Knesset since the Islamic Movement split in 1996; the National Democratic Assembly (NDA or Tajamu), established in the mid-1990s following the signature of the Oslo agreements, which won three seats in 2013; and the Arab Movement for Change, led by MK Ahmed Tibi, which, in an electoral bloc with the southern branch of the Islamic Movement, had won four seats in 2013. The Joint List won 13 seats in the 2015 Knesset election – a record representation for Arab parties[1] and two more than its component parties two years earlier.

The period immediately before and after the establishment of the Joint List involved serious discussions about the meaning and value of doing so. These discussions cannot be understood without looking at the general framework in which Palestinian political activity in Israel has developed. The Joint List is in fact an experiment whose strengths and weaknesses and prospects for success need to be examined. Below we will look at four aspects of this experiment:

1. The background of Palestinian political activity in Israel, particularly after Oslo.
2. The debate for and against the establishment of the Joint List.
3. The consequences of its formation and its electoral performance.
4. The likelihood of its continued success or its demise.

The Historical and Intellectual Context

Any discussion of Palestinian politics in Israel must be part of the lively political debate about minorities in divided societies: how minorities should deal in the public sphere with the challenges created by their subordinate status and their inability to influence the majority. The literature provides many cases of the methods that have helped minorities leverage their political power, despite their numerical disadvantage,

---

[1] A distinction needs to be made here between Arab Knesset members and those representing Arab parties. There have always been Jewish MKs from the Communist Party in the Hadash list, and Arab MKs in Zionist parties – three in the last Knesset and four in the current Knesset.

and be effective in leading change. Some minorities have opted to employ the same political actions, methods, and tools as the majority. Others follow an ethnicity-based line focused on their identity, and most of their members vote for parties that represent their community and its specific needs.

This applies to democratic societies that treat minorities as having an equal and full stake in the state and citizenship (see the discussion in Ghanem and Rouhana, 2001; Horowitz, 1985, Rouhana, 1997; Peleg and Waxman, 2013). The case of the Palestinians in Israel, however, is a complex situation created by the ethnic policies of the state, which accord superior status to the Jewish sector, supplemented by discriminatory policies that favor it. There is the additional complication of the Palestinian–Israeli dispute and the dual role of the Palestinians in Israel, as part of the Palestinian people but also citizens of Israel. There are also internal factors related to the social and cultural structure of their community, which has resulted in a serious distortion of their political development and public activity (see Ghanem, 2001; Rouhana and Ghanem, 1998; Mustafa and Ghanem, 2009).

The complex situation of the Palestinians in Israel has constricted their political behavior and ability to develop useful channels for political activity and to place their collective political action in the mainstream (see Mustafa and Ghanem, 2009). Part of this situation is due to the ethnocratic regime in Israel and the continuing strife and dispute about its intrinsic nature (see Ghanem, 2004).

The divisions have deepened in tandem with the increasing severity of the dispute among the political movements active in Palestinian society in Israel, the increasing severity of the occupation, and the mothballing of the diplomatic process between Israel and the Palestinians. The dispute about the performance of the Palestinian Authority, both domestic and foreign, has also expanded. Another factor is the Arab Spring, which exacerbated the tension and quarrels between political movements.

This situation became more acute and led to a serious regression in voter turnout by the Palestinians in Israel, to protest the restrictions on its representatives in the Knesset as well as the parties' divisions and lack of a shared program (see Ghanem and Mustafa, 2007). The parties failed to devise a serious political project that can deal with the prospects of the Palestinian community in Israel, given the challenges imposed by the Jewish majority, and the state, not to mention the international situation. The publication of the Future Vision in late 2006 provided a partial way out of this situation (see Ghanem and Mustafa, 2009a). But the Future Vision document and the popular consensus around it did not push the Palestinian politicians in Israel to form a joint slate for the Knesset or even cooperate on a more general level, despite the fact that their everyday political positions and actions are compatible or reflect only minor differences.

Based on the above, we will analyze Palestinian political activity in light of the establishment of the Joint List and try to understand how it moved from the fragmentation and deadlock to organized political action to meet the aspirations of the Palestinian citizens of Israel.

The Political Background

We understand the political background as the entirety of the conditions of the Palestinians in Israel and the political action that led to the idea of the Joint List. Although this can be traced back to the original emergence of the Palestinian minority in Israel, here we deal only with what has happened in the two-plus decades since Oslo. We begin with the general strategic reasons and then go on to the material reasons and tangible political motives that led to the creation of the Joint List.

New Israeli Policies

In the Oslo Accords, Israel and the PLO agreed on mutual recognition. On the Israeli side, this new departure required that Knesset members from Hadash and the Arab Democratic Party support Yitzhak Rabin's government. These parties were referred to as part of the "blocking majority," because they were not included in the government coalition. However, their support prevented the right-wing opposition from bringing down the government (see Ghanem, 1997b). In return for this support, the Government followed policies in areas related to the Arab citizens that were more favorable than ever in the past. But after Netanyahu's electoral victory in 1996, the peace process moved backwards and there was a retreat in the policies affecting the Palestinian community in Israel.

The relations between Palestinian citizens and the state and the Jewish majority reached a new low with the start of the Second Intifada in 2000 and the killing of 12 Arab citizens by the police and security forces. The government set up the Orr Commission to investigate the killings; it found that the main responsibility lay with the state and its leadership and recommended a change in policies towards the Palestinian minority. In fact, since then anti-Arab policies and official and popular positions have hardened (see Ghanem, 2004).

Another factor is the change in the political discourse and demands of Palestinians in Israel, as exemplified by the Future Vision document, with its opposition to the current regime and demand for cultural autonomy and recognition as a national minority. The Jewish sector and its leaders viewed these demands as a direct threat to the Jewish nature of the state (meaning the Jewish hegemony) and as reflecting a new extremism in the Palestinian minority's political awareness and demands (Jamal, 2008).

With these developments, the approach of Israel decision-makers changed and the issue of the Palestinian minority was seen as requiring radical solutions based on more stringent direct and indirect containment, greater use of force, and more severe means of control.

This was reflected in legislation that restricted the citizenship rights of the Palestinian minority, in several racist laws passed or debated by the Knesset, in the failure to indict and try police officers involved in the killing of Arab youths during the Second Intifada, and in the plans to dispossess Negev Bedouin. Palestinians were limited to demanding individual rights and improved living conditions, while those who advance collective claims that could lead to official recognition of the Palestinians in Israel as a national group with collective rights were persecuted or prosecuted. Such demands are viewed as a threat to the Jewish state and aggression against it (Jamal, 2011). There is an increasing demand among Israeli Jews to deal with the "demographic threat" posed by the Palestinian minority. One expression of this is the proposed Basic Law: Israel as the Nation-State of the Jewish People.

State policies at all levels have augmented the Palestinian citizens' sense that they face an individual or collective threat and a growing general feeling that they need to practice greater community solidarity and resistance in order to frustrate these policies and keep the state from isolating segments of the Palestinian community. The resulting desire for unity and collective action, even at the expense of individual interests, suited the masses, but triggered rivalries and divisions within the leaderships and political elite – until the Government's decision to raise the election threshold forced their hand and produced the Joint List.

The Fractured Political Elite vs. a Broad National Consensus

Considerable political pluralism developed among the Palestinians in Israel in the 1980s, reflected in the emergence of the Islamic Movement, the Progressive List for Peace, the Arab Democratic Party, and a number of regional and local organizations. The 1990s saw the fission of the Islamic Movement and emergence of its parliamentary wing (the southern branch), and the establishment of the National Democratic Alliance, the Arab National Party, and the Arab Movement for Change (Ghanem and Mustafa, 2009a).

The large Palestinian turnout in Knesset elections and presence of Arab Knesset members gave them a collective leadership and platform for expression among themselves and to other sectors in Israel, the Palestinian people, and the world in general. According to the scholarly literature, the basis of an effective collective leadership that deals with its constituents' problems effectively is membership in the Knesset (Jamal, 2011).

In fact, the parliamentary representatives were weak and divided. The High Follow-up Committee, which draws its members from the political parties and movements active in the Arab community and functions as the de facto representative organ of the Palestinian citizens of Israel, became an arena for disputes among them. Thus weakened, it was no longer able to perform effectively and achieve the goals for which it was set up: the acquisition of equality and participation in a just peace between Israelis and Palestinians. The political leadership also failed to realize and consolidate the collective vision of the Palestinians in Israel and develop means to effect change. Nor was it able to mobilize people to engage in forms of resistance that could achieve the collective goals and deal with the discrimination and racism faced by the Palestinian community as a whole or by sectors or individuals within it (Jamal, 2006).

Given the ineffectual leadership, it was left to the grassroots to develop the main components of the national consensus. This included the demand that the Palestinian issue be resolved through the establishment of a Palestinian state in the West Bank and Gaza Strip (with East Jerusalem as its capital state), alongside Israel. Opinion polls have repeatedly confirmed that the Palestinians in Israel support this proposition (see Ghanem and Mustafa, 2009a). Most Palestinians in Israel call for the establishment of a Palestinian state not only because that could lead to a solution for other Palestinians, but also it could improve their own lot (Ghanem, 2001a).

At the same time, the Palestinians in Israel call for a democratic regime in Israel, seeking change in two dimensions. First, they are asking to be included in the state and its institutions on the basis of full equality with Jews, including the allocation of resources, employment, and participation in decision-making and the political process in general. Second, they demand institutional autonomy as another facet of the equality they are demanding. They underscore the importance they attach to "recognition of their community as a national minority" by the state authorities as well as in fields that reflect their effort to escape state control, such as educational autonomy through the establishment of an Arab university and self-administration of the Arab educational system and cultural life, alongside a full range of institutions through which they can express their institutionally independent identity (Ilan and Waxman, 2011).

The vast majority of the Palestinians in Israel see their future as citizens of the state and have no interest in relocating to a Palestinian state in the West Bank and Gaza, when established. They are aware that their future will be different from that of other Palestinians. Here it bears mention that the Palestinians in Israel are largely content with the nature and level of their personal and family achievements, but dissatisfied with the community's collective achievements. They have clear demands about where they would like to be, and these aims depart widely from the current situation (see Ghanem and Mustafa, 2009a).

This consensus culminated in the publication in 2006 of the Future Vision, as a collective action plan for the Palestinians in Israel which was drawn up by independent activists and representatives of most political parties and movements. We have looked at the Future Document in Chapter 5 and repeat that surveys have found that 85% of Israeli Palestinians support the content of the Vision and believe it expresses their standpoint (Ghanem and Mustafa, 2009a).

This national consensus takes a critical and dissatisfied view of the partisan political and leadership divides and expresses the need to unify the ranks. Before the 2013 Knesset elections, 76% of Palestinians in Israel supported the established of a joint Arab list.[2] The notion

---

[2] Field research was carried out by the Stat-Net Field Research Institute in November 2012 with a sample of 450 respondents and an error margin of 4%.

continued to surge; before the elections in 2015, the Mada al-Carmel Center in Haifa found that 88% of Arab citizens supported the formation of a Joint List.[3]

The Status of Israeli Palestinians within the Palestinian National Movement

In addition to the official and institutional discrimination and popular Jewish positions against the Palestinian minority in Israel, they have been excluded from the Palestinian national movement. It may be more precise to say that the Palestinians in Israel and their political parties bear some responsibility for this exclusion, because of their attempt to emphasize the different situation of the Palestinians in Israel as compared to other Palestinians (Rekhess, 2002).

Since the PLO adopted the principle of a two-state solution in the mid-1970s, it has gradually become clear to the Palestinians in Israel that, in the existing circumstances, they do not have a realistic chance of being part of the Palestinian national movement on an equal footing with other Palestinian groups. The Palestinian national movement grew up in the diaspora, then in the West Bank and the Gaza Strip. Palestinians in Israel were left on the sidelines. In practice, the Palestinian Authority leads the political entity in the West Bank and the Gaza Strip, which are supposed to be the destination of Palestinians in the diaspora who want to return to their homeland. That is where the Palestinian Authority would create the political center for the Palestinians and where the national movement would continue to develop and build its institutions. The crisis situation of the Palestinians in Israel would become worse, because they could not be part of this structure or partners in the creation of national institutions. It may also be true that the Palestinian national movement did not want to welcome the Palestinians in Israel as equal partners, for fear of complicating the relations between the PA and Israel, where both the Jewish majority and state institutions would object to this inclusion. The Palestinians in Israel would continue to live in historical Palestine and remain on the margins of the main Palestinian developments (Ghanem and Ozacky-Lazar, 2003).

---

[3] See the presentation of the results of the Mada Al-Carmel Center's poll on the Arab48 website, www.arab48.com/?mod=articles&ID=1149809.

With this background, the Palestinians in Israel needed to develop their own collective leadership and action plan. Hence the emergence of the High Follow-up Committee, which represents the Palestinians in Israel, whereas the PLO represents all other Palestinians. The Joint List is another aspect of this situation, a vehicle for collective representation of the Palestinians in Israel as Palestinians, and not only as Israeli voters.

In addition to the strategic and general factors behind the creation of the Joint List, there were specific tactical issues related to the historical moment, and in particular:

1. Events in the Arab world: The Joint List was created against the background of the division and political fragmentation of the Arab community in Israel. In recent years there has been a growing divide between its political and ideological movements and even between the movements that compose the Joint List, due to conflicting views about developments in the Arab world. The events added to the ideological component of the ongoing rivalry among the political parties, at the expense of a discourse focused on shared values.

2. The impasse in the Follow-up Committee: The creation of the Joint List took place at the apex of the dispute among the political movements represented on the Follow-up Committee and their hot-tempered debate about the election of its leader. The disparate views of these parties brought its work to a standstill and repeatedly postponed the leadership election. When they created the Joint List, the Arab parties set aside their disputes without resolving them. A new disagreement surfaced at once, between those who were going to boycott the Knesset elections and those who signed on with the Joint List, concerning whether the selection of the new chair of the Follow-up Committee should precede the Knesset elections, as the boycotters preferred. But the issue was deferred until after the election and has spawned internal political problems that have yet to be resolved.

3. The results of the local elections: The Joint List was formed after local elections in November 2013, which adversely affected the Arab parties and movement, particularly in Nazareth. The components of the Joint List had at the time been engaged in a bitter struggle, with Hadash and the Communists on the one side and the NDA and the Islamic Movement on the other. Somehow they managed to bury the hatchet and unite in the Joint List.

The Joint List was set up in spite of the clear ideological and political differences between its components – Islamists and secularists, nationalists and Communists, left and right – and their long history of disputes. The issue was made more acute by the fact that these were "snap" elections (called early and with only a three-month notice), so there was not enough time to debate the issue of unity. The disputes between the parties of the Joint List extend to their vision of their role in the Knesset. Hadash and the Communists see this as being an opposition to the government and its policies, the NDA considers its presence in the Knesset to be a protest against Zionism itself (Zariq, 2015).

The popular demand for a joint Knesset list was part of a comprehensive strategy to organize the of the Palestinians in Israel, which also includes repairing the Follow-up Committee, rebuilding national institutions, and setting up a national fund. There are four domains here: (1) organizing their internal affairs and taking responsibility for the main challenges in various fields, notably education and the social services; (2) dealing with the authorities and the challenges imposed by the state in various areas; (3) relations with the Palestinian national movement and the Arab world and confronting attempts to exploit the Palestinians in Israel for their own purposes; and (4) dealing with globalization and creating mechanisms for welcoming international institutions and foreign authorities that wish to help the Palestinians achieve their aims.

In addition to popular pressure, the formation of the Joint List was made all but inevitable by the increase in the electoral threshold. But this does not undo the importance of its creation and its ramifications should it become the germ for the organization of collective action by the Palestinians in Israel. The Joint List is an important step in the right direction, providing it does not deteriorate into nothing more than a vehicle to protect the interests of its members, irrespective of the national interests of the Palestinians in Israel.

The Formation of the List: A Historic Moment or an Electoral Moment?

The Arabs in Israel entertain three main positions about the Joint List:

1. The Joint List is seen as a major political and electoral achievement by the Palestinian Arab citizens of Israel, in and of itself.

2. The Joint List is an important political step towards joint political action, as long as it does not simply turn into an electoral slate. This position differs from the first one is that it does not consider the list to be important per se and does not assign it historical significance simply because it has been created, but only if it proves to be part of a political strategy that transcends or seeks to transcend parliamentary activity.
3. The Joint List offers nothing new for Arab politics in Israel, particularly in the parliamentary arena.

In an article by Ibrahim Sarsur (an Islamic Movement MK until the 2015 election) about the Joint List, in which he supports the first position, he wrote that the Joint List,

alone represents the alliance of Islamic and nationalist groups and has a comprehensive project aimed at reform, ... inasmuch as it embodies the broadest unity, is most representative of the concerns of people, is closest to the issues of the public, best expresses their hopes and worries, and has the greatest wealth of experience through the expertise of its components with their long history of serving the Arab people for decades. (Sarsur, 2015).

The Joint List has increased Arab women's participation in politics, even though the number of women on its slate was not as large as some wished. It won 13 Knesset seats, two of which went to Palestinian women who are number two in their own parties: Aida Touma-Suleiman (Hadash) in the fifth slot and Haneen Zuabi (NDA) in the seventh slot. Zuabi had been the only Arab woman in the two previous Knessets. The increased representation of Palestinian women in the Israeli parliament should please those who are interested in this issue (Yahya-Yunes, 2016).

On the other hand, MK Jamal Zahalka (NDA) considers the Joint List to be a part of the struggle against the colonial Zionist project and not simply a parliamentary opposition movement:

There are those who look at the issue of unity and the Joint List as a transient situation to deal with the rise in right-wing fascism, along the lines of unified fronts (sometimes called popular fronts) created and set up by anti-fascist political parties in Europe and elsewhere, in particular by Communist and socialist parties. On the other hand, there are others, including the author of this article, who believe that self-defense, existence, and the right to freedom and justice to fight a colonial project requires the construction of a "patriotic national front" that unifies popular forces through a liberation struggle strategy against Zionism. The need for unity will exist as long as the colonial project exists and as long as the liberation project remains dormant. The idea of a "patriotic national front" does not arise from the temptation of electoral gain by bringing together different political groups but essentially by analyzing the situation and the nature of the struggle, in the context of a national liberation struggle, against the consequences of a colonial project and considering the situation we are living in to be a colonial situation. Zionism is a colonial movement garbed in nationalism and not "a representative of the bourgeoisie" in a "non-colonial" context, as some have defined it. Given that the situation is defined as being colonial and not simply "right-wing extremism," it must be opposed by forming a "national patriotic front." (Zahalka, 2015)

He adds that,

the establishment of the Joint List constitutes a special case of "unity in a time of disunity." Its establishment was not undisputed and it was not a case of jumping on the bandwagon or swimming with the tide, as Arab communities, including the Palestinian community, are currently experiencing fragmentation, the splintering of groups, division and conflict. At the same time, we have created an internal political unity. One of the main reasons for selecting the option of a single Joint List and not two lists is perhaps to protect our community from the damage done by division and political and sectarian polarization. This was expressed clearly and forcefully during all discussions and dialogue on the creation of the list. One of the main reasons that led to the creation of the list was the overwhelming popular support for the formation of a single Joint List which became intense pressure that had a big impact on the decision made by the leaders of political parties. (ibid.)

The Palestinian writer Raef Zariq adopts the second position about the Joint List. He believes that the main challenge for the Joint List is not parliamentary work but the development of common tools for action outside the Knesset. He believes that the Joint List can provide a strong foundation for joint political action in the long term; if it fails, however, it could set back political cooperation for many years. According to Zariq:

The first challenge is how to develop common working tools during the election and afterwards go beyond the election to attempt to define the scope of long-term joint and unified work. In this regard, it can be said that there are political issues and demands that all political parties agree on and it is able to provide a basis for joint work in the long term. If joint work and coordination fail in the future it will be rejected by political parties as the Joint List project will appear to simply be a measure aimed at solving the election threshold problem and [. . .]may perhaps increase the divide between the political parties and the voting public. (Zariq, 2015: 8)

The Islamic Movement, led by Raed Salah, remained faithful to its historic boycott of Knesset elections. Its newspaper, *Sawt al-Haq wal-Huriyya* (The voice of truth and freedom), has published many articles critical of the Knesset election in general and of the Joint List in particular.[4] This reflects the third position enumerated above. Salah renewed his criticism by taking on the Joint List's use of the term "the will of the people" to express its popular base. He linked the use of this term to the breakdown in the refurbishing of the Follow-up Committee because of the election. If the "will of the people" was behind the formation of the Joint List, why isn't it relevant for the Follow-up Committee?

As the Knesset elections have ended and the results have been established I will thus write without the suspicions some hold that I may have confused the Knesset elections campaign for them. Yes, I will write and say: "Some of us have entered these elections in the name of the 'will of the people' and have created an (Arab–Jewish) Joint List in the name of the 'will of the people.' How far from credible this protest in the name of the people is. If this matter was truly transparent and unbiased, why do we not run this unbiased pool in the name of everyone and use the issue of the 'will of the people' to hold a direct election of the Follow-Up Committee? Is this not the fairness required now? I do not mean immediately after one week or one month. It may take more than half a year or even a year for us to clarify the true 'will of the people' on the election of the Follow-Up Committee. When the unbiased poll clarifies the 'will of the people' on the elections for the Follow-Up Committee, it will be fair for all to respect this position and be guided by it. Otherwise history, and future generations may write that we abused the 'will of the people' on issues that determine our future." (Salah, 2015: 4)

---

[4] See, for example: Ibrahim Abu Jaber, "Inside Palestine, between Ideology and Civil Rights," *Sawt al-Haq wal-Huriyya*, March 13, 2015, p. 2. Abdul Hakim Mufid, "From the Opposition Bloc to the Forbidden to Breaking through to the Israeli Public," *Sawt al-Haq wal-Huriyya*, March 13, 2015, pp. 30–31; Abdul Hakim Mufid, "Secular Elections and Digimons," *Sawt al-Haq wal-Huriyya*, March 13, 2015, p. 28.

The Popular Committee for the Boycott of the Knesset Elections, led by Abnaa Al-Balad, boycotted the Knesset election on principle and did not change its position after the formation of the Joint List. In its view, the list was simply a list for the Zionist left wing:

The "Guaranteed Seats" list is imposed by the high election threshold to enter the Knesset, according to the official statement of the majority of the leaders of this list. It is removed in every way and form from national unity or even national partnership and the statements made by the leaders of its component parties, even at the time of announcing the agreement on it, are clear proof of what we are saying. Those gathered stated that our community is not one that is devoid of color, taste, beliefs and positions. In addition the voting public itself is not party political and self-interested and refuses to be what the leaders of this list have called "a reserve army in the Zionist camp" led by the Labor Party, Livni's Movement and those of their ilk." Our people have experienced their wars and our public has suffered from the existence of this entity for the past 67 years.[5]

The debate about the Joint List was not limited to the Palestinians in Israel. We believe that the political and geographic division of the Palestinians and poor prospects for reaching a solution that realizes the Palestinian national demands, of which the most important is the right to self-determination, made the Joint List a source of hope for all Palestinians. The Palestinian writer Elias Khoury, who lives in Lebanon, expressed this hope in an article in the Jerusalem daily *al-Quds*, "Yes to the Joint List":

It [the formation of the Joint List] comes as a clear and direct response to the fragmentation and climate of division affecting the Palestinian arena in the Occupied Territories and the diaspora. It also constitutes the reverse of the climate of disintegration in the Arab world which has devastated it with destruction and sectarian wars.

The Communists, left-wing nationalists, Islamists and independents in the Joint List are entering a battle to protect the Palestinian presence with great responsibility and an activist spirit. It should provide a sign for a change in the political situation of Palestinians and a political/cultural moment in which those who are absent or present regain their right to exist by declaring the fact that for more than 60 years their country has faced a savage campaign of elimination that uses all the tools of oppressions and racism. (Khoury, 2015)

---

[5] See the statement by the Popular Committee for the Boycott of Knesset Elections, http://m.alarab.net/Article/661160 (last accessed July 26, 2015).

Also in the broader Palestinian context, writer and scholar Hani al-Masry stated that the Palestinians in Israel are "a model to be followed" and saw the creation of the Joint List as an achievement that could have positive results for the Palestinian national movement:

The creation of the Arab Joint List to enter the twentieth Knesset election is a major step worthy of joy and a good portent that we hope will be the start of the new era whose impact will not be limited to our people living within the 1948 borders but will spread to different Palestinian groups and movements within the "liberation organization" and beyond. It could pave the way for the reconstruction and unification of the organization's institutions in partnership with different shades of the political spectrum. (Al-Masry, 2015: 15).

Yazid Sayigh, however, wrote that although the Israeli political context requires different means than those available to other parts of the Palestinian nation, this does not reduce the importance of this event for all Palestinians who see it as a way towards broader Palestinian political cooperation in which the Palestinians in Israel play an important role:

The Joint List operates in the territories of the homeland, within Israeli politics and institutions, and consequently it is difficult for Palestinian refugees in exile and those who live in the West Bank and the Gaza Strip, and even those who live in East Jerusalem, to copy the methods available to them in political activity to participate and have influence. However, it is still possible for them all to adapt and apply something similar to the Joint List; the key to this lies in a basic transformation in the method of thinking about political work. In spite of the new activism that has been sparked by the Joint List, the most probable response by the right-wing Israeli government will be to attempt to marginalize it. For this reason, the Joint List needs Palestinians in other places to take part in supplementary activities as a strong group. In turn, the Palestinian Authority, Fatah and Hamas, and the networks of Palestinian refugees and activist groups in exile can help Palestinian citizens in Israel acquire influence and impact, just as successes achieved by Palestinian citizens in Israel can support Palestinians in other places. Nonetheless there is a need for everyone to come together on a joint strategy on participation. (Sayigh, 2015)

This optimistic Palestinian view of the Joint List and its challenge to the divisions among the Palestinians, including between Hamas and Fatah and between the West Bank and Gaza, could reflect a change, albeit small, in the awareness of Palestinians outside Israel of the importance of the Palestinians in Israel and their political activity. On the other hand, the Palestinian national authorities still exploit the Palestinians in Israel as Israelis and not as Palestinians. This was demonstrated when the Palestinian president and his envoys pushed for the creation of the Joint List in order to support the Israeli left and its attempt to change the government in Israel. The important question remains: is the Joint List a change in the role of the Palestinians in Israel in Israeli politics or the start of a change in their role as Palestinians?

Formation of the List and Election Results

The Joint List was set up before the elections following a round of discussions and negotiations led by the National Accord Committee, which secured the parties' agreement to coordinate and create the Joint List. When the slate was drawn up, Hadash was allotted slots 1, 5, 8, 10, and 13; the Islamic Movement, slots 2, 6, 9, and 15; the NDA, slots 3, 7, 11, and 14; and the Arab Movement for Change, slots 4 and 12. The imperative that forced the parties to run on a single list was the rise in the election threshold, which supplemented popular pressure. The Joint List saw no need to present a united platform and issued only a program that contained basic common areas on issues such as peace, equality, and organizing the Arab community. It offered no details of its plans for after the election.

Various criticisms have also been voiced of the Joint List for excluding suitable representation of various sectors of the Arab community. Two other parties, the Arab Democratic Party (Mada) and the Arab National Party, which were part of the Arab list that ran in 2013, tried to set up a an "Arab Unity List," but dropped out of the race because they did not expect to reach the threshold.

As the election approached, the leader of the Joint List, lawyer Ayman Odeh, emerged in the Israeli and Arab media as its main spokesperson. He presented himself to the Israeli media as open and no hardliner on the civil and national issues that concern the Palestinians in Israel. Odeh emphasized individual equality and the daily rights of the Palestinians citizens in Israel. He stayed away from expressing opposition to the Jewish identity of the state and issues related to a two-state solution. He also ignored issues related to the collective rights of the Palestinians in Israel and tried not to provoke the majority. He did not bring up controversial issues such as the right of return and dismissed talk of the "historic injustice," on the grounds that he wanted to focus on the future rather than the past. On these and other issues Odeh's positions provoked widespread criticism among the Palestinian political elite in Israel and unease within the Joint List about the extent to which he represented it.

As the election approached, the List restricted itself to asserting that it represented the Palestinians in Israel, and consequently deserved their support even though it did not bother to devise an action plan for after the election. The component parties largely maintained their organizational and financial independence, and the List's organizational weakness was prominent at the local level. There was no real attempt to bring out voters.

Election day in Arab localities was unusually peaceful, because there was no rivalry between competing parties. The competition between supporters of the Joint List and those voting for Jewish parties was not intense. In this situation, turnout in the morning and early afternoon was lower than in previous elections. This changed in the evening, as calls to go to the polls boomed from mosques and car loudspeakers. Radio Shams joined this campaign. The result was a turnout unprecedented in the last decade.[6] Out of 822,052 registered Arab voters, 522,646 cast a ballot (63.4%). Ramla topped the turnout list, at 70%; the Negev trailed the pack, with 47%.

The Joint List chalked up one major electoral accomplishment and another partial accomplishment. The former was an end to the rising trend of boycotting Knesset elections that went back to 1996 (Ghanem and Mustafa, 2007) and peaked with a 47% abstention rate in 2013. The partial electoral success concerns the number of votes the Joint List received and its representation in parliament. In the 2013 elections, when the components of the Joint List competed individually, they won 9.2% of the valid ballots, which translated into 11 Knesset seats.[7] In 2015, the Joint List received 10.6% of the votes and won 13 seats (see Tables 6.1 and 6.2).[8] But these small increases did not match the expectations, especially of the leaders of the Joint List, of a much better

---

[6] Compared to the far higher turnout up to the end of the twentieth century (see Ghanem and Mustafa, 2007).

[7] See the results of the elections to the Nineteenth Knesset election on the website of the Central Elections Committee, http://votes-19.gov.il/nationalresults (last accessed July 27, 2015).

[8] See the results of the elections to the Twentieth Knesset election on the website of the Central Elections Committee, www.votes20.gov.il (last accessed July 27, 2015).

Table 6.1 *Arab voting in the 2015 Knesset elections*

List	Votes	Percentage of Arab vote (%)
Joint List	387,555	82
Zionist Union	22,812	5
Meretz	12,431	3
Kulanu	11,011	2
Yisrael Beiteinu	10,852	2
Shas	7,352	2
Likud	6,822	1
Yesh Atid	3,211	1
Arab List	2,752	1

Table 6.2 *Arab voting, by religious affiliation*

List	Druze	Percentage among Druze (%)	Muslims and Christians	Percentage among Muslims and Christians (%)
Joint List	6,492	15	381,063	89
Zionist Union	9,172	22	13,640	3
Meretz	1,547	4	10,884	3
Kulanu	6,756	16	4,255	1
Yisrael Beiteinu	7,736	18	3,116	1
Shas	2,591	6	4,761	1
Likud	3,763	9	3,059	1
Yesh Atid	2,220	5	991	0
Jewish Home	311	1	443	0
Green Leaf	175	0	338	0
Other parties	1,499	4	5,404	1
	42,262	100	427,954	100

performance, given the popular demand for its creation. In the Arab sector, 82% voted for the Joint List – record support for Arab lists. There was also saw a large drop in Arab support for Zionist and Jewish parties, continuing the trend that goes back to 1996.

The Future of the Joint List

Although the Arab public considered the establishment of the Joint List to be an essential condition for the success of its political activity and fight against discrimination by the state, and, internally, to deal with social problems and issues such as violence, and even as a means to enhance its status as part of the Palestinian people, to date most leaders and parties have underachieved with regard to their voters' aspirations. The future of the experiment will be determined by the confluence of three main factors.

The first factor is the List's achievements on the political level: its work and results in the Knesset, on matters such as budgets, land allocation, the problem of the unrecognized villages, home demolitions, and economic development. On this level, the Joint List seems to have added value as compared to its individual components and will be able to justify its existence for its voters. With respect to the Palestinian cause, it needs to devise a practical political program in support of the Palestinian demand for an independent state and in support of the participation by the Palestinians in Israel in the Palestinian national project, on the road to independence and development. The third level consists of internal issues for the Palestinians in Israel, such as community organization, the establishment of national institutions, and fighting social problems such as violence. The public's expectations of the Joint List go beyond its parliamentary work to general activity on the ground within the Arab community.

There are various reasons for the current situation that shows few if any results. The most important are the Joint List's poor performance, the absence of a realistic action plan, and the Israeli right's control of the government. This situation could undercut one of the justifications for the establishment of the Joint List – achieving meaningful accomplishments.

The second factor relates to public positions about the Joint List experiment and unity in general. As noted, public demand that the parties cooperate was the trigger for the establishment of the Joint List, and could no longer be ignored after the threshold was raised. The Joint List's ability to maintain popular support for the concept of electoral unity will be an important measure of the success of this experiment. The experiment will otherwise weaken one of the mainstays of public consciousness, namely, that Arab unity in the Knesset could effect a difference in their civil status. The Joint List's failure to maintain its popular base, both those who had voted for the parties individually and those who decided to vote for the Joint List following the previous elections, will lead to the strong return of the election boycott movement. Maintaining its popular base will require the Joint List to lead popular struggle outside the Knesset on matters of importance to the Arab community, such as the demolition of homes, the status of unrecognized villages in the Negev, violence, and the reconstruction of Arab civic and regional institutions. This would present the Joint List as a framework for social and political work and not just an electoral dodge to beat the threshold.

The third factor relates to personal disputes among leaders: Palestinian Israeli political activity over the past two decades cannot be understood without considering personal disputes and rivalries, both within and between parties. Many alliances forged over the years later disintegrated on this account. Of course such rivalries are inherent to politics; in the case of the Arabs in Israel, however, cooperation is essential, whatever the leaders' personal interests.

So the future of the Joint List experiment will very much depend on the level of the personal disputes among its members. This factor will be accentuated if it coincides with intellectual and political disputes about the political program.

The Joint List is still at the beginning of its trajectory. Clearly, however, the experiment has raised expectations of Arab political action within and outside the Palestinian community in Israel, in the Knesset and in Israel in general, as well as among Palestinians in general. On the other hand, an assessment of the List's handling of the main issues, such as devising a joint action plan, dealing with the widespread protests in Arab towns in October 2015, and countering the outlawing of Sheikh Raed Salah's Islamic Movement, suggest that the Joint List has only an electoral justification and is not an authentic framework for political cooperation.

The Joint List's weakness was also apparent in the elections for the Follow-up Committee. As noted, the expectation was that the Joint List would build up national institutions within the Arab community and extend its unity beyond parliamentary work. But three of the four parties that make up the Joint List opted to run their own candidate for the Follow-up Committee leadership. This may be natural behavior for political parties, but disappoints those who hoped that the Joint List was more than a parliamentary device.

The Joint List took no effective action in response to the banning of Sheikh Raed Salah's Islamic Movement. It did file a motion of no confidence and organized a roundtable conference in the Knesset to discuss the ban, and some Knesset members protested in a personal capacity, but the Joint List remained on the sidelines. There was also talk of a temporary walkout by Arab Knesset members, accompanied by international media and diplomatic work, but this came to naught.

Summary

The political activity of the Palestinians in Israel is accompanied by the general understanding that their position, status, and future are linked to the Palestinian–Israeli dispute, an end to the occupation of the West Bank, and a resolution of the refugee problem. This understanding has grown since the signing of the Oslo Agreements and the establishment of the Palestinian Authority, in what is regarded as the starting point for the shift from occupation to an independent state. It is not possible to go into detail here of the Palestinians' failure, increased Israeli extremism, and other developments that ended the Oslo era, and left the two-state solution in the shade; or an analysis of the schism in the Palestinian national movement and separation of the West Bank from Gaza. Both before and after Oslo there has been a lack of initiative in Palestinian political activity in Israel, and dependence on the fantasy of a political solution that would alleviate their victimization; in brief, their acceptance of a secondary historical role in the Palestinian national movement. At best they can be seen as benchwarmers.

Most Palestinian politicians in Israel accept that the problems of the constituents are subordinate to the broader struggle and do not protest the blatant interference by leaders of the national movement in their internal affairs. The main issue is their acceptance of the two-state solution envisaged by the partition plan, which is tantamount to acquiescing to second-class citizenship in Israel. This was reflected in the Joint List's electoral program, which merely combined the positions of its constituent political parties in past elections, with no real effort to devise a platform that dealt with the current challenges faced by the Palestinian community in Israel. In particular, there was the statement of support for an end to the occupation and establishment of the Palestinian state, which began: "The Joint List was created to establish unity against racism and to increase the influence and impact of the Arab people and also groups that oppose occupation and racism." There was nothing about the role of the Palestinians in Israel as Palestinians, but only as Israelis.

On the other hand, Israeli governments, and especially those led by Netanyahu, have more or less put an end to the fantasy of a two-state solution, which united the different parts of the Palestinian nation against the Judaization of the state. Netanyahu insists that the issue relates to the result of the 1948 war and not the 1967 occupation. He is recasting the Palestinian issue and its origin as it really is and not as how it is seen by the majority of Palestinian leaders and elite inside and outside Israel. Thanks to its colonial fundamentalist project, it is the Israeli government that reminds the Arab citizens of the need to change the bases of Palestinian national action and deal with the roots and not the branches.

All this calls for a real revolution in the understanding of the struggle and the role the Palestinians in Israel play in it. In other words, the status of Palestinians in Israel will not be resolved by the fantasy of a two-state solution. Any solution to the Palestinian issue will be the outcome of the successes and failures of Palestinians in Israel and the project set out in the Future Vision – which demonstrated, years before the formation of the Joint List, that there is broad national consensus among the Palestinians in Israel about the fundamental issues. They can build on this to come out of the shadows and play a central political role that pushes Israel and the Palestinian national movement towards a fair historical solution that deals with the impact of the Nakba and not the occupation. The Joint List may be the start of this change. However, this requires far more effort than its members are currently making. They have not yet realized that the Joint List is the start of the process of change and not its end, with their Knesset seats guaranteed.

Conclusion

The Future of the Palestinians in Israel

The Oslo Accords between Israel and the PLO signaled the start of a track that was supposed to lead to a resolution of the "Palestinian Problem." Conspicuously missing from this track is any consideration of the future and political status of the Palestinian citizens of Israel (Ghanem, 1996; Haider, 1997). The PLO did not raise this issue with the Israelis; the Israelis consider it an internal affair and will not negotiate about it with outside parties. So a somewhat odd situation emerged: while efforts were being made to reach a comprehensive solution to the outstanding issues between Israel and the Palestinians, the question of the Palestinian minority in Israel remained marginalized.

The exclusion of the future status of the Palestinians in Israel from the peace process and the Palestinian national movement's total neglect of their predicament as second-class citizens in the Jewish state prodded them to act on their own behalf. The increased strength of the Israeli right since Oslo and its subsequent control of the government, with the parallel standstill in the political process, has worsened the tenuous existence of the Palestinian minority in Israel and made a solution to their distress even more important. This tension has become strikingly evident in recent years, following the publication of *Future Vision of the Palestinian-Arabs in Israel*, which calls for a fundamental change in the status of Palestinians in Israel, a change in the basic principles of Israeli citizenship.

As early as the 1950s, and even more so after Oslo, the Palestinians in Israel embarked on a gradual and linear development process. The increased demographic weight of the Palestinian minority, its greater cohesion, and better leadership has led the Palestinian minority to assert their demand for equality.

The future of the Palestinians in Israel is related to their two major spheres of affiliation, Israel and the Palestinian national movement.

First, with regard to the future relationship between Israel and its Palestinian citizens: in principle, the Palestinians in Israel are coalescing around their demand for collective rights. The Future Vision document states a clear demand for transforming Israel from a Jewish ethnic state to a binational, democratic State (Ghanem and Mustafa, 2009a).

The Palestinians in Israel are not satisfied with their collective status. As they seek to preserve their Arab Palestinian identity, they also aspire to obtain full citizenship in the state and its institutions. In addition, they seek to attain institutional self-rule, so as to ensure their right to manage their unique interests in the fields of education, culture, and religion. They pursue these goals as an integral part of the state and as Israeli citizens. As such, they demand equal rights with the Jewish majority. Ultimately, such self-rule is based on the model of consensual democracy, which ensures true partnership in government, resources, and the process of decision making for both nationality groups in the country.

Although Israel has managed to project an open democratic image, mainly because of its competitive electoral system and freedom of speech, it has effectively become a state controlled by one ethnic group at the expense of its own minority citizens and residents. Judaization remains the main foundation of the Israeli ethnocratic regime, with continuing Jewish settlement, a clear hierarchy between Jewish and Palestinian–Arab citizens, free access to the contested land by world Jewry while Palestinians are barred from returning, and military control of the occupied Palestinian territories (Ghanem, Rouhana, and Yiftachel, 1999).

Given the relationship between the Palestinian minority and the state with its Jewish majority, any democratization process may involve two paradoxical developments. On the one hand, Israel's ethnicization policies have intensified since Oslo. Israel maintains the inferior status of its Palestinian citizens through discrimination in various spheres and at various levels so as to maintain the status quo and prevent the Palestinians from achieving equality (Ghanem, 1998; Ghanem and Mustafa, 2009a). The Jewish majority is in favor of the ethnic state and supports these policies towards the Arab minority (Ghanem, 2003; Smooha, 2005). This support guarantees that the ethnocracy can continue to function.

The different levels of change across the divide between the state and the Palestinian minority could lead the future relationship in two opposite options. We might see an increase in the restrictions imposed on Palestinian citizens and a strengthening of the ethnic components of the state at the expense of democracy in a way that brings the regime in Israel closer to "Herrenvolk democracy." But there might be a gradual transformation towards an egalitarian democracy that accords equal status to both national communities.

A discussion of the various options for the transformation of the relationship between the Palestinians in Israel on one hand and the Jewish majority and the state on the other must take account of a number of basic attributes of the Palestinians in Israel and of the Jewish majority. These attributes seem to set fundamental limits on any discussion of this issue and will continue to be with us if there are no revolutionary developments in the state or in the Arab–Israeli and Jewish–Palestinian conflict.

First, the Palestinians in Israel have no clear and distinct status today. If no formula is found that is acceptable to a majority on both sides, this situation will continue to trouble the state authorities, the Jewish majority, and the Palestinian minority itself.

Second, the Palestinians in Israel have acquiesced in their minority status and divergent fate from the rest of the Palestinians. An overwhelming majority accept Israel as a fact and a political entity and wish to continue being its citizens, even as they reject its Jewish–Zionist character. On the Jewish side, most accept the existence of the Palestinians among them, but reject any recognition of them as a national minority and see the Jewish–Zionist character of the state as an existential need (Smooha, 2005). Thus both sides fundamentally accept coexistence between Jews and Palestinians in Israel but each seeks a different format for this coexistence in the future.

Third, the majority of the Palestinians in Israel, while making peace with their minority status, have developed a complex identity, compounded of Palestinian nationality and Israeli citizenship. As a minority that has not assimilated and differs from the Jewish majority in its culture, language, social customs, and many other aspects, total Israelization and surrender of their national distinctiveness is no real option. On the other hand, their Palestinian identity is unique within the Palestinian national movement.

Fourth, the State of Israel is a centralized polity where power is concentrated in the hands of institutions or actors elected on a country-wide basis, such as the Knesset and the Government. These are the institutions that must pass any future decision about special arrangements for the Palestinians in Israel. All these institutions are totally dominated and controlled by Jews. In such a situation it is unrealistic to expect that the Palestinians in Israel could carry the vote in the debate on the issue without the support of a large number of Jews, especially in light of the fact that the Palestinians in Israel constitute a disadvantaged minority that is located on the political, economic, and social periphery. Hence the Palestinians in Israel must invest special effort in changing the Jews' attitude towards them and their demands.

Finally, the majority of the Israeli Jews view the Palestinians in Israel as hostile and affiliated with the enemy because of their rejection of the Jewish–Zionist character of the state and its objectives and because of the history of the Arab–Jewish conflict (Smooha, 2005). Any attempt by the Palestinians in Israel to modify their current status without the assistance of a major Jewish group will merely reinforce Jewish perceptions of the Palestinians in Israel.

Any future resolution of the status of the Palestinians in Israel must take account of these facts. Such an arrangement must accord priority to the development of a "civic state" on two levels – the bond among citizens and the link between citizens and the authorities – where what counts is the civic affiliation and not the ethnic–national affiliation. This is what must prevail in the debate about Israel as the state of the Jewish people or as binational state.

With regard to the Palestinians in Israel vis-à-vis the Palestinian National Movement: the literature on the relations between the Palestinians in Israel and the Palestinian national movement reveal that the former have been marginalized by the latter (Al-Haj, 1993, 1997; Ghanem, 1996). Because the national movement does not view them as part of the "Palestinian issue" and does not include them on the national agenda or the Palestinian political future, they never raise their issues at the negotiating table (Ghanem, 1996).

The relations between Palestinians in Israel and the rest of the Palestinian people and its organizations has always been a sensitive topic, in the individual and communal sense. In the context of the long hostility between the Zionist movement and the Palestinian national movement, the status of the Palestinians in Israel has always posed a threat to the Israeli authorities and the Israeli Jewish public. The PLO was considered a terrorist organization and any contact with it by Israeli citizens illegal and tantamount to treason. Although some Palestinians in Israel were in contact with the PLO before the signing of the Oslo agreement in 1993, the subsequent process facilitated the establishment of closer relations with the Palestinians of the West Bank and Gaza Strip and with the PLO and Palestinian Authority.

From the ample literature discussing the political stance taken by Palestinians in Israel with regard to the peace process of the early 1990s, it is clear that it was based on their civil status as citizens and not on their collective national identity. They offered strong support to the process because they saw it as a way to improve their civil status in Israel (see Reiter, 1995).

However, there is a gap between the self-identification of the Palestinians in Israel as Palestinians and the PLO as the leadership of the Palestinian people. Although most Palestinians view the PLO as the sole legitimate representative of the greater Palestinian community, including the Palestinians in Israel, neither the PLO nor the Palestinians in Israel have ever claimed that the PLO represents the Palestinians in Israel. This is despite the syllogism that runs as follows: (a) the PLO is the sole legitimate representative of the Palestinian people; (b) the Palestinians in Israel are an integral part of the Palestinian people as a whole; thus (c) The PLO represents the Palestinians in Israel. Hence, once Israel launched public negotiations with the PLO, the conundrum of the relations between the Palestinians in Israel and the Palestinian national movement resurfaced as an issue that was far more complex than had been anticipated.

Even though the status of the Palestinians in Israel is part of the Palestinian issue as a whole, the peace process between Israel and the PLO has totally ignored it. This avoidance complements the exclusionary approach that the PLO adopted long ago with regard to the Palestinians in Israel, as manifested by the conspicuously low-profile interaction between the two sides. The Palestinians in Israel played no role in the establishment of the national and political institutions of the Palestinians in the 1960s.

Moreover, the Palestinian national movement did not consider their problems to be a priority on the national agenda. Israel considered all issues related to the Palestinians in Israel to be an internal Israeli affair; the PLO implicitly accepted this stance. The Palestinians in Israel themselves chose not to apply pressure on the subject, an understanding that the inclusion of such a thorny issue might undermine the peace process as a whole and harm their relations with the state. This situation persists today, although the Palestinian leadership has gradually increased its intervention in the affairs of the Palestinian citizens of Israel.

This intervention became evident when the PLO sought mutual recognition with Israel, especially after the Madrid conference in 1991. The PLO leadership attempted to utilize the Palestinians in Israel to serve its own political ends, most notably by lobbying Arab voters to support the leftist Zionist parties (Rouhana and Ghanem, 1998).

The Palestinian national movement's exclusion of the Palestinians in Israel from the national discourse has spread from the pragmatic political level and endeavor to realize its political project through negotiations, to the cultural level of social awareness that shapes collective identity and future aspirations. This is despite the direct interaction the Palestinians of Israel and those of the West Bank and Gaza after 1967 and the development of the Palestinian political discourse, including that of resistance to occupation, since Fatah gained control of the national movement.

The discourse has effectively shrunk and refers only to the Palestinians in the West Bank and Gaza Strip, and, to a lesser degree, those in the diaspora, while ignoring the Palestinians in Israel. The term "the occupied territory" has gradually morphed from referencing all of historic Palestine to only the parts occupied in 1967. And except for general slogans alluding to the steadfastness of the Palestinians in Israel as historically part and parcel of the Palestinian struggle, the community has been excluded from the discussions, conferences, and seminars discussing the Palestinian future.

Even the critical studies and political writings that question the efficacy of the Oslo Accords and the peace process still consider the occupation to include only the land occupied in 1967, although some make passing reference to the need to consider the Palestinians in Israel. Almost all these works adopt the political stand that the Palestinians in Israel are a domestic Israeli issue. Thus the Palestinians themselves have made a strong contribution to the entrenchment in the Palestinian consciousness of the idea that the occupation did not begin in 1948 but only as a result of the 1967 war (e.g., Farsakh, 2008; Makdisi, 2008).

This implicit agreement between the different parties – the PLO, most of the Palestinian elite outside Israel proper, Israel, and some of the Palestinian elite inside Israel – has rendered this group and their problems invisible at the Palestinian level. It became clear to the Palestinians in Israel that their problems with the state were theirs alone. Over time, they came to realize that they have no real chance of becoming part of the national Palestinian movement on an equal footing with other Palestinians.

After Oslo, the main energies of the Palestinian national movement were directed to establishing self-rule and institutions in the West Bank and Gaza. The Palestinians in Israel were irrelevant and had been further marginalized.

Looking Ahead

The future of the Palestinians in Israel depends on several variables. Some of them are related to the minority's ability to capitalize on developments at the international, state, and internal Palestinian levels, including the progress of the peace process and the success or failure of the establishment of a Palestinian state alongside Israel. More important, however, is their ability to deal with their unique situation and advance from dependency and reaction to proactive implementation of their own vision and a place at the center of critical developments. This would require preparatory work on several levels, of which the most essential is the drafting of a collective national program that reflects their needs.

The rise to power of the Israeli "New Right" raises basic questions that must be addressed, including the new Israeli approach to the Palestinian problem in general and the status of Israeli Palestinians in particular. This developments requires the Palestinian elites in Israel to search for new directions. Two major trends appear to be dominant today among Arab leadership, including in the Follow-up Committee and the Joint List. One direction stresses the need to further the integration of the Palestinian minority into Israel and to forge a political bloc with the Israeli left. Its most prominent representative is MK Ayman Odeh, the head of the Joint List, who advocates a positive approach towards the majority and its representatives and adopts the rhetoric and style of the American civil rights activist Martin Luther King. The other direction, championed by the Islamic Movement and some members of the Joint List, features those who believe that the Arab minority should withdraw from Israeli national politics and consolidate its own "enclaves" as a national minority.

Both ideas enjoy support among the Arab public. According to a survey conducted by sociologist Sammy Smooha in May–June 2015, 75.7% of Israeli Arabs agreed or tended to agree that "the Joint List should talk to the authorities and Jewish parties in order to advance the interests of the Arab population"; 57.6% of the Palestinians in Israel agreed or tended to agree that "the Joint List should talk to the authorities and Jewish parties in order to advance the interests of the Arab population." On the other hand, 42.3% disagreed or tend to disagreed with this option. Moreover, 29.3% of Arabs supported illegal demonstrations, 32.5% supported a boycott of Knesset elections, and 18.5% supported the use of all means, including violence, to further the Arabs' struggle for equal rights. And 54.0% of the respondents justifies launching their own intifada should their situation not improve substantially.[1]

The future of these two camps depends mainly on how the governments of Israel deal with two basic concerns of the Palestinian minority in Israel: the future of the conflict with the Palestinians and the prospects for a peace process and the establishment of a Palestinian state alongside Israel; and the policy towards the Israeli Palestinian citizens themselves. Both processes will have an impact on whether more egalitarian and open policies that support integration and equality, or much harsher policies and the closing of the horizon for equality and integration, are adopted.

---

[1] Sammy Smooha. *Still Playing by the Rules: Index of Arab-Jewish Relations in Israel 2015*, 19.

Bibliography

Abbas, A. A. 1988. *Formative Evaluation of the Electoral System Change on Elected of Local Municipalities Heads in Arab Society in Israel.* Haifa: University of Haifa (Hebrew).

Abulof, Uriel. 2008. "Back to the Future": A Comparative Ethical Look at Israeli Arab Future Vision Documents." *Israel Studies Forum* 23(2): 29–54.

Abunimeh, Ali. 2006. *One Country: A Bold Proposal to End the Israeli-Palestinian Impasse.* New York: Henry Holt.

Abu-Raiya, Issam 1989. "Developmental Leadership: The Case of the Islamic Movement in Umm-al-Fahm, Israel." MA thesis, Clark University.

2004. "The 1996 Split of the Islamic Movement in Israel: Between the Holy Text and Israeli-Palestinian Context." *International Journal of Politics, Culture, and Society* 17(3): 439–455.

2005. "Concrete Religions versus Abstract Religions: The Case of the Split in the Islamic Movement in Israel." *Megamot* 43(4): 682–698 (Hebrew).

Abu-Zaher, N. 2008. *"Civil Society" Between the Descriptive and the Normative: Deconstructing a Conceptual Muddle.* Ramallah: The Palestinian Institute for the Study of Democracy (Arabic).

Adalah. 2007. *Democratic Constitution.* Shafa`amr, Adalah: The Legal Center for Arab Minority Rights in Israel.

Agbaria, Ayman K. and Mohanad Mustafa. 2011. "Two States for Three Peoples: The 'Palestinian–Israeli' in the Future Vision Documents of the Palestinians in Israel." *Ethnic and Racial Studies*: 1–19.

Agbaria, Ayman and Mohanad Mustafa. 2012. "Two States for Three Peoples: The 'Palestinian–Israeli' in the Future Vision Documents of the Palestinians in Israel." *Ethnic and Racial Studies* 35(4): 718–736.

2014. "The Case of Palestinian Civil Society in Israel: Islam, Civil Society and Educational Activism." *Critical Studies in Education* 55(1): 44–57.

Al-Haj, Majid. 1986. "Adjustment Patterns of the Arab Internal Refugees in Israel." *International Migration* 24(3): 651–674.

1988. "The Sociopolitical Structure of the Arabs in Israel: External vs. Internal Orientation." In John E. Hofman, ed., *Arab-Jewish Relations in*

Israel: A Quest of Human Understanding. Bristol, IN: Wyndham Hall, 92–123.

1993. "The Impact of the Intifada on the Arabs in Israel: The Case of Double Periphery." In Akiva Cohen and Gadi Wolsfeld, eds., *Framing the Intifada: Media and People.* New Jersey: Albex, 64–75.

1995. *Education, Empowerment and Control: The Case of the Arabs in Israel.* Albany, NY: SUNY Press.

1997. "Identity and Orientation among the Arabs in Israel: The State of Double Marginalization." *State, Government and International Relations,* 43–44: 103–122 (Hebrew).

2006. *The Palestinian Education in Israel.* Beirut: Center for Arab Unity Studies (Arabic).

Al-Haj, Majid and Henry Rosenfeld. 1990. *Arab Local Government in Israel.* Boulder & London: Westview Press.

Al-Hout, Bayan-Nowehid. 1986. *Political Institutions and the Political Leadership in Palestine 1917–1948.* Beirut: Institute for Palestine Studies (Arabic).

Al Khalidi, Walid. 1998. *So as Not to Forget.* Beirut: Palestinian Studies Institution (Arabic).

Ali, Nuhad. 2004. "Political Islam in an Ethnic Jewish State: Its Historical Evolution, Contemporary Challenges and Future Prospects." *Holy Land Studies* 3(1): 69–92.

2006. "Religious Fundamentalism as Ideology and Practice: The Islamic Movement in Israel in Comparative Perspective." Doctoral dissertation, University of Haifa.

2007. "The Concept of the Independent Society of the Islamic Movement." In Elie Rekhess, ed., *The Arab Minority in Israel and the 17th Knesset Elections.* Tel Aviv: Tel Aviv University, 100–110.

Al-Masry, Hani. 2015. "1948 Palestinians: An Example to Follow." *al-Safir,* January 27, p. 15.

Alon, Y. 2007. *Changes in Characteristics of the Third Sector in the last Decade.* Bier Shiva: Ben Gurion University (Hebrew).

Amara, Mohammad. 1998. "The Clan in Arab Politics: Accommodated to Changing Patterns." In Elie Rekhess, ed., *The Arabs in Israeli Politics: Identity Dilemmas.* Tel Aviv: University of Tel-Aviv, 91–98 (Hebrew).

1999. "Option of Hard Status Quo." In Sara Ozacky-Lazar, As'ad Ghanem, and Ilan Pappe, eds., *Seven Roads: Theoretical Options for the Status of the Arabs in Israel.* Givat Haviva: Institute for Peace Research, 123–154 (Hebrew).

Amara, Mohammad and Mustafa Kabha. 2005. *Identity and Affiliation: The Project of the Affiliation of the Basic Terms of the Arab Students.* Tamra: Ibn Khaldun Society.

Anheier, Helmut K. 2001a. "Dimensions of the Third Sector: Comparative Perspectives on Structure and Change." *Journal of Youth Studies* 4(2): 1–23.

2001b. "Foundations in Europe: A comparative Perspective." Civil Society Working Papers 18. London: London School of Economics.

Anheier, H., M. Glasius, and M. Kaldor. eds. 2003. *Global Civil Society*. Oxford: Oxford University Press.

Arian, Asher. 1990. *Politics and Regime in Israel*. Tel Aviv: Zmura Bitan (Hebrew).

1998. *The Israeli Second Republic: Politics and Regime in Israel*. Tel Aviv: Zmura Bitan (Hebrew).

Ariele, S. et al. 2006. *Injustice and Folly: On the proposals to Cede Arab Localities from Israel to Palestine*. Jerusalem: The Floersheimer Institute for Policy Studies (Hebrew).

Aronowitz, Stanley. 1992. *The Politics of Identity: Class, Culture, Social Movements*. New York: Routledge.

Balbetchan, Y. 2008. "Trends in Registration of New Third Sector Organizations in 2007." *A`lon* 30: 3 (Hebrew).

Barakat, Halim. 2000. *The Modern Arab Society*. Beirut: Center for Arab Unity Studies (Arabic).

Barzilai, G. 2003. *Communities and Law: Politics, and Cultures of Legal Identities*. Michigan: University of Michigan Press.

Bashir, Nabih. 2008. *Arab Localities and Their Local Government in Israel*. Shafa'amer: The Galilee Society.

Bäuml, Yaer. 2002. "The Military Role and the Process of Canceling, 1958–1968." *Hamezrah Hahadash* 23: 133–156 (Hebrew).

2007. *A Blue and with Shadow: The Israeli Establishment`s Policy and Actions among Its Arab Citizens: The Formative Years: 1958–1968*. Haifa: Pardes (Hebrew).

Beckford, J. A. 2000. "Religious Movements and Globalization." In R. Cohen and S. M. Rai., eds., *Global Social Movements*. London: Athlone Press, 165–183.

Bell, Daniel. 1989. "American Exceptionalism Revisited: The Role of Civil Society." *The Public Interest* (95): 38–56.

Bendix, Reinhard. 1969. *Nation-Building and Citizenship: Studies of Our Changing Social Order*. New York: Doubleday.

Benziman, U. 2006. *Whose Land Is It? A Quest for a Jewish–Arab Compact in Israel*. Jerusalem: The Israel Democracy Institute (Hebrew).

Berthoud, Oliver. 2001. *NGOs: Somewhere between Compassion, Profitability and Solidarity*. Managua: Envio.

Binder, Leonard. 1964. "National Integration and Political Development." *American Political Science Review* LVIII: 622–631.

Bishara, Azmi. 1998. *The Fragmented Political Discourse and Another Studies*. Ramallah: Muwaten Center (Arabic).

Bishwapriya, Sanyal. 1997. "NGOs' Self-Defeating Quest for Autonomy." *Annals of the American Academy of Political and Social Science* 554: 21–32.

Brake, Salem. 2005. "The Local Druze's Municipalities Election, the Municipalities Crises between Clan Politics and Modern Administration." *State and Society*, 5(1): 1105–1146 (Hebrew).

Brichta, Avraham. 1998. "The Weakness of Parties in Local Government." In Dani Koren, ed., *The Demise of Parties in Israel*. Tel Aviv: Hakibbutz Hameuchad, 263–273 (Hebrew).

2001. "Transformation on Local Government in Israel: 1950–1998." In Abraham Brichta and Bedhazur Ami, eds., *The Elections for Local Municipalities in Israel 1998*. Tel Aviv: Ramut, 199–214 (Hebrew).

Brinkerhoff, Jennifer, Stephen C. Smith, and Hildy Teegen. 2007. *NGOs and the Millennium Development Goals: Citizen Action to Reduce Poverty*. London: Palgrave Macmillan.

Bukay, David. 2004. *Muhammad's Monsters: A Comprehensive Guide to Radical Islam for Western Audiences*. Green Forest, AR: Balfour Books.

2008. *The Arabs in Israel – From Alienation to Extermination: The Coming of Intifadat al-Nakba*. Ariel Center for Policy Research.

Burton, John. 1990. *Conflict: Human Needs Theory*. New York: St. Martin's Press.

Cohen, L. 2007. "With Angry." *Eretz Aheret* 39: 58–61. (Hebrew).

Cohen, Rannan. 1989. *Political Development of Israeli Arabs Through their Votes in Elections 1948–1984*. Tel Aviv: Tel Aviv University (Hebrew).

1990. *In the Thicket of Loyalties: Society and Politics in the Arab Sector*. Tel Aviv: Am Oved (Hebrew).

2006. *Strangers in Their Homeland: Palestinians. The Jews and the State*. Tel Aviv: Tel Aviv University (Hebrew).

Committee of Arab Local Authority Heads in Israel. 2006. *Future Vision of the Palestinian-Arabs in Israel*. Nazareth: Committee of Arab Local Authority Heads in Israel.

Coston, M. J. 1998. "A Model and Typology of Government-NGO Relationships." *Nonprofit and Voluntary Sector Quarterly* 27(3): 358–382.

Dekmejian, H. 1995. *Islam in Revolution: Fundamentalism in the Arab World*. Syracuse, NY: Syracuse University Press.

Dessouki, Hassan. 1982. "The Islamic Resurgence: Sources, Dynamics, and Implications." In Dessouki Hassan, ed., *Islamic Resurgence in the Arab World*. Westport, CT: Praeger.

Deutsch, Karl W. 1953. *Nationalism and Social Communication: An Inquiry into the Foundation of Nationality*. New York: Technology Press of MIT and John Wiley and Sons.

1961. "Social Mobilization and Political Development." *American Political Science Review* 55: 493–514.

1969. *Nationalism and Its Alternatives*. New York: Alfred A. Knopf.

Deutsch, Karl W. and William J. Foltz. 1963. *Nation-Building*. New York: Atherton Press.

Doron, Gedron. 1996. "Two Civil Societies and One State: Jews and Arabs in the State of Israel." In A. R. Norton, ed., *Civil Society in the Middle East*. Leiden, The Netherlands: Koninklijke Brill NV.

Eisengang-Kna, P. 2004. *Basics of Local Goverment*. Ranana: The Open University (Hebrew).

Emerson, Rupert. 1960. "Nationalism and Political Development." *Journal of Politics* XXII: 137–149.

Evan Chorev, Nadav. 2008. *Palestinian NGOs for Civic and Social Change in Israel: Mapping and Field*. Jerusalem: The Van Leer Jerusalem Institute.

Farah, J. 2007. "Wake Up: You Are Not in Europe Anymore." *Eretz Aheret*, 39: 38–43. (Hebrew).

Farsakh, Leila. 2007. "Time for a Bi-national State" in *Monde Diplomatique*, March. At www.monde-diplomatique.fr/2007/03/FARSAKH/14565

ed. 2008. "Commemorating the Nakba, Evoking the Nakba." Boston: University of Massachusetts.

Fernando, Jude L. 1997. "Nongovernmental Organizations, Micro-Credit, and Empowerment of Women." *Annals of the American Academy of Political and Social Science* 554: 150–177.

García-Aguilar, José L. 1999. "The Autonomy and Democracy of Indigenous Peoples in Canada and Mexico." *Annals of the American Academy of Political and Social Science* 565: 79–90.

Ghanem, As'ad. 1995. "The Municipal Leadership among the Arabs in Israel: Continuity and Change." *Hamizrah hehadash* 15 (Hebrew).

1996. "The Palestinians in Israel, Part of the Problem not the Solution: The Issue of Their Status during Peacetime." *State, System and International Relations* 41–42: 132–156 (Hebrew).

1997a. "The Palestinians in Israel Are Part of the Problem and Not of the Solution: Their Status in the Age of Peace." *Medina, Memshal Vayahasim Benleumiem (State, Government, and International Relations)* 41–42: 123–154. (Hebrew).

1997b. "The Limited Efficiency in Parliamentary Politics of the Arab Minority in Israel: The Elections for the Thirteenth and Fourteenth Knessets." *Israeli Affairs* 4(2): 72–93.

1998. "State and Minority in Israel: The Case of Ethnic State and the Predicament of Its Minority." *Ethnic and Racial Studies* 21(3): 428–447.

1999. "A Bi-National, Palestinian-Israeli State, in all the Land of Palestine/Eretz Yisrael and the Status of the Arabs in Israel within This Frame."

In Sarah Ozacky-Lazar, As'ad Ghanem, and Ilan Pappe, eds., *Theoretical Options for the Future of the Arabs in Israel*. Givat Haviva: Institute for Peace Research, 271–303 (Hebrew).

2001a. *The Palestinian Arab Minority in Israel: A Political Study*. Albany, NY: SUNY Press.

2001b. "The Palestinians in Israel: Political Orientation and Aspirations." *International Journal of Inter-Cultural Relations* 26: 135–152.

2006. "Israel and the 'Danger of Demography." In Jamil Hilal, ed., *Where Now for Palestine*. London: Zed Books, 98–116.

2004. "About the Situation of the Palestinian–Arab Minority in Israel." *Medina Vahevra (State & Society)* 4(1): 165–180.

2005. "The Bi-National Solution for the Israeli-Palestinian Crisis: Conceptual Background and Contemporary Debate." In Mahdi Abdul-Hadi, ed., *Palestinian–Israeli Impasse*. Jerusalem: PASSIA, 19–44.

2009. "The Bi-National State Solution." *Israel Studies* 14(2): 120–133.

Ghanem, As'ad and Mohanad Mustafa. 2007. "The Arabs in Israel Boycott the 16th Knesset Elections: Towards the Study of the Political and Ideological Meanings." *Holy Land Studies* 6(1): 51–74.

2008. "The Future Vision as a Collective Program for the Palestinians in Israel." In Sarah Ozacky-Lazar and Mustafa Kabha, eds., *Between Vision and Reality: The Documents of the Future Visions for the Arabs in Israel 2006–2007*. Jerusalem: The Civic Reconciliation Forum, 83–96 (Hebrew).

2009a. *Palestinians in Israel: Indigenous Group Politics in the Jewish State*. Ramallah: Madar (Arabic).

2009b. "Coping with the Nakba – The Palestinians in Israel and the 'Future Vision' as a Collective Agenda." *Israeli Studies Forum* 24(2): 52–66.

Ghanem, As'ad and Mohanad Mustafa. 2011. "The Palestinians in Israel: The Challenge of the Indigenous Group Politics in the 'Jewish State.'" *Journal of Muslim Minority Affairs* 31(2): 177–196.

2014. "Explaining Political Islam: The Transformation of Palestinian Islamic Movements." *British Journal of Middle Eastern Studies* 41(4): 335–354.

Ghanem, As'ad and Muhanad Mustafa. 2007. "The Palestinians in Israel and the 2006 Knesset Elections: Political and Ideological Implications of the Election Boycott." *The Holy Land Studies* 6(1): 51–73.

Ghanem, As'ad and Sarah Ozacky-Lazar. 1994. *The Arab Local Government Elections, November 1993: Results and Analysis*. Givat Haviva: Institute for Peace Research (Hebrew).

1996. "The Arab Vote in the Elections to the 14th Knesset, 29 May 1996." Tel Aviv University, The Moshe Dayan Center for Middle

East and African Studies, The Program on Arab Politics in Israel: Tel Aviv.

2003. "The Status of the Palestinians in Israel in an Era of Peace: Part of the Problem but Not Part of the Solution." In Alexander Bligh, ed., *The Israeli Palestinians: An Arab Minority in the Jewish State.* London: Frank Cass, 263–289.

Ghanem, As'ad and Nadim Rouhana. 2001. "Citizenship and the Parliamentary Politics of Minorities in Ethnic States: The Palestinian Citizens of Israel." *Nationalism & Ethnic Politics* 7: 66–86.

Ghanem, As'ad, Nadim Rouhana, and Oren Yiftachel. 1999. "Questioning 'Ethnic Democracy.'" *Israel Studies* 3(2): 253–266.

Ghanem, As'ad, Ahmad Shiekh, Mohamad Khalailee, and Sawsan Rizek. 2015. *Palestinian Arab Localities in Israel and Their Local Authorities.* Shafaamr: The Galilee Society.

Gidron, B. and Y. Elon. 2007. *Patterns and Changes in the Third Sector in Israel in the two last Decade.* Bier Shebaa: Ben Gurion University (Hebrew).

Guillermo de Los Reyes and Antonio Lara. 1999. "Civil Society and Volunteerism: Lodges in Mining Communities." *Annals of the American Academy of Political and Social Science* 565: 218–224.

Gurr, Ted-Robert. 1993. *Minorities at Risk: A Global View of Ethnopolitical Conflict.* Washington, DC: US Institute of Peace Press.

Haddad, Y. 1992. "Islamists and the 'Problem of Israel': The 1967 Awakening." *Middle East Journal* 46: 266–285.

Haidar, Aziz. 1990. *The Arab Population in the Israeli Economy.* Tel Aviv: International Center for Peace in the Middle East.

1991a. *The Arab Population in the Israeli Economy.* Tel Aviv: International Center for Middle East Peace (Hebrew).

1991b. *Needs and Welfare Services in Arab Sector in Israel.* Tel Aviv: International Center for Middle East Peace (Hebrew).

1997. *The Palestinians in Israel in Light of the Oslo Agreement.* Beirut: The Palestinian Studies Institution (Arabic).

2005. *Arab Society in Israel: Populations, Society, Economy.* Jerusalem: Van Leer Institute and Hakibbutz Hameuhad (Hebrew)

Haklai, Oded. 2004a. "Helping the Enemy? Why Transnational Jewish Philanthropic Foundations Donate to Palestinian NGO's in Israel." *Nation and Nationalism* 14(3): 581–599.

2004b. "Palestinian NGOs in Israel: A Campaign for Civic Equality or 'Ethnic Civil Society'?" *Israel Studies* 9(3): 157–168.

2009. "State Mutability and Ethnic Civil Society: The Palestinian Arab Minority in Israel." *Ethnic and Racial Studies* 32(5): 864–882.

2011. *Palestinian Ethnonationalism in Israel.* Philadelphia, PA: University of Pennsylvania Press.

Hanafi, Sari and Linda Tabar. 2005. *The Emergence of a Palestinian Globalized Elite – Donors, International Organizations and Local NGOs.* Jerusalem: Jerusalem Institute of Jerusalem Studies and Muwatin.

Harari, Yoram. 1978. *Elections in Arab Society 1977.* Givat Haviva: The Center for Arab Studies (Hebrew).

Hashem, Mazen. 2006. "Contemporary Islamic Activism: The Shades of Praxis." *Sociology of Religion* 67(1): 23–41.

Hilhorst, Dorothea. 2003. *The Real World of NGOs: Discourses, Diversity and Development.* London: Zed Books.

Horowitz, Donald. 1985. *Ethnic Groups in Conflict.* Berkeley, CA: University of California Press.

Hroub, Khalid. 2004. *Hamms: The Thought and the Political Actions.* Beirut: Institute for Palestine Studies (Arabic).

Ibrahim, Saad-Edin. 2004. *Egypt, Islam and Democracy.* Cairo: The American University in Cairo Press.

Israeli, Raphael. 2002. *Arabs in Israel: Friends of Foes?* Jerusalem: ACPR Publishers.

Israeli, Rafi. 2008. *Arabs in Israel: Friends or Foes?* Nisan: Ariel Center for Policy Research.

Jabareen, Yousef. 2007. "Non-Governmental Organizations as a Political Alternative – Critical Assessment." In Elie Rekhess, ed., *The Palestinian Minority in Israel and the 17th Knesset Elections.* Tel Aviv: Tel Aviv University, 93–99 (Hebrew).

Jabberi, Muhammad 'Abed, 1993. "Problematic of Democracy and Civil Society in the Palestinian Homeland." *Al-Mastakabal al-Palestiniani* 115 (167): 4–15 (Arabic).

Jamal, Amal. 2005. *Deliberations on Collective Rights and National State.* Haifa: Mada Al-Carmel Press.

2006. "Arab Leadership in Israel: Ascendance and Fragmentation." *Journal of Palestine Studies* 35(2): 1–17.

2008. "The Political Ethos of Palestinian Citizens of Israel: Critical Reading in the Future Vision Documents." *Israel Studies Forum* 23(2): 3–28.

2011. *Arab Minority Nationalism in Israel: The Politics of Indigeneity.* New York: Routledge.

2017. *Arab Civil Society in Israel: New Elites, Social Capital and Oppositional Consciousness.* Tel Aviv: Hakibbutz Hameuchad (Hebrew).

Jansen, G. H. 1979. *Militant Islam.* London: Pan Books.

Juergensmeyer, M. 2000. *Terror in the Mind of God: The Global Rise of Religious Violence.* Berkeley, CA: University of California Press.

Kaufman, E. 1999. "Option Israeli State." In Sara Ozacky-Lazar, As'ad Ghanem, and Ilan Pappe, eds., *Seven Roads: Theoretical Options for the Status of the Arabs in Israel*. Givat Haviva: Institute for Peace Research, 201–242 (Hebrew).

Keane, J. 1988. *Civil Society and the State*. New York: Verso.

    2004. *Civil Society: Old Images, New Visions*. UK: Polity Press and Blackwell Publishers Ltd.

Keck, Margaret and Kathryn Sikkink. 1998. *Activists Beyond Borders: Advocacy Networks in International Politics*. Ithaca, NY: Cornell University Press.

Khalidi, Rashid. 1997. *Palestinian Identity: The Construction of Modern National Consciousness*. New York: Columbia University Press.

Khamaisi, Rasem. 1999. "The Option of Separation: Irredenta, Independence or Transfer." In Sara Ozacky-Lazar, As'ad Ghanem, and Ilan Pappe, eds., *Seven Roads: Theoretical Options for the Status of the Arabs in Israel*. Givat Haviva: Institute for Peace Research, 155–200 (Hebrew).

Khatib, Kamal. 2015. "Mutterings about the Elections." *Sawt al-Haq wal-Huriyya*, February 27, 2015, p. 5 (Arabic).

Khoury, Elias. 2015. "Yes to the Joint List." *al-Quds*, March 9, 2015 (Arabic).

Kimmerling, Baruch and Joel Migdal. 1993. *Palestinian: The Making of a People*. Cambridge, MA: Harvard University Press.

    2003. *The Palestinian People: A History*. Cambridge, MA: Harvard University Press.

Kretzmer, David. 1992. *The Legal Status of the Arabs in Israel*. Boulder, CO: Westview Press.

    2002. *The Occupation of Justice: The Supreme Court of Israel and the Occupied Territories*. Albany, NY: State University of New York Press.

Kumar, K. 1993. "Civil Society: An Inquiry into the Usefulness of an Historical Term." *The British Journal of Sociology* 44(3): 375–395.

Kymlicka, Will. 1995. *Multicultural Citizenship: a Liberal Theory of Minority Rights*. Oxford: Clarendon Press.

Landau, Yakov. 1993. *The Arab Minority in Israel – Political Aspects*. Tel Aviv: Am Oved (Hebrew).

Lewis, Bernard. 1988. *The Political Language of Islam*. Chicago, IL: University of Chicago Press

    1993a. "Islam and Liberal Democracy." *Atlantic Monthly*, February.

    1993b. *Islam and the West*. Oxford: Oxford University Press.

Lijphart, Arnold. 1977. *Democracy in Plural Societies*. New Haven, CT: Yale University Press.

Lijphart, Arend. 1984. *Democracies*. New Haven, CT: Yale University Press.
1999. *Patterns of Democracy*. New Haven, CT: Yale University Press.
2002. "The Wave of Power Sharing." In Andrew Reynolds, ed., *The Architecture of Democracy*. New York: Oxford University Press, 37–54.

Lustick, Ian. 1980. *Arabs in the Jewish State: Israel's Control of a National Minority*. Austin, TX: University of Texas Press.

Mada al-Carmel. 2007. *Haifa Declaration*. Haifa: Mada al-Carmel.

Makdisi, Saree. 2008. *Palestine Inside Out – An Everyday Occupation*. New York & London: Norton.

Malik, Ibrahim. 1990. *The Islamic Movement in Israel: Between Fundamentalism and Pragmatism*. Givat Haviva: Institute for Arab Studies.

Mamdani, M. 2002. "Good Muslim, Bad Muslim: A Political Perspective on Culture and Terrorism." *American Anthropologist* 104: 766–775.

Mann, M. 1999. "The Dark Side of Democracy: The Modern Tradition of Ethnic and Political Cleansing." *New Left Review* 253: 18–45.

Mannaa', Adel. 2000. "An Identity in a Crisis: The Arabs in Israel in Light of the Agreement between Israel and the PLO." In Ruth Gavison and Daphna Hacker, eds., *The Arab Jewish Polarization in Israel*. Jerusalem: Israel Democracy Institute (Hebrew).

Mar'i, Sami. 1988. *Identity, Co-existence and Curriculum*. Haifa: The Follow-up Committee for Arab Educations (Arabic).

Mayer, Thomas. 1988. *The Awaking of Muslims in Israel*. Givat Haviva: Center of Arab Studies (Hebrew).

Mehra, Rekha. 1997. "Women, Empowerment, and Economic Development." *Annals of the American Academy of Political and Social Science* 554: 136–149.

Melson, Robert and Howard Wolpe. 1970. "Modernization and the Political Communalism: A Theoretical Perspective." *American Political Science Review* 64: 1112–1130.

Melucci, A. 1985. "The Symbolic Challenge of Contemporary Movements." *Social Research* 52: 790–816.

Miari, Mahmoud. 1986. "The Development of Political Identity for the Palestinians in Israel." *The Social Sciences Magazine (Kuwait University)* 14(1): 215–233 (Arabic).
1992. "The Identity of the Palestinians in Israel: Is it Israeli-Palestinian?" *Palestinian Studies Journal* 10: 40–60 (Arabic)

Moaddel, Mansoor. 2002. "The Study of Islamic Culture and Politics: An Overview and Assessment." *Annual Review of Sociology* 28: 359–386.

Muslih, Muhammad. 1993. "Palestinian Civil Society." *Middle East Journal* 47(2),

Mustafa, Mohanad. 2002. *The Arab Palestinian Student Movement in Israeli Universities*. Um El Fahem: Center of Contemporary Studies (Arabic).

2008. "Democratization, Politization and Leadership: The Arab Local Politics in Israel." In Asad Ghanem and Faisal Azaiza, eds., *The Arab Local Government in Israel in the Beginning of 21th Century*. Jerusalem: Carmel, 87–114 (Hebrew).

2013. "Political Participation of the Islamic Movement in Israel." In E. Rekhess and A. Rudnitzky, eds., *Muslim Minorities in Non-Muslim Majority Countries*. Tel Aviv: Tel Aviv University, 95–113.

Mustafa, Mohanad and As'ad Ghanem. 2009. "The Empowering of the Israeli Extreme Right in the 18th Knesset Elections." *Mediterranean Politics* 15(1): 25–44.

Najam, A. 2000. "The Four-C's of Third Sector – Government Relations Cooperation, Confrontation, Complementarily and Co-optation." *Nonprofit Management & Leadership* 10(4): 375–396.

Nakhleh, Khalil. 1978. "Cultural Determination of Palestinian Collective Identity." *New Outlook* 18: 31–40.

1979. *Palestinian Dilemma: National Consciousness and University Education in Israel*. Belmont, MA: Association of Arab-American University Graduates.

1990. *Volunteer Organizations in Palestine*. Jerusalem: Palestinian Thought Group (Arabic).

Neuberger, Benyamin. 1995. "Trends in the Political Organizations of The Israeli Arabs." In Elie Rekhess and Tamar Yegnes, eds., *Arab Politics in Israel at a Crossroad*. Tel Aviv: Tel Aviv University, 35–46 (Hebrew).

Oakeshott, Michael. 1996. *The Politics of Faith and the Politics of Skepticism*. New Haven, CT: Yale University Press.

O'leary, Brendan. 2002 "The Belfast Agreement and the British-Irish Agreement: Consociation, Confideral Institutions, a Federacy, and a Peace Process." In Andrew Reynolds, ed., *The Architecture of Democracy*. Oxford and New-York: Oxford University Press, 293–355.

Orr Committee Report. 2003. *Commission of Inquiry into the Clashes Between Security Forces and Israeli Citizens in October 2000*. Jerusalem: Israel Government.

Ozacky-Lazar, Sara and As'ad Ghanem. 1996. "Arab Voting for the Fourteenth Knesset." *Sekirot* 19, Givat Haviva: Institute for Peace Research (Hebrew).

Ozacky-Lazar, Sara, As'ad Ghanem, and Ilan Pappe, eds. 1999. *Seven Roads: Theoretical Options for the Status of the Arabs in Israel*. Givat Haviva: Institute for Peace Research.

Ozacky-Lazar, Sara and Mustafa Kabha, eds. 2008. *Between Vision and Reality: The Documents of the Future Visions for the Arabs in Israel 2006–2007*. Jerusalem: The Civic Reconciliation Forum (Hebrew).

Pappe, Ilan. 1998. *Ethnic Cleansing in Palestine.* Beirut: The Palestinian Studies Institution (Arabic).

2011. *The Forgotten Palestinians.* New Haven, CT: Yale University Press.

Payes, Shanny. 2003. "Palestinian NGOs in Israel: A Campaign For Civic Equality in a Non Civic State." *Israel Studies* 8(1): 60–90.

2005. *Palestinian NGOs in Israel: The Politics of Civil Society.* Library of Middle East Studies. London, New York: Tauris Academic Studies.

Peled, Yoav. 1992. "Ethnic Democracy and the Legal Construction of Citizenship: Palestinian/Citizens of the Jewish State." *American Political Science Review* 86(2): 432–443.

Peleg, Ilan, 2007. *Democratization the Hegemonic State.* Cambridge: Cambridge University Press.

Peleg, Ilan and Dov Waxman. 2011. *Israeli Palestinians: The Conflict Within.* New York: Cambridge University Press.

Peres, Yochanan. 1970. "Modernization and Nationalism in the Identity of the Palestinian Minority." *The Middle East Journal* 24: 479–492.

Peres, Yochanan and Nira Yuval-Davis. 1968. "On the National Identity of the Palestinian Minority." *New East* 18(1–2): 106–111 (Hebrew).

1969. "Some Observations on the National Identity of the Palestinian Minority." *Human Relations* 22: 219–233.

Petter, D. 2007. "Important Strategic Debate." *Hagada Hasmulit (The Left Bank)*, January 17. (Hebrew). See: http://hagada.org.il/2007/07/20/ויכוח-אסטרטגי-חשוב/

Philips, Anne. 1995. *The Politics of Presence: The Political Representation of Gender, Ethnicity and Race.* Oxford: Clarendon Press.

Rabinowitz, Danni. 2001. "de Tocqueville in Um El Fahem." In Yoav Peled and Adi Opher, eds., *Israel: From Mobilized to Civil Society.* Tel Aviv: Hakibbutz Hameuchad, 350–360 (Hebrew).

Rabinowitz, Dan. and Abu Baker Khawla. 2002. *The Stand Tall Generation: The Palestinian Citizens of Israel Today.* Jerusalem: Keter (Hebrew).

Reiter, Yitzhak. 1995. "Between a Jewish State and a State for all its Residents: The Status of the Arabs in Israel in Peacetime." *Ha-mizrah he-hadash* 16: 45–60 (Hebrew).

ed. 2005. *Dilemmas in Arab-Jewish Relations in Israel.* Tel Aviv: Schocken Press (Hebrew).

Rekhess, Elie. 1985. *The Arab Village in Israel: A Renewing National and Political Center.* Tel Aviv: Dayan Center (Hebrew).

1986. "Between Communism and Arab Nationalism: Rakah and the Arab Minority in Israel, 1965–1973." Ph.D. dissertation, Tel Aviv University (Hebrew).

1989. "The Arabs in Israel and the Arabs in the West Bank and Gaza Strip: Political Affinity and National Solidarity, 1967–1988." In Aharon Lish, ed., *The New East: Special Issue on the Arabs in*

Israel, Between Religion and National Awakening. Jerusalem: Magnes Press, 165–191 (Hebrew).

1993. *The Arab Minority in Israel: Between Communism and Arab Nationalism.* Tel Aviv: Tel Aviv University.

1998. "Political Islam in Israel and Its Connection to the Islamic Movement in the Territories." In Elie Rekhess, ed., *The Arabs in Israeli Politics: Dilemmas of Identity.* Tel Aviv: Tel Aviv University, 73–84.

2002. "The Arab of Israel after Oslo: Localization of the National Struggle." *Israel Studies* 7(4): 1–44.

2007. "The Evolvement of the Arab-Palestinian National Minority in Israel." *Israel Studies* 12(3): 2–28.

Rouhana, Nadim. 1993. "Accentuated Identities in Protracted Conflicts: The Collective Identity of the Palestinian Citizens in Israel." *Asian and African Studies* 27: 97–127.

1997. *Identities in Conflict: Palestinian Citizens in an Ethnic Jewish State.* New Haven, CT: Yale University Press.

1999. "Option of Bi-national State." In Sara Ozacky-Lazar, As'ad Ghanem, and Ilan Pappe, eds., *Seven Roads: Theoretical Options for the Status of the Arabs in Israel.* Givat Haviva: Institute for Peace Research, 243–270 (Hebrew).

Rouhana, Nadim and As'ad Ghanem. 1998. "The Crises of Minorities in Ethnic States: The Case of Palestinian Citizens in Israel." *International Journal of Middle East Studies* 30(3): 321–346.

Roy, Oliver. 1994. *The Failure of Political Islam.* Cambridge, MA: Harvard University Press.

2006. *Globalized Islam: The Search for a New Ummah.* New York: Columbia University Press.

Rubinstein, A. 2007. "The Silence of the Left." *Ma`arev*, January 5.

Rueschemeyer, Dietrich. 1976. "Partial Modernization." In J. J. Loubser, R. C. Baum, A. Effrat, and V. M. Lidz, eds., *Exploration in General Theories in Social Science.* New York: Free Press, 756–772.

Sa'abn, Amid. 2004. *The Arab Citizens' Boycott of the Israeli Knesset Elections 2003.* Haifa: Mada al-Carmel.

Saban, E. 1999. "Option of the Zionist Paradigm Border." In Sara Ozacky-Lazar, As'ad Ghanem, and Ilan Pappe, eds., *Seven Roads: Theoretical Options for the Status of the Arabs in Israel.* Givat Haviva: Institute for Peace Research, 79–122 (Hebrew).

Salah, Ra'ed. 2000. "The Political Experience of the 1948 Palestinians – The Religious Stream." Position paper presented at the conference "Palestinian Political Organizations in the 20th Century," Cairo.

2001. "Towards an Independent Society." *Sawt al-Haq wal-Huriyya*, July 13, p. 5.

2002. "The Elections and Us." *Sawt al-Haq wal-Huriyya*, November 29, p. 5.

2006. "Towards an Independent Society." *Sawt al-Haq wal-Huriyya*, March 30, p. 5.

2015. "The High Follow-Up Committee and the Will of the People." *Sawt al-Haq wal-Huriyya*, March 20, p. 4.

Salla, M. E. 1997. "Political Islam and the West: A New Cold War or Convergence?" *Third World Quarterly* 18: 729–742.

Sarsur, Ibrahim. 2005. "The Islamic Movement and the State." In Yitzhak Reiter, ed., *Dilemmas in Arab-Jewish Relations in Israel*. Tel Aviv: Schocken, 242–249 (Hebrew).

2015. "The Arab Joint List: The Start, Not the End," Al-Qariya website, February 18, 2015. At www.kufur-kassem.com/news-17-139757 .html (accessed July 25, 2015).

Savas, E. S. 2000. *Privatization and Public Private Partnership*. New York: Chatham House.

Sayigh, Yazid. 2015. "What Will the Joint List Offer Palestinians?" *Al-Hayat*, April 2, 2015. At ‏ما الذي تقدمه "القائمة المشتركة" للفلسطينيين؟‏ (accessed July 28, 2015).

Schueftan, D. 2007. "Future Vision Writers Did Not Want to Integrate in Israeli Society, But to Destroy it." *Eretz Aheret*, 39: 49–51 (Hebrew).

Shabi, Ariela and Roni Shaked. 1994. *Hamas: from Believing in God to Terrorism*. Tel Aviv: Keter (Hebrew).

Shafir, Gershon and Yoav Peled. 2002. *Being Israeli: The Dynamics of Multiple Citizenship 16*. Cambridge: Cambridge University Press.

Shamgar, Meir. 2005. *A Constitution by Consensus*. Jerusalem: Israel Democracy Institute

2006. *The Israel Democracy Institute's Proposal for a Constitution by Consensus*. Jerusalem: The Israel Democracy Institute (Hebrew).

Shils, Edward. 1991. "The Virtue of Civil Society." *Government and Opposition* 26(2): 3–20.

Smooha, Sammy. 1983. "Minority Responses in a Plural Society: A Typology of the Arabs in Israel." *Sociology and Social Research* 67(4): 436–456.

1984. *The Orientation and Politicization of the Arab Minority in Israel*. Haifa: University of Haifa.

1989a. *Arabs and Jews in Israel*. Vol. 1. Boulder and London: Westview Press.

1989b. "The Arab Minority in Israel: Radicalization or Politicization." In Peter Medding, ed., *Israel: State and Society*. Oxford: Oxford University Press, 59–88.

1990. "Minority Status in an Ethnic Democracy: The Status of the Arab Minority in Israel." *Ethnic and Racial Studies* 13(3): 389–413.

1992. *Jews and Arabs in Israel*. Vol. 2. Boulder and London: Westview Press.

1998. "Ethnic Democracy: Israel as an Archetype." *Israel Studies* 2(2): 198–241.

1999. *Autonomy for Arabs in Israel?* Beit Berl: The Institute for Israeli Arab Studies.

2002. "The Model of Ethnic Democracy: Israel as a Jewish and Democratic State." *Nation and Nationalism* 8(4): 475–503.

2005. *Index of Arab-Jewish Relations in Israel, 2004*. Haifa: University of Haifa.

2008. "The Arab Vision of Transforming Israel Within the Green Line into Bi-national Democracy." In Sarah Ozacky-Lazar and Mustafa Kabha, eds., *Between Vision and Reality: The Documents of the Future Visions for the Arabs in Israel 2006–2007*. Jerusalem: The Civic Reconciliation Forum, 126–139 (Hebrew).

Smooha, Sammy and As'ad Ghanem. 1998. *Ethnic Religious and Political Islam among the Arabs in Israel*. Haifa: University of Haifa.

2000. "Political Islam among the Arabs in Israel." In Theodor Hanf, ed., *Dealing with Difference: Religion, Ethnicity and Politics: Comparing Cases and Concepts*. Baden-Baden: Nomo, 143–173.

Smooha, Sammy and Theodor Hanf. 1992. "The Diverse Modes of Conflict-Regulation in Deeply Divided Societies." *International Journal of Comparative Sociology* 33(1–2): 26–47.

Sultany, N. 2004. *Israel and The Palestinian Minority*. Haifa: Mada al-Carmel.

Tami Steinmetz Centre for Peace Studies. 1995. *Peace Index 1995*. Tel Aviv: Tami Steinmetz Centre for Peace Studies (Hebrew).

Tamimi, Azam. 2007. "Islam and Democracy from Tahtawi to Ghannouchi." *Theory, Culture and Society* 24(2): 39–58.

Taylor, Charles. 1992. *Multiculturalism and the Politics of Recognition*. Princeton, NJ: Princeton University Press.

1994. "The Politics of Recognition." In Amy Gutmann, ed., *Multiculturalism: Examining the Politics of Recognition*. Princeton, NJ: Princeton University Press.

Voll, J. O. 1982. *Islam: Continuity and Change in the Modem World*. Boulder, CO: Westview Press.

Walzer, Michael. 1991. "The Idea of Civil Society." *Dissent* 38(2): 293–304.

Waxman, Dov, and Ilan Peleg. 2008. "Neither Ethnocracy nor Bi-Nationalism: In Search of the Middle Ground." *Israeli Studies Forum* 23(2): 55–73.

Witt, Steve W. ed. 2006. *Changing Roles of NGOs in the Creation, Storage, and Dissemination of Information in Developing Countries*. Munich: Saur.

Wuthnow, R. 1980. "World Order and Religious Movements." In A. Bergeson, ed., *Studies of the Modern World-System*. New York: Academic Press, 57–75.

Yaffa Research Institute. 1990. *Catalogue of Arab Voluntary Societies and Organizations in Israel*. Nazareth: Yaffa Research Institute (Arabic).

Yahia-Younis, Tagreed and Hana Herzog. 2005. "Gender and Clan Discourse Role: Preliminary Elections in the Clans to Determine Candidates in Local Authorities in Arab-Palestinians Localities in Israel." *State and Society* 5(1): 1077–1104 (Hebrew).

Yahya-Yunes, Tagreed. 2015. "The Joint List – Genderism Readings." JADAL 25(December): 25–30.

Yakobson, Alexander and Amnon Rubinstein. 2003. *Israel and the Family of Nations: Jewish Nation-State and Human Rights*. Tel Aviv: Schocken (Hebrew).

Yiftachel, Oren. 1997. "Israeli Society and Jewish-Palestinian Reconciliation: 'Ethnocracy' and Its Territorial Contradictions." *Middle East Journal* 51(4): 505–519.

2000. "Ethnocracy, Democracy and Geography: Notes on the Judaization of the Land." *Alpayim* 19: 78–105 (Hebrew).

2006a. *Ethnocracy: Land and Identity Politics in Israel/Palestine*. Philadelphia, PA: University of Pennsylvania Press.

2006b. "Neither Two States, Nor One: the Evolving Political Geography of Israel/Palestine." *Arab World Geographer* 8(3): 125–130.

Yiftachel, Oren and As'ad Ghanem. 2004. "Understanding 'Ethnocratic' Regimes: the Politics of Seizing Contested Territories." *Political Geography* 23(6): 647–676.

Yishai, Yael. 1991. *Land of Paradoxes: Interest Politics in Israel*. Albany, NY: State University of New York Press.

1998. "Civil Society in Transition: Interest Politics in Israel." *Annals American Academy of Political and Social Science* 555(1): 147–162.

Zahalka, Jamal. 2015. "The Joint List – A Joint Front or National Alliance." *Jadal* 25(December): 31–35.

Zariq, Raef. 2015. "Joint List: Question of Unity and Conflict." *Palestinian Studies Journal* 102: 7–11.

Zeidan, Elias and As'ad Ghanem. 1999. *Donations and Voluntary Work among the Palestinian-Palestinian Society in Israel*. Beer-Sheva: Israel Center for Third Sector Research, Ben-Gurion University (Hebrew).

Zureik, Elia. 1979. *The Palestinian in Israel: A Study in Internal Colonialism*. London: Routledge and Kegan Paul.

Index

9 781108 701051